Management for Professionals

The Springer series *Management for Professionals* comprises high-level business and management books for executives. The authors are experienced business professionals and renowned professors who combine scientific background, best practice, and entrepreneurial vision to provide powerful insights into how to achieve business excellence.

More information about this series at http://www.springer.com/series/10101

Claudio Franzetti

Pricing Export Credit

A Concise Framework with Examples and Implementation Code in R

 Springer

Claudio Franzetti
Zürich, Switzerland

ISSN 2192-8096   ISSN 2192-810X   (electronic)
Management for Professionals
ISBN 978-3-030-70284-7   ISBN 978-3-030-70285-4   (eBook)
https://doi.org/10.1007/978-3-030-70285-4

This Springer imprint is published by the registered company Springer Nature Switzerland AG.
The registered company address is: Gewerbestrasse 11, 6330 Cham, Switzerland

To the dreamers who believe in internationalism and my family Rita, Francesco, Bibiana and Lorenzo.

The low-hanging fruits always get picked first—and if one is lucky—somebody else will climb the ladder later to finish the job for you.

    Michael Gonter, OECD Export Credit Division

The "unsung giants" of international finance are the world's export credit agencies.

    Delio E. Gianturco

Economists are usually accused of three sins: an inability to agree among themselves; stating the obvious; and giving bad advice. In the field of international trade, they would be right to plead not guilty to all three.

    The Economist

Ceci n'est pas une pipe.

    René Magritte

Preface

The issue of pricing export credit can be seen in a very wide frame encompassing World War I and the time after until today. The name of the game is the International Organisation whose beginning is traced to the Peace of Westphalia in 1648 as origin of the modern international system: external powers should avoid interfering in another country's domestic affairs. What is an international organisation? (Fomerand 2017) states:

> An international organization (IO) is an ordering principle and a method of conducting international relations. It may refer to formal institutions set up by more than three sovereign states through multilateral treaties to achieve, with the support of a permanent secretariat, shared interests, and desirable objectives.

On January 8, 1918, President Woodrow Wilson delivered to the US Senate a speech proposing the famous 14 points as a blueprint for later peace negotiations. He proposed inter alia the removal of trade barriers between nations, the "self-determination" for oppressed minorities, and a world organisation that would provide a system of collective security for all nations. Point 3 reads as follows:

> The removal, so far as possible, of all economic barriers and the establishment of an equality of trade conditions among all the nations consenting to the peace and associating themselves for its maintenance.

During the conference in Versailles, most of the 14 points were dismissed by the other leaders. Nonetheless, in the covenants to the treaty the so-called League of Nations was established. It was the first worldwide intergovernmental organisation whose principal mission was to maintain world peace. Very unfortunately, the USA never ratified the peace treaties nor became member of the League of Nations.

Obviously, the League failed to prevent another World War. The three pillars of international economic co-operation were identified as (1) trade liberalisation, (2) freedom of capital and (3) fixed exchange rates. Especially, the third was not satisfactorily addressed, thus leading to high tariffs and other damaging competitive policies for decades. The Great Depression in the thirties was the longest, broadest and deepest depression of the last century.

In 1944, at a mainly British-American conference in Bretton Woods it was agreed to create three multilateral institutions: (1) a monetary authority, the *International*

Monetary Fund, (2) a development bank named *International Bank for Reconstruction and Development* (World Bank) and (3) an international trade organisation. The third failed to be established due to the refusal of the USA. In 1947, the less ambitious *General Agreement on Tariffs and Trade* (GATT) was born.

Nonetheless, the GATT experienced an increasing influence through its so-called rounds, often named by the country of meeting, e.g. Uruguay round in 1986. There, the name was changed to *World Trade Organisation* (WTO). The next round in Doha encompassed over 150 countries trying to agree on tariffs and non-tariff barriers, agriculture, labour, environmental issues, intellectual property and so forth. After years, the round was declared dead in 2015.

As an aftermath a multitude of bilateral and regional multilateral agreements have been established, eventually generating stalemate. The USA and the EU could not agree on the Transatlantic Trade and Investment Partnership (TTIP); furthermore, the USA withdrew from the Trans-Pacific Partnership (TPP) Agreement.

Under Chinese leadership, some sub-global international organisations or agreements were established, e.g. the Asian Infrastructure Investment Bank, the Comprehensive Economic Partnership or the belt-and-road initiative. The centre of gravitation with respect to international organisations has moved eastwards. How things are changing is further documented by the signing of the *Regional Comprehensive Economic Partnership* (RCEP), on 15th November 2020. It is a free trade agreement encompassing 15 nations around China and concerns almost 30% of global trade. The USA and India are not members.

Another stream of organisations flows from the World Bank: They made room to the Marshall Plan for the reconstruction of Western Europe following the end of World War II. The *Organisation for European Economic Cooperation* (OEEC) was established in 1948 to run the US-financed Marshall Plan. In 1961, this institution turns into the *Organisation for Economic Co-operation and Development* (OECD) when the USA and Canada joined, followed by Japan soon after. Today, there are 36 member countries worldwide.

When contemplating the aim of the OECD according to article 1 of its Convention, one may have serious doubts whether these goals are still appropriate. There is no concern for ecological issues. It reads:

> The aims of the Organisation for Economic Co-operation and Development (hereinafter, called the "Organisation") shall be to promote policies designed:
>
> (a) to achieve the *highest sustainable economic growth* [author's emphasis] and employment and a rising standard of living in Member countries, while maintaining financial stability, and thus to contribute to the development of the world economy;
> (b) to contribute to sound economic expansion in Member as well as non-member countries in the process of economic development; and
> (c) to contribute to the expansion of world trade on a multilateral, non-discriminatory basis in accordance with international obligations.

Over the last couples of decades, the world and trade has changed massively. New players have emerged, and the OECD members' share of trade has decreased. Tvardek (2011, 14) summarises, "One of the outcomes of the post-World War II policy framework is the rapid growth of export-driven developing economies.

Enlightened co-operative policies governing trade, competition, and development have all contributed to this growth. These growth and development successes now require that this enlightened co-operation effort be extended to a new set of global economic partners".

SaceSimest (2020), the Italian export credit agency, summarises one of the latest international initiatives:

> The International Working Group on Export Credits (IWG) was established in 2012 subsequent to a joint initiative of the United States and China. The IWG is an international forum with the aim of negotiating a set of common rules on Export Credits to be shared by both OECD and emerging countries such as Brazil, China, India and South Africa, which are not part of the OECD Arrangement.

It should have become evident that pricing export credit insurance is a very important issue within this very complex international setting. Its common rules free trade from competing on financial terms and subsidies and allow for competing on quality and services provided. Pricing need not implement the most sophisticated scientific approach available, but should not be less complex than useful, but as comprehensive and transparent as possible in order to be able to serve as a discussion material within these multilateral discourses and have a chance to reach some consensus.

Pricing insurance is one of the most important tasks of actuaries. They are often quite practical people. Nonetheless, some affinity with the language of mathematics is needed. As you will see, pricing rests on some acceptable principles. This exposition is free from political "fudge factors" that may be applied later.

This book is also intended to give a fresh view on a matter that has mainly been discussed in a closed group within a framework like the OECD.

The author hopes, against the evident odds, that this small treatise may fall on fertile ground and foster a discussion on this minute, yet very important topic. As Swiss professional in this complex network of national interests, we would very much like to think that we can be seen as credible bona fide brokers.

This book is also about climbing the ladder to pick high hanging fruits.

Zürich, Switzerland   Claudio Franzetti
April 29, 2021

References

Fomerand, J. F. (2017). *The evolution of international organizations as institutional forms and historical processes since 1945: Quis custodiet ipsos custodies?* https://oxfordre.com/internationalstudies/view/10.1093/acrefore/9780190846626.001.0001/acrefore-9780190846626-e-87/version/0.

SaceSimest (2020). *International working group on export credits (IWG).* https://www.sacesimest.it/en/International-Relations/international-working-group-on-export-credits-(iwg).

Tvardek, S. (2011). Smart rules for fair trade: Why export credits matter. In OECD (Ed.), *Smart rules for fair trade: 50 years of export credits* (pp. 12–17) Paris: OECD. [Online; accessed 15-April-2020].

Contents

List of Figures

List of Tables

Motivation

1

This chapter is actually about two motivations. Why is there and should be export support, and having answered that, why a comprehensive pricing framework is needed. To anticipate the second: globalisation and the advent and raise of new players in production and export puts pressure on old agreements of the main players of the past. The new situation must be reflected in such an important framework.

1.1 Benefits of International Trade

Most economic theories on trade and international trade state in general that trade is beneficial. This means that the contrary, e.g. economic sanctions or boycotts, is detrimental for the targeted country or entity. We expand on both topics.

Economics is mainly focused on the entire economic activity of big communities, hence the classic "Wealth of Nations". The wealth of nations can profit as whole, while the distribution within the nation may be uneven and may produce winners and losers. Therefore looking only at the big picture may hide internal disparities that can lead to societal problems and to a difficult search of a sustainable equilibrium. The epitome of this problem is the contrast between competitive manufacturers and non-competitive farmers. There has long existed a hard dilemma between free trade and protectionism. This has been a reason for the failure of the Doha round of the WTO.

1.1.1 Advantages

1.1.1.1 Principle of Comparative Advantage

This term was first mentioned by Adam Smith when arguing about specialisation. Smith is known for his trade theory of absolute advantages. In 1817, David Ricardo

Fig. 1.1 Comparative advantages lead to trade. The Portuguese winemaker exports his wine and imports English cloth getting 1.16 units, while buying Portuguese cloth is more expensive, i.e. yields only 0.9 units

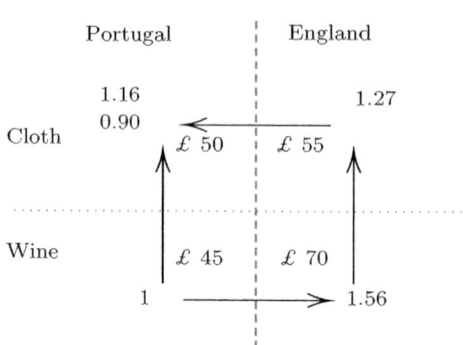

developed his comparative trade theory (Ricardo 1817) after having made a fortune with financing the Napoleonic war.

His example (Ricardo 1817, 119–123) concerns England and Portugal with respective production of cloth and wine. Suppose Portugal can produce a certain quantity of cloth for unit labour cost of £50 and wine for £45; England needs £55 and £70, respectively. This means that Portugal has absolute price advantages. Nonetheless, the relative terms of the products (*terms of trade*) are $50/55 = 0.91$ for cloth and $50/70 = 0.71$ for wine.

As Fig. 1.1 shows, countries should produce what they are relatively better and cheaper doing and then trade. This leaves both countries better off. Specialisation also increases total output. A similar theory proposed by Heckscher and Ohlin in 1919 states that the benefits of international trade can be reaped when each country puts the most effort into exporting resources that are domestically naturally abundant. All countries benefit when they import the resources they naturally lack. This view is not so relevant today as it is based very much on commodities. Supply chain dependence, e.g. for pharmaceutical ingredients, shows that international division of labour can have massive drawbacks when the political framework is shaky.

1.1.1.2 Increased Competition

Opening up markets to foreign suppliers increases competition and broadens the market. The absence of trade and its pressure on prices can lead to monopolies or oligopolies that can impose higher profits while pricing also their slack hampering productivity and efficiency.

Industries that benefit from economies of scale can enlarge their production due to broader markets and thus lower their prices.

Furthermore, trade also increases the variety of products on offer. This is beneficial to consumers.

1.1.2 Disadvantages

First, free trade eliminates jobs in domestic industries that cannot compete globally and leads to outsourcing by means of relocation of service centres, research and development offices and production to countries with a lower cost base.

The *Optimal Tariff Theory*, re-proposed around 1940, argues that a country that is a large importer of a particular good can shift the economic burden of an import tariff from domestic consumers to foreign suppliers if the country is a primary buyer from many competing suppliers (*monopsony*). Thus, in a supply that is relatively inelastic or insensitive to price changes, forces exporters to lower their pre-tariff prices when facing a tariff increase. Thus importing countries can capture revenue that exporters previously received.

By raising tariffs, they can significantly reduce world demand, cutting the world price of the good and tilting the terms of trade in their favour.

A second example of purposefully restricting trade, which came to prominence in the 1980s, is *Strategic Trade Policy* (Krugman 1986). In an industry with economies of scale, the imposition of a tariff, by reserving the home market for a domestic firm, allows the firm to cut its costs and possibly to undercut foreign rivals in overseas markets. This might work in industries like aircraft, semiconductors and cars.

In summary, most theories say: *trade is good*. But there is looming the apprehension that, especially where very heavy economies oppose small ones, government intervention with tariffs may even better the terms of trade. Trade has distributional side effects.

1.2 Trade Statistics

We want to come to a feeling of how important trade is in the world economy. Therefore, we look at some statistics for economic activity and trade. As trade consists of export and import, one's export being an other's import, on a consolidated global scale these figures should equal.

1.2.1 Economic Activity

The economic activity is often epitomised by the Gross National Product of an economy or country. The relative comparison is hampered by the fact that the exchange rates do not mirror the buying power in different countries. Just for getting a coarse overview we take statistics commonly denominated in USD.

Figure 1.2 shows the relative importance of the 20 major economies measured in USD terms. The worldwide GDP is 85.91 Trillion USD, or 85.91E12, for the year 2018. The corresponding figure for the world in terms of *Purchase Power Parity* (PPP) in current international USD is 136.03 Trillion USD (see Fig. 1.3).

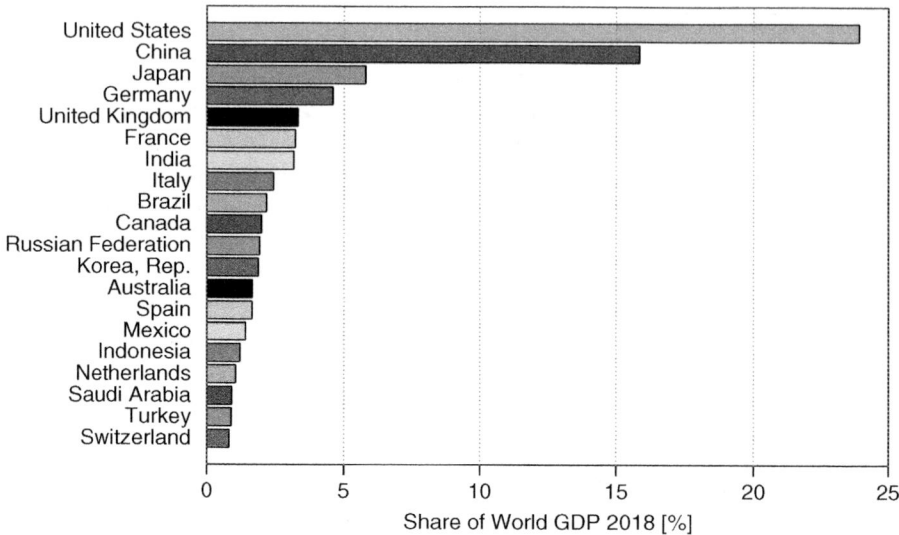

Fig. 1.2 Largest economies by share of world GDP 2018 in USD terms (Source: World Bank)

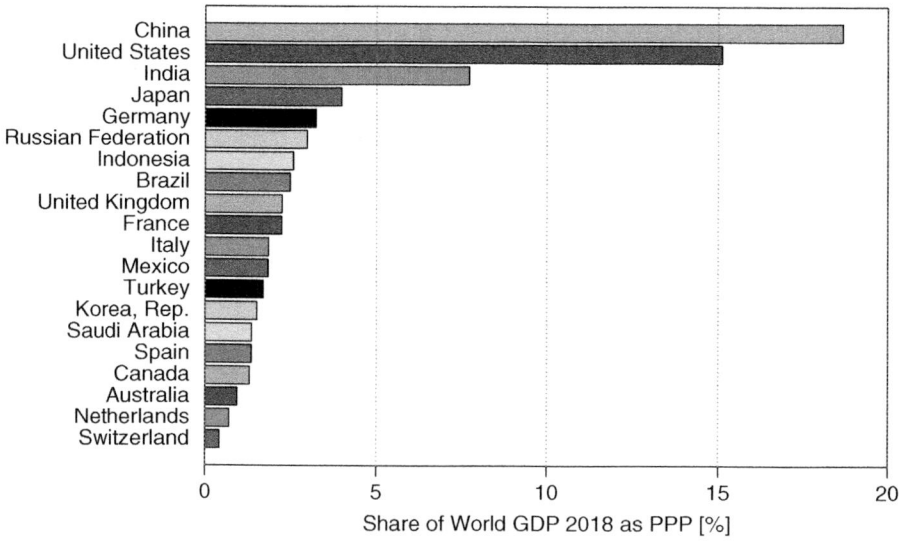

Fig. 1.3 Largest economies by share of world GDP 2018 in PPP terms (Source: World Bank)

1.2.2 Flow Statistics

A first overview of the global trade is given by the statistics of the World Bank. Worldwide exports and imports net to zero. Therefore, the share of exports is the same as the share of imports. A general difficulty is posed by the fact that there is no common value standard. Crossing the borders means often a change in currency

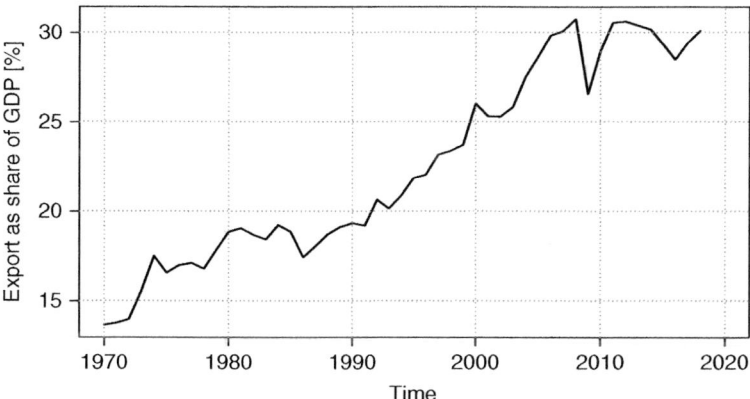

Fig. 1.4 Global exports as share of GPD (Source: World Bank)

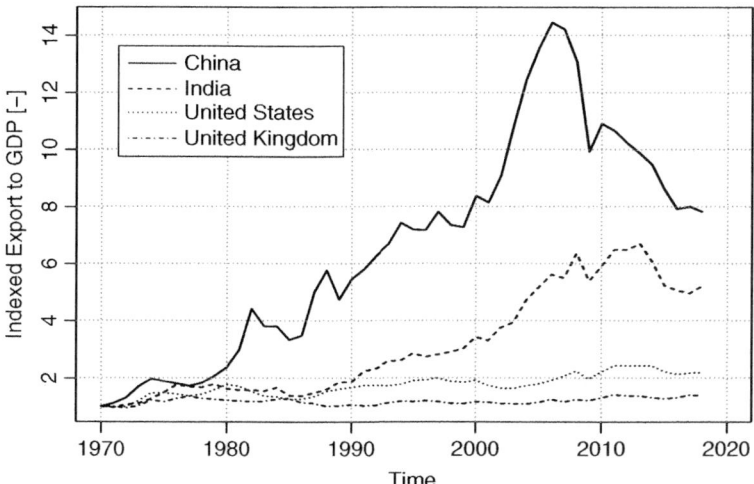

Fig. 1.5 Indexed exports as share of GPD. The series is normalised to values of 1970. (Source: World Bank)

that uses to float. One solution is taking the most widely used currency, i.e. the USD, or trying an adjustment known as Purchase Power Parity that compares the prices of local goods. In such terms the ranking of the major economies is inverted, now China leading the USA.

Figure 1.4 shows the frantic increase of global export during the last 50 years: it has more than doubled. This goes hand in hand with a stronger integration and dependencies of economies and specialisation of products. If we consider some economies, viz. "old" and "new" ones, we can see a very uneven picture (Fig. 1.5). China is the champion followed by India. The USA and UK did not expand any more. The classical analysis of an economy rests on the *balance of payments*.

Actually it is not a balance as known in accounting. It is not a point-in-time statement but a flow account for a given period of time. The balance of payment consists of two parts:

- the current account and
- the capital and financial account.[1]

For these accounts there are standardised versions from the International Monetary Fund, which are revised more or less every decade. The last version is from 2008 (IMF 2009), the penultimate from 1996 (IMF 1996). Changes are induced inter alia by new financial products.

There are two ways of presenting the balance of payments, either as formula or as table. The formula description is as follows (IMF 1996, 158–166):

$$\text{Current Account Balance} = \text{Financial and Capital Account Balance}, \qquad (1.1)$$

in more detail:

$$\begin{aligned} \text{CAB} &= X - M + NY + NCT = NKA + RT \\ &= S - I, \end{aligned} \qquad (1.2)$$

where

CAB	Current account balance,
X	Exports of goods and services,
M	Imports of goods and services,
NY	Net income from abroad,
NCT	Net current transfers,
NKA	Net capital and financial account (i.e. all capital and financial transactions, excluding reserve assets),
RT	Reserve asset transactions,
S	Saving,
I	Investment.

The *current account* CAB shows flows of goods, services, primary income and secondary income between residents and nonresidents of an economy.

The *financial account* shows net acquisition and disposal of financial assets and liabilities.

"The *capital account* shows credit and debit entries for nonproduced nonfinancial assets and capital transfers between residents and nonresidents. It records acquisitions and disposals of nonproduced nonfinancial assets, such as land sold

---

[1] In older compilation these two accounts were shown separately.

Table 1.1 Current account balance (balance of payments) and net trade 2019 for some selected countries

Country	CAB	Net trade in goods and services
Brazil	−49.5	5.6
China	141.3	164.1
Euro area	357.8	436.6
France	−18.5	−27.5
Germany	274.8	225.0
India	−26.9	−70.4
Italy	58.9	61.4
Japan	184.5	4.6
Korea	60.0	53.8
Switzerland	86.2	83.6
United Kingdom	−106.9	−33.1
United States	−498.4	−616.4

Amounts in USD Billion (Source: World Bank)

to embassies and sales of leases and licenses, as well as capital transfers, that is, the provision of resources for capital purposes by one party without anything of economic value being supplied as a direct return to that party" (IMF 2009, 9).

Table 1.1 shows some data referring to the current account. They may serve as crude proxies for the major exporting and importing economies. The biggest difference is between the USA and Germany.

1.2.3   Berne Union

The *International Union of Credit and Investment Insurer*, short "Berne Union", also gathers data from its members that are also export credit agencies ECAs. The union is organised in four different sections, i.e. short term up to 1 year, middle to long term longer than 1 year, investment insurance and the Prague Club. It has 83 member companies and ECAs. As is quite understandable given the competitive situation there are no data about premia. The most interesting statistics is about the share of international trade insured by the BU members and its composition with regards to the first three aforementioned categories. While the middle- to long-term section may be identified mainly with ECAs we cannot deduce the short-term business from ECAs.

The scarce and approximate data can be seen in Table 1.2. Because OECD defines short term as shorter than 2 years and the Berne Union means by short term less than 1 year, there is a mismatch between OECD data and Berne Union data. Moreover, the Berne Union reports only ECA data of members that are not identical with the OECD members. But for a course interpretation it suffices nonetheless.

First, the data shows that ECAs have a major short-term business that is not regulated. Secondly, the difference in default ratio, i.e. the ratio between claims paid and new commitments, is of an other order, even when adjusted for the tenor. For middle- to long-term MLT business we see 218 bp, while for short-term ST we

Table 1.2 Volume data from Berne Union and OECD for 2018

	Berne Union			OECD
	New commitments	Claims paid	Ratio [bp]	New commitments
Middle- to long-term ECA	151.4	3.3	217.8	57
Short term	2222.3	2.6	11.6	*94.4*
Investment	87.2	0.52	59.2	–
Total/Average	2460.8	6.399	26.0	151.4

Amounts are in USD billion, figures in italics are estimates (Source: Berne Union and OECD)

have only 12 bp. It becomes evident why there is a clear split between private credit insurance and governmental credit agencies.

Thirdly, the volumes of private credit insurance are much bigger than state business. Even though the data is not complete we can infer that ECAs make up for approximately 10% of credit insurance cover but 50% of risk. Figure 1.6 shows the official volume of new ECA cover by years that falls under the OECD Arrangement. This is middle- to long-term credit split between general exports and exports covered under sector understandings, e.g. ships, aircraft etc. The core volume is approximately 40 billion USD.

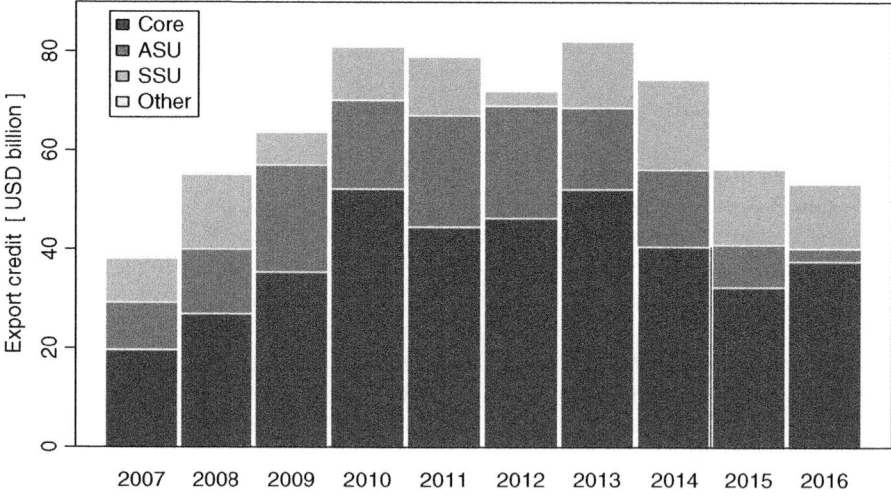

Fig. 1.6 Officially supported export credit volume by year from OECD countries. Core means all export credits besides Aircraft (ASU), ship (SSU) and credit from concessional finance abiding to the rules of the Arrangement. The figures include only middle- to long-term credits. Officially supported short-term business is not covered by the Arrangement (Source: OECD)

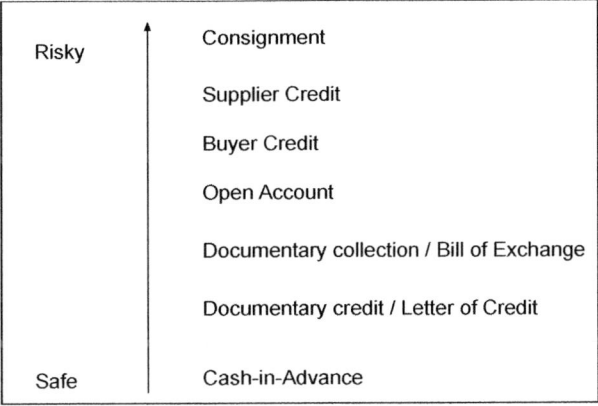

Fig. 1.7 The relative riskiness of payment methods to exporters; for importers the risk is inverted

1.2.4 Payment Methods

In trade there are several methods of payment involved. The payment is the responsibility of the buyer in a sales contract. Delivery and payment have a temporal relationship that creates a situation of credit when the two are not simultaneous. Figure 1.7 shows the main payment methods and their riskiness from the point of view of the exporter. For the importer it is exactly the other way round.

Some payment methods involve third parties, e.g. financial institutions, and their services. The simplest scheme of modern trade is given in Fig. 1.8.

There are three main payment methods, as depicted in Fig. 1.9:

1. cash-in-advance,
2. on open account and
3. bank intermediated.

The first two make up approximately two thirds. Bank intermediated can be further divided in payment through *documentary collection* and *letters of credit* and others.

1.2.5 Special: Projects

Infrastructure projects are special cases of export as the work will be partly executed in a foreign country with the help of domestic contractors, lenders and sponsors. Export here is more than just the crossing of borders by goods. The simplest depiction of an export is shown in Fig. 1.8. It is a relationship between supplier or exporter and buyer or importer. Banks are at least involved with remitting the money.

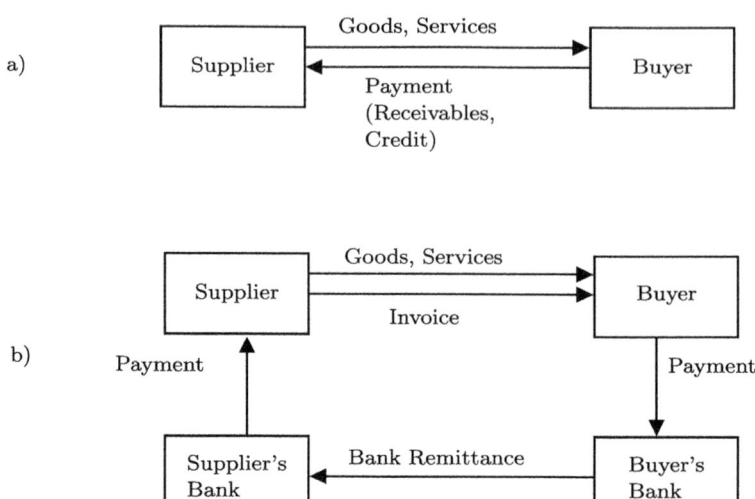

Fig. 1.8 The scheme above (**a**) is the general setting of an export contract that stipulates the delivery and the payment between a supplier (exporter) and a buyer (importer). The payment involves mainly banks and their transfer system (**b**). This situation is typical for an open account method

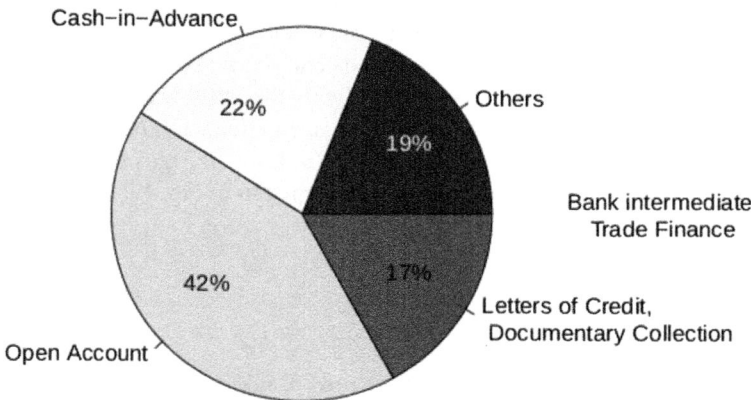

Fig. 1.9 The payment methods used in trade finance are either cash-in-advance and open account or bank intermediated payment methods. One half consists in letter of credit or documentary collection. These figures stem from an estimate of the IMF of 2009 (Franzetti 2018, 382). Similar figures can be found in Caprio (2013, 202)

A definition for *Project Finance* reads (Wikipedia contributors 2020): "Project finance is the long-term financing of infrastructure and industrial projects based upon the projected cashflows of the project rather than the balance sheets of its sponsors". The preferred contracting agreement for building an infrastructure is called *Engineering, Procurement, Construction* or short EPC. The EPC contractor,

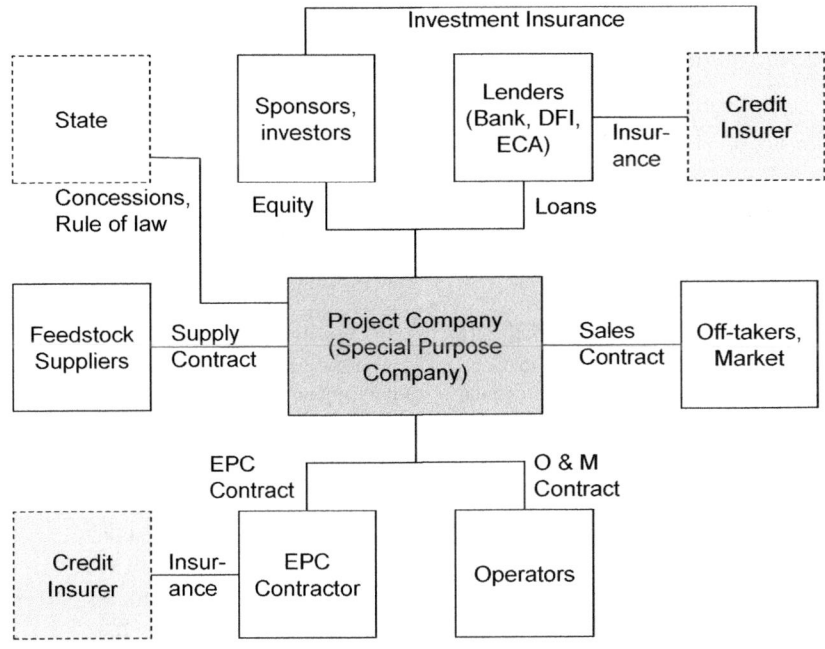

Fig. 1.10 Typical project structure; the credit insurer has several possibilities to contribute cover

obviously, will accomplish the detailed design of the project, procure the necessary equipment and materials and then build and deliver a functioning infrastructure or facility to the buyer that then can be commissioned. Normally the EPC contractor has to deliver the project within a set date and budget, commonly known as a *Lump Sum Turn Key* contract. Such contracts place the risk for delay and budget overdraft on the contractor (Fig. 1.10).

Project lending involves most often a special purpose company SPC in order to remove the project from the balance sheet and segregate risks as depicted in Fig. 1.11 (Table 1.3).

The financing of the project, besides equity of sponsors, rests on three groups of institutions, i.e.

- commercial banks,
- export credit agencies and
- multilateral agencies.

Multilateral agencies are established by intergovernmental agreements and are therefore independent of any single country member. They are meant to promote international and regional economic co-operation by means of direct lending, political insurance and equity participation. They focus on supporting projects

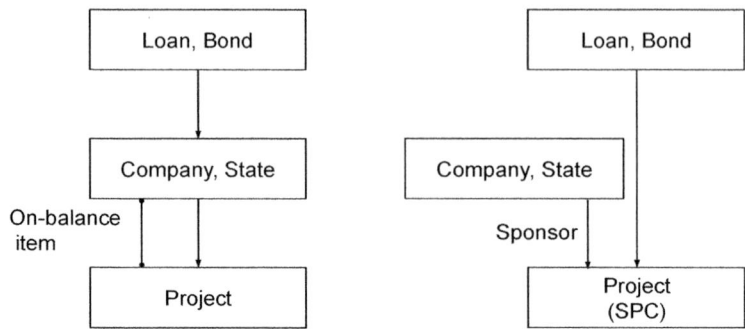

Fig. 1.11 Project lending either on-balance or for a special purpose company. States often do not have a double-entry accounting system but a so-called cameralistics (Franzetti 2018, 368)

Table 1.3 Global loans in project finance by sectors for 2018 (Source: Project Finance International)

	Sector	Volume (Mill. USD)
1	Power	137,627
2	Oil and Gas	54,069
3	Transportation	50,514
4	PPP	13,288
5	Mining	7632
6	Telecommunications	7391
7	Water and Sewerage	4790
8	Petrochemicals	3537
9	Industry	2705
10	Waste and Recycling	1133
	Total	282,685

The same year 130 bonds were issued with an amount of 46,137 million USD

with a definite developmental scope. Table 1.4 shows exposures for ECAs and multilaterals.

In Table 1.3 we see the sectors that are the most involved in project finance as ranked by the loan volume. In 2018 Power was far higher than Oil and Gas and Transportation.

Example 1.1 (Sergipe). Figure 1.12 shows the structure of financing for a power project in Brazil. Through a financing vehicle in Luxembourg that issues SERV guaranteed notes to the market it becomes feasible for the Brazilian electricity company CELSE to tap into a more liquid market outside Brazil for financing. The face value of the notes is BRL 3,201,500,000 that corresponds at the time of writing to EUR 562 million or USD 611 million. From Fig. 1.12 we learn that two additional lenders are involved, i.e. the Inter-American Investment Corporation, IDB Invest and the International Finance Corporation, IFC, a member of the World Bank Group.

Table 1.4 Project finance exposure by multilateral institutions 2018 (Source: Project Finance International)

	IDFI	Direct Lending	Guarantees	Exposure	Deals No
1	KEXIM/ K-Sure	1718	1048	2767	8
2	China Export Import Bank	2560		2560	2
3	JBIC/Nexi	2051	373	2424	7
4	CESCE	500	1250	1750	2
5	IFC/World Bank/MIGA/IBRD	1496		1496	18
6	SERV		1484	1484	2
7	EKF	183	855	1038	7
8	Sinosure		1012	1012	1
9	ADB	869		869	6
10	IDB Invest/IDB	740	113	853	13
11	UKEF	700		700	1
12	CABEI	450		450	1
13	Proparco	447		447	10
14	FMO	409		409	14
15	DEG	393		393	10
16	Euler Hermes/ UFK	75	300	375	3
17	OPIC	313		313	4
18	CDC	307		307	5
19	EIB	230		230	4
20	EBRD	222		222	9
	Sub-total	13,663	6435	20,099	127
	Grand Total	14,721	6558	21,279	

The ranking has a high volatility by years. The SERV exposure is connected with the aforementioned power project in Brazil and might be a once in lifetime event

The IDB Invest Loan Agreement comprises (a) the IDB Invest Loan amounting to USD 38 million; (b) the IDB Loan in an amount of BRL 664 million (projected) and (c) the China Fund Loan in an amount of USD 50 million. IFC is contributing a loan in BRL equivalent of up to USD 200 million.

The EPC contractor is GE Switzerland, a corporation organised and existing under the laws of Switzerland. This motivates the participation of GE Capital as sponsor and SERV as credit insurer. △

There are four main prerequisites for an infrastructure project:

- sustainable economics,
- identifiable risks,
- accessible financing and
- political stability.

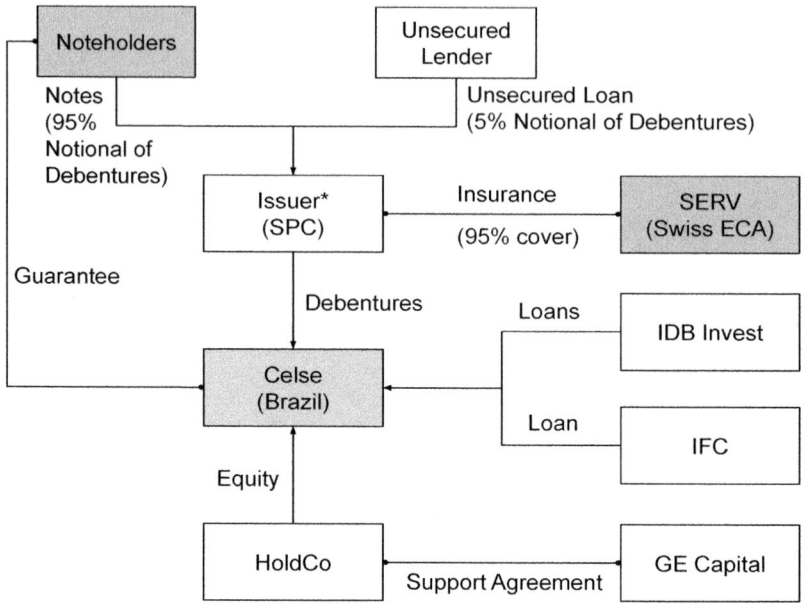

*) Swiss Insured Brazil Power Finance SARL
(Luxembourg)

Fig. 1.12 Financing structure of a power project in Brazil. The financing of CELSE, a Brazilian electricity company, uses equity, loans and debentures passed on to a financial SPC. The latter issues notes on the capital market and contracts a loan. The ECA insures the SPC against credit events of the debentures. It is an on-balance financing (Goldman Sachs 2018, 93). What you do not see is the Swiss supplier, i.e. GE Switzerland

There must be a clear and sustainable business case for the output of the infrastructure to be build, an exhaustive overview of risks and mitigants as well as political stability, e.g. force majeure. Then financing can be made available.

The phases can be stylised into six steps, bound to documents, as follows:

1. request for expression of interest,
2. request for qualification,
3. request for proposal,
4. bid submission and selection,
5. commercial negotiations ("commercial close") and
6. financial agreements ("financial close").

Figure 1.10 shows the common structure of a project and the possibilities of credit export support. Either the supplier or exporter can be supported directly or by insuring or lending to the project company as buyer or rather employer.

As Fig. 1.12 shows typically, also development finance institutions are very often involved in the financing of infrastructure projects that need support.

Project finance can be characterised as cashflow based limited recourse financing. The cashflow is the sole financial source to back the project. As soon as proceeds are generated they will be distributed according to the so-called waterfall. It starts with (1) expenditures for operations, (2) debt service, (3) reserves and then (4) dividends.

An important concept are cover ratios that may be used as covenants in the loan agreements. To show the cashflow focus we just look at one out of many (Vinter 1998, 150) to the Project Life Cover Ratio that puts the net present value of the expected cashflows over the life of the infrastructure in relation to the outstanding debt, i.e.

$$\text{PLCR} = \frac{\text{NPV(Cashflows)}}{\text{Outstanding Debt}} > 1.75. \tag{1.3}$$

The present value will be evaluated every 6 month.

There are legions of publications in this field. Therefore we do not go farther into details here. For readers interested in the different roles in a project we reference Epec (2014).

1.2.5.1 Financing

Financing infrastructure projects long relied on syndicated bank loans. Then project bonds emerged. As of 2018 the ratio between loans and project bonds is approximately 282/46 or more than 6 (see Table 1.3). Although there is a much deeper capital market banks still dominate. This is even more true in Europe where banks have a strong hold.

The EU started twice an initiative to promote bonds also to stimulate the market. "The initiative is designed to enable promoters of infrastructure projects to attract additional private finance from institutional investors such as insurance companies and pension funds" by providing credit enhancement to project companies. The bonds will be issued by the project companies themselves and the European Investment Bank provides credit enhancement in the form of a subordinated financial instrument in order to support the senior debt issued by the project company.

Project bonds are issued by the SPV and sold to banks or bond investors. The bond can be a straight bond, whose creditworthiness depends on the cashflow performance of the vehicle, or a secured bond with a higher priority than the credit enhancement.

Due to their characteristics, i.e. relatively low risk and long maturities, these bonds are good investment opportunities for insurance companies, pension funds etc. who thus can match their liabilities. For further arguments see Della Croce and Gatti (2014) and Fig. 1.13 therein.

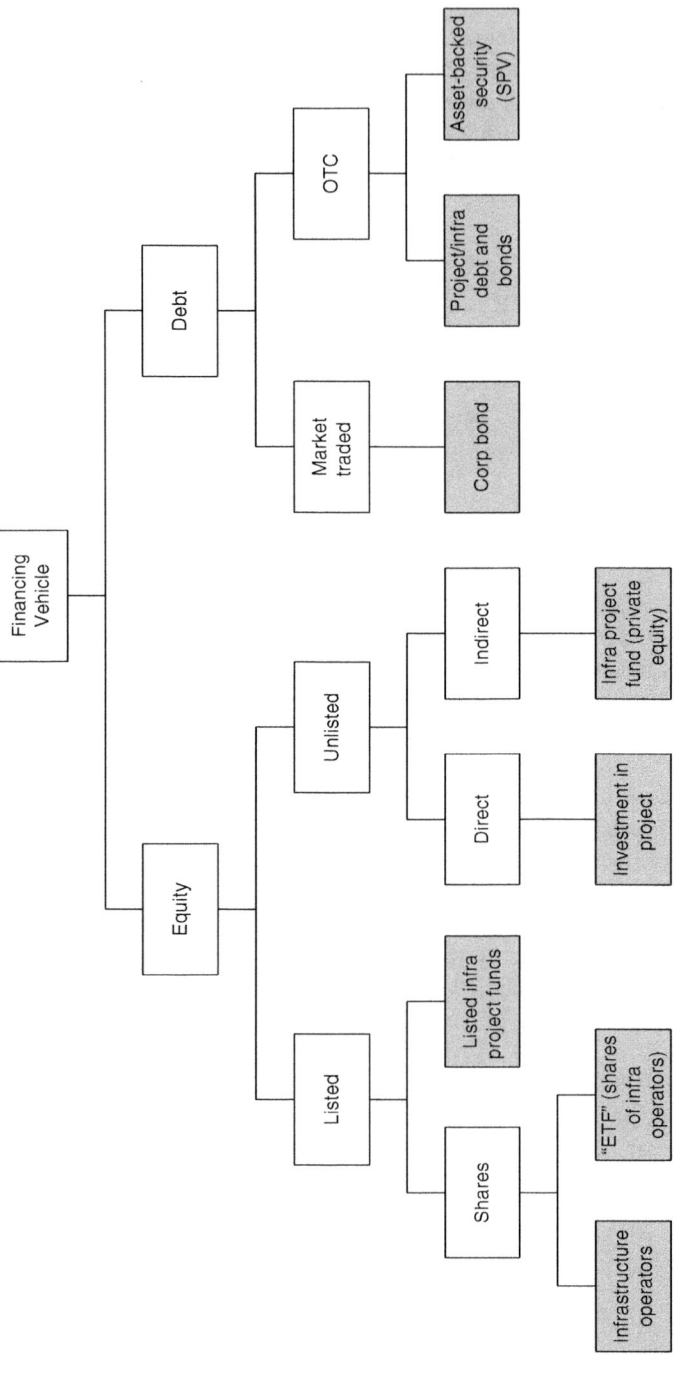

Fig. 1.13 Different channels to infrastructure investments available to the private sector (Della Croce and Gatti 2014, 126)

References

Caprio, G. (2013). *The evidence and impact of financial globalization*. London Waltham, MA: Elsevier.

Della Croce, R., & Gatti, S. (2014). Financing infrastructure—International trends . *OECD Journal: Financial Market Trends, 2014*(1), 123–138. OECD, Paris. https://www.oecd.org/finance/Financing-infrastructure-international-trends2014.pdf.

Epec (2014). *Role and use of advisers in preparing and implementing PPP projects*. Report, European PPP Expertise Centre EPEC, European Investment Bank, Luxembourg.

Franzetti, C. (2018). *Investmentbanken: Geschäftsfelder, Akteure und Mechanismen.* Wiesbaden, Germany: Springer Gabler.

Goldman Sachs (2018). SwissInsBrPFin 9,85 16/07/2032 Rule 144A—US870880AA90. *Luxembourg Stock Exchange*. [Accessed 2020-04-17].

IMF (1996). *Balance of payments manual*. Technical report, International Monetary Fund, Washington. https://www.imf.org/external/np/sta/bop/BOPman.pdf.

IMF (2009). *Balance of payments and international investment position manual*. Technical report, International Monetary Fund, Washington. https://www.imf.org/external/pubs/ft/bop/2007/pdf/BPM6.pdf.

Krugman, P. (1986). *Strategic trade policy and the new international economics*. Cambridge, Mass: MIT Press.

Ricardo, D. (1817). *On the principles of political economy and taxation*. London: J. Murray.

Vinter, G. (1998). *Project finance: A legal guide*. London: Sweet & Maxwell.

Wikipedia contributors (2020). *Project finance—Wikipedia, the free Encyclopedia*. https://en.wikipedia.org/w/index.php?title=Project_finance&oldid=942602054. [Online; accessed 15-April-2020].

Export Credit Industry

2

In this chapter we would like to summarise basic knowledge of export, trade finance, that is bank products, export credit agency products and credit as well as fundamentals of finance and its core concepts.

2.1 Export

The meaning of exports is quite simple: Exports are goods and services that are produced in one country and sold to buyers in another. Projects are special cases of this general definition. Exports, together with imports, make up international trade. One's export is another's import.

The goods must pass borders between countries. On each side of the border – on land or between ports or airports – there may be some customs officers with a wide range of duties. Up to now, trade is heavily dependent on documents and paperwork.

2.2 Credit

The Romans made the distinction between *credere* and *putare*, both meaning believe. The first notion is a transcendental act, e.g. believe in gods, while the second means guessing, thinking without precise knowledge. Credere stems from "give the heart" or "put at one's heart". Thus credit has this implication: I give you something because there is a moral obligation you to give it back to me.

© The Author(s), under exclusive license to Springer Nature Switzerland AG 2021
C. Franzetti, *Pricing Export Credit*, Management for Professionals,
https://doi.org/10.1007/978-3-030-70285-4_2

2.2.1 Credit as Situation

The modern notion of credit may have different meanings. On the one hand it is the *situation* that a supplier having delivered or a creditor having lent awaits to be paid or repaid. Figure 2.1 shows four typical situations. Situation (d) is selling for cash. The exchange of goods and money is simultaneous. There remains only the risk of the quality or performance of the good. No other credit will be generated.

Situation (c) is selling and invoicing. The payment is due only some short period later, often 30 – 90 days after delivery. These receivables may be sold at a discount to a factor. Liquidity is stressed only for a short period of time.

In (b) we have a payment in advance. Until the point in time of delivery there is the risk to the buyer that the supplier does not honour his or her duty to deliver the good. The buyer must trust the seller, while the seller makes a promise to the buyer.

Situation (a) is the basis for export credit insurance, viz. the supplier delivers and grants credit terms. We will see later that export credit agencies insure both the situations (a) and (b). In Fig. 2.2 we see the two dominant risk classes in trade, viz. the credit risk and the performance risk. We would consider performance risk also to be a special credit risk.

On the other hand, credit is a generic term for *inter alia* debt or a *loan*, a receivable or a security, e.g. a bond. It could also be lending one's own *creditworthiness* through a guarantee or a letter of credit. This is a typical bank business.

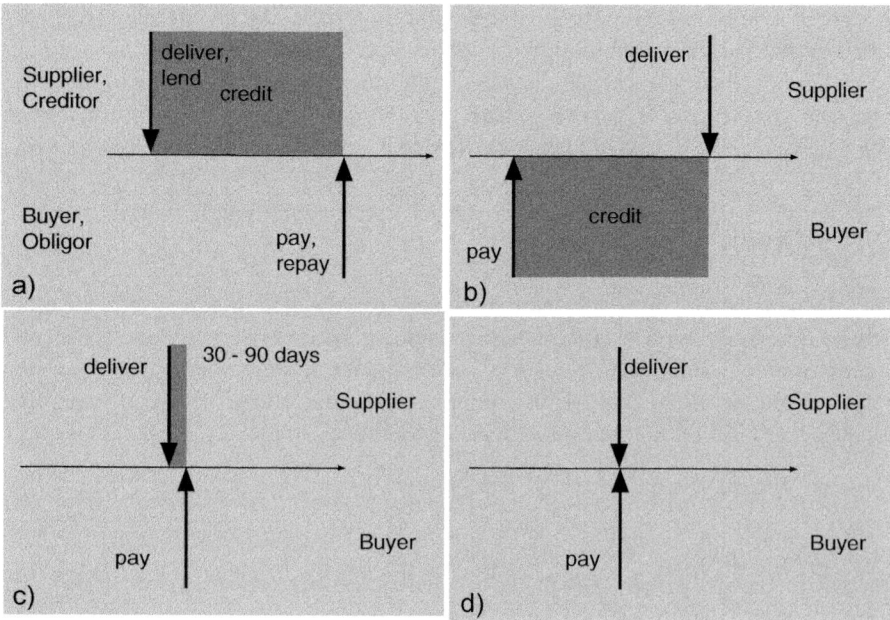

Fig. 2.1 Typical credit risk situations in Export. If delivery and payment are not synchronous, there will be credit

Fig. 2.2 Advance payment versus progress payment. These two types of payments occur in the phase before delivery or acceptance of the export good or construction. With an advance payment the buyer incurs a performance risk, while with a progress payment the supplier has the credit risk of not being paid for the work done

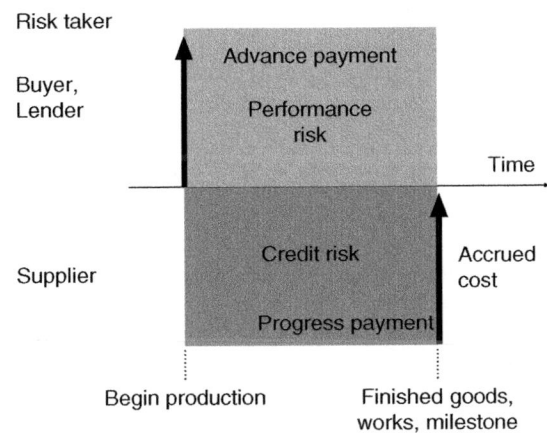

2.2.2 Credit as Future Cashflows

In narrow monetary sense credit can be defined as future cashflows promised. These promises must take some form through documentation. Where and how are these promises documented? This is a non-exhaustive list:

- a commercial contract,
- a loan agreement,
- a promissory note,
- a bill of exchange or draft,
- wrapped in a letter of credit or documentary credit,
- an insurance policy,
- a guarantee,
- a receivable,
- an invoice etc.

The list may depend on jurisdiction and definition of terms, the countries' traditions and legal system. But the principle is evident. Some forms of documentation need typically a bank, e.g. letter of credit, and some can be stipulated between contracting parties without third parties, e.g. bill of exchange. A private stipulation can be avalised by a bank.

These documentations may contain more than just the cashflow definition. They may contain instructions, supporting evidence, contingencies, references, accessories etc.

Now credit insurers, faithful to their name, must cope with these cashflows and thus with their documentation. In pricing we will base our theory on the cashflows from the different products like insuring cashflows from commercial contract, supplier credit, from loans, buyer credit and so forth.

If the contingency is the non-payment of a principal obligation by the debtor, then we have some kind of surety interest or guarantee that means a lending of the creditworthiness of the guarantor.

2.3   The Emergence of Credit Insurance

Before credit insurance came credit in the form of a security called *bill of exchange*. It was invented by the time of the Champagne fairs in the thirteenth century by Italian merchants. According to the UK Bills of Exchange Act 1882 it means: "A bill of exchange is an unconditional order in writing, addressed by one person to another, signed by the person giving it, requiring the person to whom it is addressed to pay on demand or at a fixed or determinable future time a sum certain in money to or to the order of a specified person, or to bearer" There can be a qualified acceptance if such conditions are stated in the bill. With such instruments it was possible to live up to the motto: "Buy now, pay later". The first known marine insurance contract dates from 1347, issued in Genoa (SwissRe 2017, 9).

Going back to pre-Greek times the Roman knew the *bottomry contract (fenus nauticum)*, a maritime contract by which the owner of a ship borrows money for equipping or repairing the vessel and, for a definite term, pledges the ship as security. It is stipulated that if the ship be lost in the specified voyage or period, by any of the perils enumerated, e.g. *pericula maris*, the lender shall lose his or her money (Britannica 2020). A similar contract creating a security interest in the cargo is called a respondentia. Although not a proper insurance contract, it is what we now would call a *insurance-linked bond*. It is also a pre-import credit with collateral. Figure 2.3 shows the mechanics. The loan to the captain is not a general debt but restricted to the collateral.

Credit insurance was discussed in 1820 as "A plan for the establishment of a British commercial insurance company, for the protection of trade" (Bate and Earle 1820), leading to the establishment of the British Commercial Insurance Company with the purpose of insuring "against losses sustained by merchants, manufacturers, traders, and others by bankruptcy and insolvency of their debtors". In this cited booklet we find many good practices that are still valid. It proposes to set the

Fig. 2.3 Bottomry contract, schematically. It is an insurance-linked bond. The advance is not a general debt but is only tied to the ship

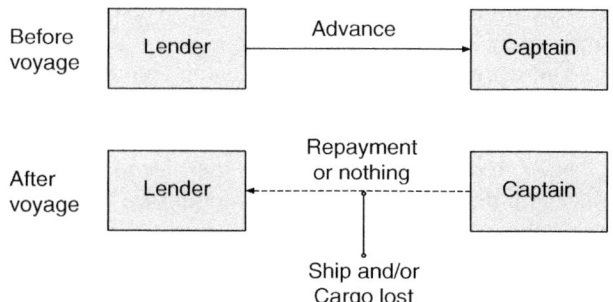

premium at a flat rate of 1s per pound covered. This corresponds to a rate of 5%. Jus (2013, 7) reports the oldest credit insurance contract known to be a policy from 1831 issued by the Riunione Adriatica di Sicurtà in Trieste, now part of Allianz. The first century in credit insurance business has been ruinous because of the inherent moral hazard and other behavioural risks, the lack of appropriate bankruptcy laws, sparse information etc. (Julius 1905, 11:620).

During the First World War the British government grew anxious with regard to the post-war trade situation. Foreseen problems to resume the status ante it decided in 1919 to experiment and adopt a scheme of financing credit up to a maximum of £26 million as a guarantee against "abnormal" risks. The newly created Export Credit Department, later ECGD, considered applications up to 80% of the cost of goods. The first ECA was born.

During the slump after the war many industrialised nations recognised the need for governmental stimulation of trade. The twenties saw a mushrooming of guarantee and insurance schemes in Belgium, Denmark, the Netherlands, Finland, Germany, Austria and Italy, France and Spain, and Norway (Gianturco 2001, 41).

In Germany, after the hyperinflation and the stabilising of the currency, the industry was completely depressed. In 1925/26 the German government acknowledged that private credit insurers for domestic business, i.e. mainly Hermes Kreditversicherungsbank Berlin, could not cope with exports and its inherent political risk. In 1926 a general agreement was stipulated having Hermes fronting credit insurance policies to exporters that were 100% reinsured by the government (Hamann and Habicht 1966, 199).

The Great Depression and the so-called New Deal lead to the establishment, in the USA, of the Export–Import Bank in 1934. It was organised by Franklin D. Roosevelt with the goal "to aid in financing and to facilitate exports and imports and the exchange of commodities between the United States and other Nations or the agencies or nationals thereof". The Export–Import Bank became an independent agency in 1945. It helped finance the reconstruction after World War II. Also in 1934, Switzerland launched "Exportrisikogarantie" as a governmental programme.

As we can clearly understand ECAs and credit insurance companies are the offsprings of crisis.

Although the government-backed export support must not convey subsidies, this is often insinuated. Neo-liberal thinkers deny a role of the state in this business all together or tolerate it only because of other countries having it. A pandemic may change some views.

2.4 Export Credit Agencies

Export credit agencies, in short ECAs, are a special sub-group of credit insurers, because they insure on state account or are a governmental agency. They insure only export-related credits, are subsidiary to and complementing the commercial insurance market, are potentially tied to international agreements, etc.

2.4.1 Insurability

Their rarely disputed domain is export credit for the middle term, i.e. between two and five years, and long term between 5 years and longer. Most commercial credit insurers do not serve these terms.

For short term – in the ECA world defined as shorter than 2 years – ECA can insure those risks that are shun by the private sector. This is mainly the case for risks and countries that are too exposed to perils of trade. Some ECAs require the presentation of two negative replies from private insurers. ECAs try to stay on good terms with domestic private insurers concerning insurability. Insurability varies with time and circumstances.

Short-term business must be much leaner in operations than middle- to long-term business. Cost efficiency translates in more comprehensive cover often for pools of risk and less for single risks. There are more so-called framework cover and *whole turnover polices*.

It goes without saying that the general principles of an insurance apply (see list on page 31), e.g. fortuitous event, homogeneous cover amounts, potential statistical estimation etc. For small insurer with very large customers there may be a problem with regard to a large single risk. Generally, one single exposure, or exposure minus insurance premium, should not exceed 15–25% of the insurer's equity or risk bearing capital. Such provisions also apply to banks within the Basel capital framework (BCBS 2018): "The large exposures framework sets prudent limits to large exposures, whereby a large exposure is defined as the sum of all exposures of a bank to a single counterparty that are equal to or above 10% of its Tier 1 capital. The limit is set at 25% of Tier 1 capital".

2.4.2 Eligibility

Governments of state define the potential beneficiary of export credit support on the basis of directives or laws etc. In addition OECD members participate in the agreement that defines also eligibility.

First, applicants should be domestic supplier or lender, mainly corporations and seldom private persons. There must be an export transaction with a minimum domestic content or with a so-called national interest. Traditionally, the purpose of ECAs was also to support work places. Here the ECA world is divided into these two philosophies. Domestic content can be a minimum of 50% of value added of the export value. *Export value* must not be confused with *contract value* that might include local costs. For middle- to long-term cover an advance payment of 15% of the export value is mandatory in the OECD framework.

Figure 2.4 depicts a situation where there is a foreign agent or an own subsidiary by which the goods are delivered. The foreign subsidiary is not eligible for cover. One can think of a pharmaceutical company dispatching drugs. With an "if-and-when" clause the domestic supplier's payment is contingent on the payments to

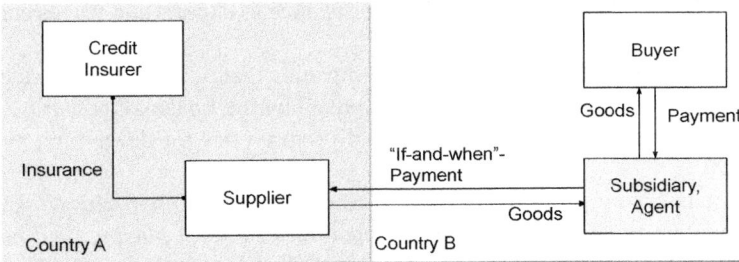

Fig. 2.4 Export via foreign agent. By means of a strong clause it is possible to shift the risk to the domestic exporter and make the situation insurable

the agent. Technically this can be achieved by assigning the receivable upon non-payment to the supplier. The question arises naturally what happens if the subsidiary is paid but the proceeds cannot be transferred? Now the risk is the own subsidiary and not the buyer.

Some kind of goods may not be eligible for cover, e.g. military equipment and agricultural commodities. Some goods like ships and aircraft or infrastructure projects are governed by additional rules. Operational lease where the leased good is not sold at the end cannot be covered, whereas financial lease can. The distinction between operational and financial can be hard to assess.

With respect to countries there are both limitations generally and concerning tenors. There are two categories whereby richer countries are more restricted in tenors. Then there is a special case with the European Union.

Moreover, there are sanctions by the own government and by foreign states. In the first case it is obvious not to insure and this may not be possible because an export permit will not be issued by the government's export controls. The second situation may be more of a game theoretical issue. Foreign sanctions may also be a credit event, especially when the acceptance of repayment is not possible anymore.

2.5   Rationale for Export Support

Classical liberals, i.e. the follower of the Scottish forebear, liked to think that *laissez-faire* is the best economic policy. Government intervention is only acceptable if there are massive distortions or problems in the market. Now there is evidence that export credit agencies, on state account or as corporations belonging to the state, have survived quite a long stretch. There has been enough time to come up with six well known rationales for support. We follow Gianturco (2001, 35) closely in the arguments for economic support.

First, it is a response to imperfections in the capital market that distort assistance to exports.

Second, it is a market deficiency that biases middle- to long-term credit and favours short-term lending.

Third, there is a close linkage between assistance to exports and wages and fiscal policies.

Fourth, it is a help for new and small companies that develop new products also for new markets. These stakeholders are shunned by the financial industry.

Fifth, ECA support is a surrogate for aid programmes for developing and poor countries.

Sixth, it is a way to meet the competition offered by other nation's ECA. In order to contain predatory behaviour the creation of a *level playing field* becomes very important. Now this argument hinges on the fact that the same result could be achieved if all nations would desist from using ECA and providing export support.

From game theory it is known that the strategy "tit for tat" is often the most successful.

It is not really a secret that economies compete with one another and that export means expansion, improvement and enrichment for an economy. Therefore, the least convincing argument, i.e. sixth, is the most compelling argument.

During the debate of reauthorisation of the US Exim Bank in 2015 we could read arguments, from politicians mainly, like these:

> Critics argue that the bank isn't necessary. They claim its main beneficiaries are big companies and that its offerings largely amount to corporate welfare and distort the export marketplace. And, they say, many of the small companies the bank claims to have helped are actually big.

But also academia has investigated the issue. One research finds (Agarwal and Wang 2017): "Our results cast doubt on the ubiquitously positive claims made by the [US Exim] Bank and its supporters, yet also provide policy lessons for countries that are either in the inception stages of establishing their own ECAs or are now placing greater importance on ECA financing in encouraging exports". Another study (Freund 2016) claims: "Overall, the results show that EXIM financing leads to a 3–6 percent increase in trade. The result that only lags, and not leads, are significant suggests this is a causal effect".

The rational for export support comes down to the worldview: how does economy work and what are the goals of all human endeavours. Pure economics will never be in a position to answer such questions alone.

But, it is a general trend that ECAs try to extend their offer with new products, enlarge the customer base and try to grow, at least in the public perception.

2.6   Moral Hazard

There are behavioural risks of applicants inherent in insurance. The most obvious risk is that the insured relents in his or her endeavour to contain arising risks due to the fact that there is a cover that indemnifies a potential loss. The insured's efforts are not well observable and become evident, if ever, after the loss. Thus insurance creates disincentives to take care. Among the insured there may be big differences in behaviour.

The astute insurance company tries to minimise this situation. But it cannot be remedied only by higher premium margins. An applicant who is close to the brink does not care about the amount of the premium because in case of a negative business outcome the company is bankrupt and the problem is then with the creditors. Those willing to pay a high premium can be suspected of being "bad" obligors.

Anticipating the result of the discussion we posit that banks do not mainly price for risk but rather effect a credit rationing. This result is due to Stiglitz and Weiss (1981) in their often discussed publication.

2.6.1 Asymmetric Information and Signalling

The insurance company starts with an average loss experience and cannot easily discern the good from the bad insureds. Such an average penalises the good risks and favours the bad ones. Because for the latter the insurance is cheap there is a risk of *adverse selection*. Insurance company and applicants have asymmetric information.

For the insurance company it is very onerous and expensive to investigate the quality of the applicant. If the applicant is able and willing to provide reliable information in order to discriminate from the average, this should be beneficial for both parties.

2.6.2 Deductibles and Contract Design

In order to keep the interest of insurance company and insured aligned there are several contract designs that are used. The most common is a deductible or first loss position. The insured should participate to the loss. The most important design parameter is the extent of the deductible. If it should be substantial and effective, it needs to be commensurate with the possibilities to mitigate the loss.

In middle- to long-term credit insurance, deductibles are rather high. The OECD arrangement foresees an advance payment of 15%, and thus a cover of 85% of the export value is left for cover. With a deductible the insured must be enough resilient to survive the own losses. Suppliers normally know their buyers and have potentially a yearlong relation. Therefore suppliers may be in a position to exert some influence. Banks on the other side have some potential to harm buyers. Buyers will much less enter into legal battles with a bank than with suppliers because of the huge legal capacity of banks and the fact that bank products are better enforceable than sales contracts.

Under a credit insurance policy the insured has some important duties. Specifically the supplier has more duties than a lending institution.

2.6.3   Collateral

Posting collateral is a typical bank attitude. Collateral does not lead automatically to lower premia. Often it is only a prerequisite for cover. Studies from bank lending show that spreads are higher with general loans that supply collateral.

There are different types of security interests which can be applied by lenders depending on the collateral. The major forms of creating a charge on assets are:

- pledge,
- hypothecation,
- lien,
- mortgage and
- assignment.

The differences are with the status of possession, the assets charged, e.g. current, movable, fixed etc., legal framework and the like.

With a pledge the lender holds the actual possession and either returns them or sells them off in order to recover the outstanding principal and the interest.

Hypothecation is used when the charge is on movable assets, but the possession of such movable security stays with the borrower. In an event of default, the lender must take the possession or seize the asset before he or she can recover the principal and interest.

Under a lien, the lender can hold up the asset, e.g. property or machinery, against the credit. The lender is not allowed to sell the asset. The lender can retain the security until the loan amount is discharged.

With a mortgage the legal ownership of the asset can be transferred to the lender if the borrower defaults. The obligor remains in the possession of the asset. Mortgages are mainly used for immovable assets that are permanently fixed to the earth.

Assignments create charges on the assets or proceeds thereof held in the books. Examples of assignment include proceeds of credit insurance policies and receivables. Assignment must not be confused with transfer of title where a complete substitution of one party by the transferee takes place. Therefore, assignment of proceeds of a contract is not the same as assignment of a contract.

It shows that interest rates on secured loans are higher than on unsecured loans, confirming that guarantees are not sufficient to completely offset their higher riskiness (Pozzolo 2002).

Then there is also the fact that monetising the collateral can be very time consuming and onerous.

2.7   Export Credit and Investment Insurance

On a very high level the two notions can be equated to investing in a foreign loan or bond versus investing in foreign equity. While the first produces, or should produce, fixed repayments in time, the latter has, besides dividends, no certain proceeds as it is in the nature of equity as risk capital of a venture. Therefore, investment insurance will cover only political and no commercial risk. The political events are three (Stephens 1999, 26):

- confiscation, expropriation and nationalisation,
- losses from war and civil war (political violence) and
- inability to convert, transfer and remit profits and dividends.

Often the business of investment insurance is separate from export credit insurance, either in different agencies or at least in different divisions. Just to name two: in the USA there is the US International Development Finance Corporation (former Overseas Private Investment Corporation OPIC) next to the US Exim Bank, and in Germany the C&L Deutsche Revision doing investment insurances on behalf of the Federal Republic. The volumes are also much smaller with investments. And most prominent, investment insurances do not fall into the *OECD Arrangement* and can thus be priced at own judgement.

The subject matter of political risk insurance need not be only equity (see Fig. 2.5). It may cover:

- equity,
- loans,
- inventories,
- plant and equipment and
- permission and licence cancellation.

Investment insurance is fortified by bilateral agreements between states called *Bilateral Investment Treaties*. There are more than 2000 such agreements in force. By definition a BIT is: "An agreement made between two countries containing reciprocal undertakings for the promotion and protection of private investments

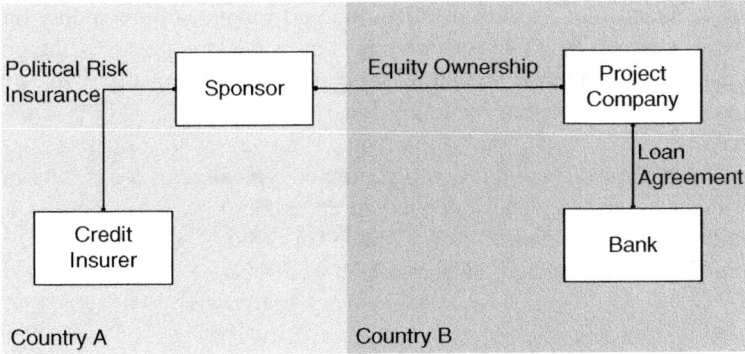

Fig. 2.5 Investment insurance scheme. Here the cover concerns an equity ownership of a sponsor in a project abroad. Bilateral investment treaties may mitigate the political risk

made by nationals of the signatories in each other's territories. These agreements establish the terms and conditions under which nationals of one country invest in the other, including their rights and protections". UNCTAD[1] gives the details with every agreement published. With these treaties an investment insurance indirectly ties in the government.

For our purpose of pricing export credit we cannot learn a lot from this branch because it is not systematic. For further insight see Gianturco (2001, 98–106).

2.8   Guarantee and Insurance

export credit agencies are organised in different forms. We know three common patterns:

- on state account,
- by a state owned insurance corporation or
- by a state owned bank corporation.

Departments of government often outsource operations of the credit insurance business to either commercial insurances or mandated management companies. In the first case the state may issues reinsurance policies. Because insurance companies and banks are highly regulated and locally licensed they can issue only certain type of instruments, e.g. policies, guarantees or letters of credit. US banks generally do not issue bank guarantees but use standby letters of credit that are intended to fulfil the same function. Therefore we understand by insurance and guarantee a certain *pattern*.

2.8.1   Nature of Guarantee and Insurance Policy

In English law, a guarantee is a contract whereby the person (the guarantor) enters into an agreement to pay a debt or effect the performance of some duty by a third person who is primarily liable for that payment or performance. For the guarantee there must exist a principal subsiding obligation. In ancient times the guarantor expressed his or her consent by letter, thus letter of credit. This is a traditional guarantee or surety interest. Such a guarantee is a *secondary* obligation.

But in international trade finance, a guarantee typically has a different meaning. It rather means a *primary* and independent undertaking by the guarantor to pay if the conditions of the guarantee are satisfied. This kind of guarantee is prefaced by the words "bank" or "demand" (Czarnocki et al. 2020).

---

[1] https://investmentpolicy.unctad.org/international-investment-agreements.

When comparing insurance and guarantees we mean the traditional notion. When speaking of contract guarantees we mean *bank guarantees*.

An insurance contract is known as policy ("promise") that promises the insurance company to compensate the insured in the event of a covered loss for a premium. The insured must have an insured interest. This kind of contract belongs to the so-called aleatory agreements. Long established insurance principles encompass the following (Wikipedia contributors 2020):

1. large number of similar exposure units,
2. definite loss, the loss takes place at a known time, in a known place and from a known cause,
3. accidental loss, the event that constitutes the trigger of a claim should be fortuitous or at least outside the control of the beneficiary of the insurance,
4. substantial loss,
5. affordable premium,
6. calculable loss and
7. limited risk of catastrophically large losses.

Insurance premia need to cover both the expected cost of losses plus the cost of issuing and administering the policy, adjusting losses and supplying the capital needed to reasonably assure that the insurer will be able to pay claims (Wikipedia contributors 2020).

Insurable losses are ideally independent and non-catastrophic, meaning that the losses do not happen all at once and individual losses are not severe enough to bankrupt the insurer. Insurers may prefer to limit their exposure to a loss from a single event to some small portion of their capital base, on the order of 5%.

In the event of loss the insured interest as contract is subrogated to the insurance company. *Subrogation* is the assumption by a third party, e.g. such as an insurance company, of another party's legal right to collect a debt or damages.

Guarantees or policies, viz. their rights, can be *assigned*. This means that these contracts as a whole or their proceeds may be transferred to the assignee. For insurance policies an assignment of the right to recover under the policy is more appropriate than an assignment of the policy itself. The prerequisite is that there is no express prohibition or restriction on the assignment of any right or interest under the terms of the policy. The assignment is documented in an agreement.

Export credit support is given by guarantees or insurance products in the case of so-called pure cover providers. Direct lenders, on the other hand, incorporate the credit risk support in a loan or a credit security.

It is generally assumed, also in the OECD minimum premium system, that a guarantee is more valuable than an insurance contract.

2.8.2 Commonalities

From an economic point of view there are several financial instruments delivering a very similar credit risk outcome. These are:

- guarantees,
- insurance policies and
- credit default swaps.

They are instances of what Roman law names as *aleatory contract*. Kagan (2020) defines: "An aleatory contract is an agreement whereby the parties involved do not have to perform a particular action until a specific, triggering event occurs. Events are those that cannot be controlled by either party, such as natural disasters and death".

Or, alternatively (Gigerenzer et al. 1989, 3): "Jurists defined such agreements as the exchange of a present and certain value for a future, uncertain one – staking a gamble, purchasing an annuity, taking out an insurance policy, bidding on next year's wheat crop, or buying the next cast of a fisherman's net".

The notion of *uncertainty* and *randomness* is at the very heart of the insurance principle.

The credit default swap as an instrument is not analysed any further. As a traded market instrument it will prove important to benchmark pricing of credit support instruments, i.e. insurances and guarantees.

In essence, a guarantee pays for the debt of a third party in case the latter is delinquent on his or her obligation. The insurance indemnifies the loss on an insured interest. If the insured interest is a debt and the insured risk is non-payment, then the two instruments have almost the identical effects.

2.8.3 Differences

Besides these commonalities there are important legal and regulatory differences. Guarantees are issued by banks, insurances or other natural or incorporated persons. Insurance policies are only allowed to insurance companies, or even more restrictive, certain insurance policies are allowed only to special insurance companies. Credit default swaps are typical market products, i.e. credit derivatives, issued by banks or markets and bought by both speculators and end users.

Insurance policies are treated differently from guarantees in the financial reporting. Financial guarantees may have to be marked to market.

Guarantees are agreed by two parties with a distinct beneficiary, very much alike to life insurance, and a distinct payout.

Export credit insurance is most akin to property and casualty insurance. Here the protection conveyed by the policy is at maximum the damage experienced by the policy holder and not a fixed payout. Schematically,

$$\mathbb{C}_G(P_1, P_2, B, X, \pi, \ldots) \Longleftrightarrow \mathbb{C}_{LI}(P_1, P_2, B, X, \pi, \ldots) \tag{2.1}$$

$$\mathbb{C}_{CI}(P_1, P_2, -, \min(X, D), \pi, \ldots) \Longleftrightarrow \mathbb{C}_{P\&CI}(P_1, P_2, -, \min(X, D), \pi, \ldots), \tag{2.2}$$

where $\mathbb{C}$ stands for a contract, the index for either guarantee, life insurance, credit insurance or a property/casualty insurance. P_1 and P_2 are the parties to the contract, B is a beneficiary and X or $\min(X, D)$ is the payout, either fixed or capped by the effective damage D. The beneficiary could be one of the parties. The premium or commission is π.

This scheme, summarised in Fig. 2.6, could help people more familiar with banking to learn from the analogy. It may help to sharpen the attention for the fact that it makes a difference whether an export support is an insurance or a guarantee. A main difference is the payment of the two instruments, its timing. While guarantees, especially bank guarantees, may pay on demand, insurance claims need to be assessed and representations have to be reconsidered. Guarantees live by the motto: "pay now, argue later".

A guarantee is best suited in a tri-party constellation, whereas an insurance is used in a bilateral agreement (Fig. 2.6).

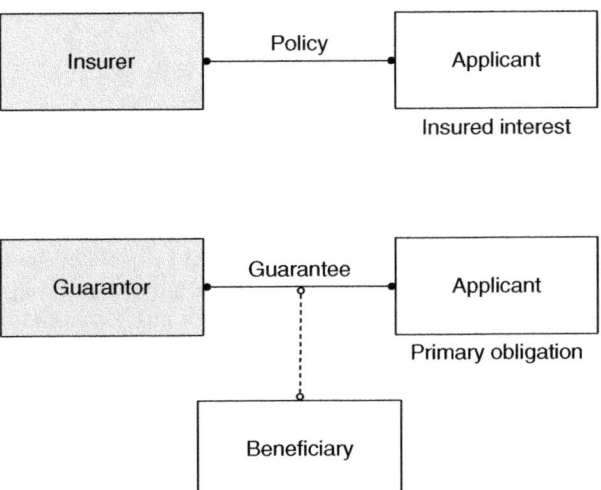

Fig. 2.6 Schematic different between policy and guarantee. The beneficiary may be the applicant

2.9   Banks' Export Products

Banks are always, up to now at least, involved in exports. The least they would do is
to remit money from a buyer's account to a supplier's account. This is assumed in the
following implicitly. Exporting on credit terms without a bank means documenting
the payments with bills of exchange, drafts, promissory notes or similar financial
documents. But even here the banks are used for collection of the money.

The reader will discover again and again that everything revolves around one
party to believe and trust and the other to promise. The word "policy" in insurance
policy stems from Latin word *policere* that means to promise.

Banks can intermediate trust because they know their customers and they know
the other banks. Therefore, they can bridge the risky relationship between the
supplier and buyer as depicted in Fig. 2.7. This is a massively simplifying and raising
efficiency in credit.

2.9.1   Documentary Collection

With documentary collections banks act as intermediaries to the exchange of
payment for title documents. Banks are not obliged to pay as is the case under a
documentary credit. Thus, collection is just a *service* of financial institutions. Banks
are no party to the risks.

The commercial documents consist of invoices, bills of lading and similar,
documents of title or other qualifying documents.

There are two common conditions for release of the documents:

• documents against payment ("sight collection") and
• documents against acceptance ("term collection").

In the first case, commercial documents may be released only if the buyer makes
payment in exchange for documents. Here, the domestic supplier is exposed to the
credit risk of the foreign buyer and the political risk of the buyer's country.

In the second case, documents may be released only if the buyer *accepts* the
accompanying bill-of-exchange or promissory note, thereby assuming an obligation
to pay at a specified future date. Here, the supplier is also exposed to the credit risk
of the foreign buyer and the political risk of the buyer's country.

Fig. 2.7 Banks intermediate
trust, because they know each
other and their own
customers. Thus export
partner F and T need not
know and assess each other

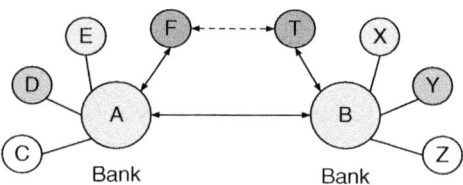

Documentary collection is of course more economical and less complicated than letters of credit for the applicant, but riskier for the supplier due to the potentially weak creditworthiness of the buyer. The credit risk stays with the supplier unless the buyer's bank has avalised, i.e. guaranteed, the bill.

Documentary collection is used when supplier and buyer have a well established relationship, there is no doubt about the buyer's willingness or ability to pay and the political and economic conditions of the buyer's country are stable with no restrictive foreign exchange controls.

2.9.2 Letters of Credit and Documentary Credit

A letters of credit is a method of payment commonly used in international trade, whereby the issuing bank promises to pay the supplier, provided the supplier complies with the terms and conditions of the instrument. A letter of credit is referred to, especially outside the United States, as a *documentary credit*.

Irrevocable letters of credit cannot be cancelled or amended without the consent of all involved parties, i.e. supplier, buyer and the issuing bank. The letter can be "confirmed" by a domestic bank (see Fig. 2.8). This means that the supplier will be paid by the confirming bank which in turn will seek payment from the issuing bank. Thus credit risk and country risk can be mitigated because the supplier can rely upon the creditworthiness of the confirming and issuing bank in lieu of the creditworthiness of the buyer.

Analogously to the documentary collection, there are two and more ways of handling the presentation of the documents. Either payment upon presentation of certain documents (sight) or payment at a future date after documents has been accepted under the letter of credit (term). Such term letters of credit can be discounted after acceptance of bills of exchange thereby making liquidity available.

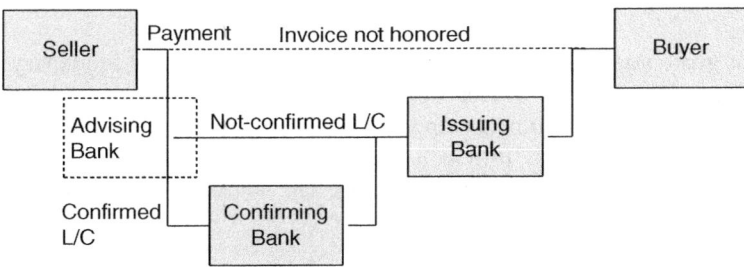

Fig. 2.8 The guarantee structure of standby letters of credit. Standby means that it is a secondary payment mechanism, i.e. the buyer did not pay according to terms. The advising or notifying bank may be the same institute doing the confirmation

Documentary credit can comprise different types of credit:

- sight credit,
- deferred payment credit,
- acceptance credit with bill of exchange,
- red clause credit with advances,
- transferable credit, for sub-suppliers,
- revolving credit for partial deliveries etc.

The guarantor's obligation may be independent of the existence or continuation of a contractual relationship between the principal and the beneficiary. Then the guarantee is abstract or non-accessory or a primary obligation.

The underlying document is often a *bill of exchange*. It may be used both in documentary collections and in documentary credit. With documentary collections, the bill of exchange can be used only when the acceptance is stipulated, whereas in documentary credit it can be used in almost all kinds of credit except when deferred payment is chosen (time draft). It can be drawn on a bank that is specified in the credit. It does not give additional payment guarantee to the beneficiary.

An alternative to drawing on the bank is the *avalised bill of exchange*. Here the drawee is the buyer and debtor who has his or her bank stamping the words "pour aval" on the reverse of the accepted bill and duly signing it. The effect is almost identical with a guarantee. This bill may be discounted. The margin is often much lower than that with a letter of credit but still in the proximity of 1–2 % p.a.

There are initiatives to simplify or to modernise documentary credits by introducing the so-called Bank Payment Obligation. The advertising says: "The BPO delivers equivalent business benefits to those previously obtained through a commercial letter of credit, while eliminating the drawbacks of manual processing associated with traditional trade finance".

2.9.3   Payment Guarantee and Standby Letter of Credit

Payment guarantees and especially standby letters of credit are secondary obligations. This means that the buyer should have paid according to the commercial contract but has not. Contingent upon this non-payment the issuing bank or the confirming bank will pay, provided the supplier complies with the terms and conditions of this guarantee or letter of credit. The wording of a payment guarantee may read as follows:

> We, XYZ Bank, irrevocably guarantee that we pay you, upon first demand, irrespective of the validity and legal effect of the aforementioned contract and waiving any objections or defence arising from the same, any amount X up to a maximum of Y upon presentation of your duly signed demand for payment including a declaration from you that you (i) have supplied the object of the aforementioned contract to the Purchaser in compliance with the contract, and (ii) have received no payment from the Purchaser upon maturity for the amount provided for by this guarantee.

Table 2.1 Typical wording of a standby letter of credit

Issued by:	Issuing Bank
Applicant:	Applicant
Beneficiary:	Beneficiary
Advising bank:	Advising Bank
Instructions to Advising bank:	Notify the Beneficiary we issue the following **Standby letter of credit**.

For account of our customer, the Applicant, we hereby establish and issue our irrevocable standby letter of credit in favour of the Beneficiary, for an amount not to exceed [currency and amount].

Credit is available against presentation of the following documents:

1. Beneficiary's demand in writing purportedly signed stating:

> A. *The amount drawn is equal to a payment due to us in respect of merchandise and services provided by us to the Applicant.*
>
> B. *The Applicant has failed to fulfil its obligation to us in respect of our terms of sale. An attached copy of our commercial invoices, billed by us on an open account basis, remain unpaid [. . .] days after the dates of the invoices.*
>
> C. *The amount of this drawing will be applied against indebtedness recorded on our books in the name of the Applicant.*

2. A draft (bill of exchange) and

3. A signed copy of the invoices referred to in 1.B which are dated at least [. . .] days prior to the date of the drafts.

All banking charges outside of the country of the Issuing bank are for the account of the Beneficiary.

Partial drawings are permitted.

Confirmation: [with/without].

This standby letter of credit is effective immediately and expires on [date] at the counters of Issuing bank in [location].

Four parties are mentioned, a supplier as beneficiary, a buyer as applicant and the two respective banks. With the demand for payment two additional documents must be attached: a draft (bill of exchange) and the invoice. The LOC is a payment mechanism and not a payment instrument like a draft

Table 2.1 on page 37 shows a template of a SLOC, the common abbreviation. It stipulates what documents and titles must be provided. Here the following have to be presented:

1. a written demand,
2. a bill of exchange or draft and
3. the signed copy of the invoice.

From the said it can be concluded that the term "letter of credit" can be confusing and could easily be avoided.

Since the standby letter of credit can be valid for years (evergreen clause) it reduces the cost of separate letters of credit for each transaction with a certain client.

2.9.4 Loans, Facilities and Lines of Credit

Credit agreements are part of contract law. This means that there are ample possibilities of structuring loan agreements, only limited by banking regulations or codes of obligation. Attempts to harmonise contract law in the EU, albeit its Roman law basis, were not very successful. This is just to underline the fact that there is a vast variability in loan agreements globally.

Market-traded debt, e.g. notes, bonds etc., is on the contrary strongly standardised. The middle-ground is filled with syndicated loans that may be transferred into collateralised loan obligations. Tirole (2009, 103), a Nobel laureate, writes: "Loan agreements are a source of confusion and misunderstanding to many bankers". The main objectives of the parties to the loan are to be found in Table 2.2.

Table 2.6 on page 58 may serve as a table of content of a sophisticated loan agreement. It tries to define in a self-contained manner the rules and expectations, control mechanisms and facts surrounding the credit.

A *loan* in finance is the lending of money by one or more individuals, organisations, or other entities to other individuals, organisations etc. Lending means to give for temporary use on condition that the same or its equivalent be returned with interests. The loan is accompanied by a document evidencing the debt.

Table 2.2 Principal objectives in negotiating a loan (CGAP 2006, 3)

Borrower	Lender
• Ensure funds will be available when needed. • Obtain funds at the most advantageous financial terms possible e.g., the lowest interest rate possible. • Provide for the repayment of the loan over a period that will not place an undue burden on it. • Ensure it can comply with all other terms of the loan agreement (such as financial covenants) in its ordinary course of business.	• Set out the conditions under which it will be obligated to disburse funds under the loan agreement. • Enable it to monitor the borrower's financial situation and, when necessary, to take remedial action if the borrower experiences serious financial difficulties. • Provide itself with a legally enforceable claim to its funds, or access to other remedies, if the borrower defaults.

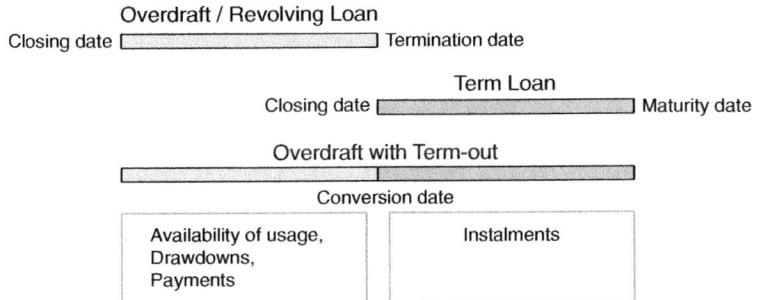

Fig. 2.9 Loan schemes. An overdraft with an exercised term-out option is in effect a series of two different types of loan. The pricing and handling of the two loans are significantly different

There are two archetypes of loans (Wikipedia contributors 2019), viz.:

- *term loans*, which are repaid in set instalments over the term or
- *revolving loans* or *overdrafts* where up to a maximum amount of money can be drawn and used at any time, and interest is paid periodically on the drawn amount.

The time from commit date to termination date of an overdraft is called *availability period* or *commitment period*. Syndicated revolving loans may contain a so-called swing line as a sub-limit whereby a lender makes a very short term, not more than 5 days, loan, in smaller amounts, on shorter notice, and with a higher interest rate than is otherwise available for revolving credit loans (Fig. 2.9).

Overdrafts most often contain the provision called *term-out option*. The clause may read: "The borrower may convert the outstanding overdraft to a term loan effective on (...) provided that the borrower shall have delivered (...) a written notice electing the conversion prior to the termination date and no event of default exists on the notification date or on the termination date". The term-out will allow the borrower to convert borrowings into a term loan at a given *conversion date*. Under the option, borrowers may take what is outstanding under the facility and pay it off according to a predetermined repayment schedule. Often the spreads ratchet up if the term-out option is exercised.

In our export context we start with *credit*, a situation where one party, the creditor, provides money or resources to another party, the debtor, and the second party does not reimburse the first party immediately but promises either to repay or to return those resources at a later date.

While the supplier extends credit to the buyer as agreed in the commercial contract, the bank may grant credit as a term loan to the buyer or the buyer's bank. In addition the bank or financial institution may open an overdraft account for the purpose of pre-financing the export, i.e. as a *working capital facility* or *packing credit*. In export finance there are most often *collateral* requirements to mitigate risk and to organise recourse.

2.9.5   Pre-export Payment Facility and Packing Credit

The pre-export payment facility may be used to support exports of long-lead manufactured capital goods that necessitate extensive customisation. Such transactions
often require the foreign buyer to make periodic partial payments to a supplier
during the manufacturing period, i.e. prior to shipment of the finished product. Such
a facility enables the supplier to finance some of its production costs before final
delivery in accordance with the payment terms in the commercial contract with
the foreign buyer. This facility complements the long-term financing to the foreign
buyer. See Fig. 2.10.

Obviously, there need to be an irrevocable commercial contract. A so-called
packing credit is provided to exporters or sellers to finance the goods' procurement
before shipment. The domestic bank will grant a loan against the deposit of a
documentary credit as the collateral. The advance is provided to purchase raw
materials, process, manufacture, pack, market and transport the required goods and
services. The borrower is required to present documents to the lender before the
latest shipment and expiry date. Should he fail to do so as agreed, then the bank can
ask for refund (Luk 2011, 122). In some countries it is possible to share a packing
credit say of a merchant or export house with its manufacturers and sub-suppliers.

In a *red clause credit* the applicant instructs the issuing bank of a documentary
credit to include clauses, in early times typed in red, to finance the beneficiary, i.e.
supplier, to some percentages of the credit before shipment. In an undertaking the
supplier promises to ship the goods in accordance with the documentary credit. The
financing bank has a right of recourse to the instructing bank for the outstanding
plus interest. Yet another variant is to have the supplier draw some bills of exchange
on the bank of the buyer together with an undertaking to deliver the goods (Luk
2011, 224).

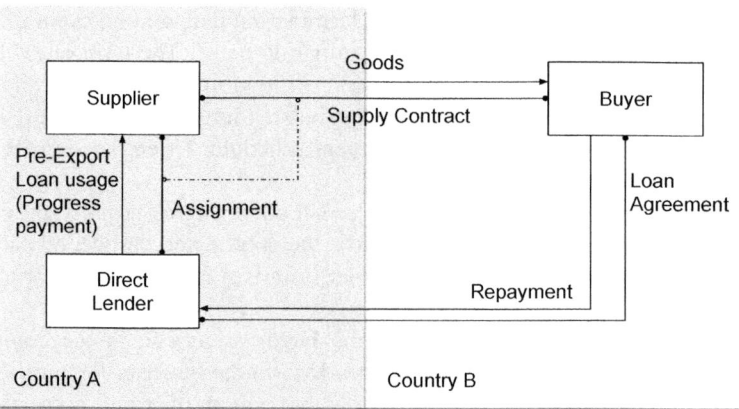

Fig. 2.10 Schema of pre-export payments. The credit insurer as direct lender advances progress
payments debiting the loan with the buyer

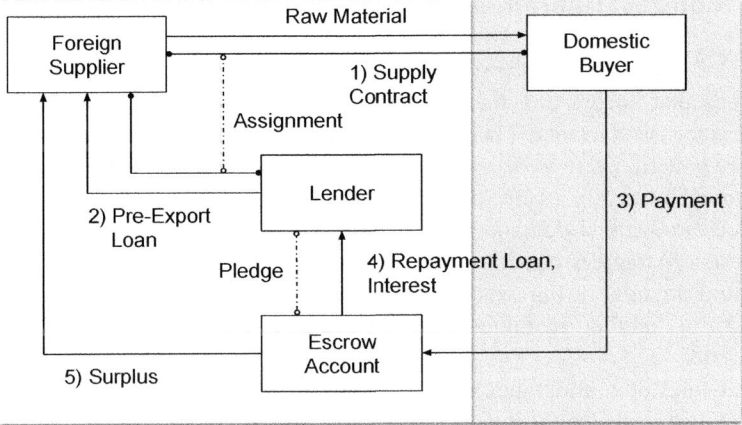

Fig. 2.11 Pre-export financing for import, here typically for buying crude oil

A pre-export credit is also used for import, especially of raw material. Some countries have strategic programmes for buying vital goods and have their Export–Import Bank supporting it. Figure 2.11 shows the typical structure.

2.9.6 Working Capital Loan

Working capital is a term from accounting meaning the difference from current assets minus current liabilities, or simply net current assets. It is equivalent to *operating liquidity*. Financing liquidity is expensive because it can indicate a bad management, seasonality of the business or extraordinary situations, e.g. an extraordinarily large contract or strong expansion of business. Most borrowers must post assets as collateral for such credits. Working capital loans for exporters can use a guarantee from an ECA in order to induce domestic lenders to include export-related collateral in the loan, e.g. materials, equipment, supplies, labour and other inputs to fulfil export orders and to profit from higher advance rates. Materials would be advanced to 75% instead of 25%, work-in-progress inventory would become eligible as collateral etc.

Such a facility can be established both specifically for a single export transaction and as a multi-transactions facility where financing for several transactions may be advanced.

The combination of working capital loan and buyer credit is very similar to the situation of an overdraft with term-out as depicted in Fig. 2.9. The difference is that there is a change in debtor with the first scheme, and the cover rate might differ. With construction works or infrastructure projects the latter is used in combination with advance payment guarantees (see next chapter).

2.9.7   Contract Guarantees

In trade of capital goods there have been traditionally several types of contract guarantees that accompany the life of the sales contract fulfilment, from tender to the expiry of warranty. These are specific products that follow of course the guarantee pattern, i.e. two parties and one beneficiary (see Fig. 2.12). The guarantees are intended to testify to the principal's ability to carry out the contract. These guarantees are bank or demand guarantees, see Sect. 2.8.1.

Contract guarantees bear the risk of being unduly called for other reasons than contractual defaults of the exporter ("unfair calling"). Some credit insurers cover such risks by another guarantee where the beneficiary can be the exporter or the issuing bank.

A drawback of contract guarantees is the fact that the issuing institutions, mainly banks, require *cash collateral* from the applicant. This strains suppliers because often needed *liquidity* is reduced. By means of a counter-guarantee from yet another party, e.g. an ECA, such requirements can be alleviated.

Here is a comprehensive list of guarantees, also called bonds, that are used in export. The beneficiary is the buyer:

- Bid bond/tender guarantee: The purpose is to cover the risk that the company submitting a tender will not abide by its offer or deliver the required performance.
- Advance payment guarantee: Issued when the buyer pays the contract price or part thereof in advance and requires security for a refund if the goods are not delivered, or if the delivery is not in accordance with the contract. The guarantee amount can reduce with the value of each partial shipment following

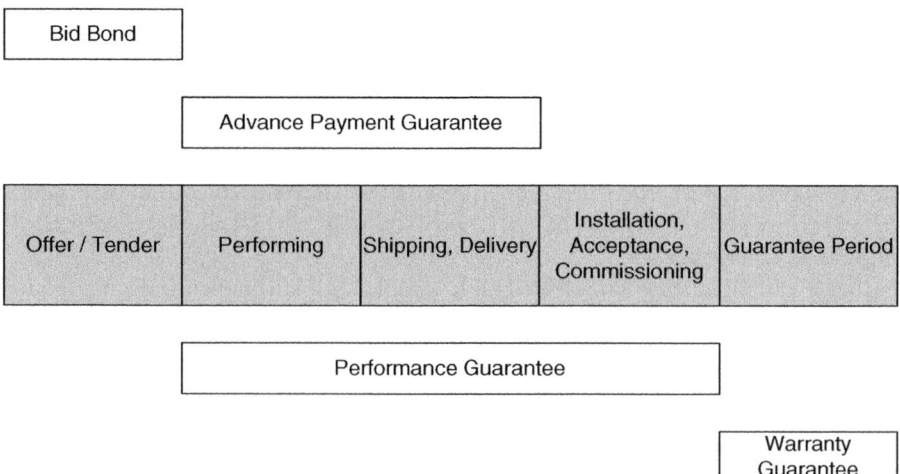

Fig. 2.12 Usage of contract bonds in trade. One bond or guarantee is returned on issuance of a new guarantee

unconditional acceptance of the qualifying documents. ECAs do insure this kind of credit risk only in conjunction with other covers.

- Performance guarantee: It secures the supplier's contractual obligations.
- Warranty guarantee: It covers the buyer after goods are delivered or work is completed during any agreed warranty period.
- Retention money guarantee: It ensures that the correct repayments are made if the supplier fails to meet its contractual obligations during the warranty period.

Retention guarantees are also used in construction contracts where *interim payments* (milestone payments) are executed on presentation of certificates for work done by the contractor. Simultaneously, a retention guarantee is issued by the contractor's bank at the benefit of the employer.

2.9.8   Receivables Discounting

Receivables discounting or monetisation is the purchase of *open account* receivables by a bank that provides cashflow support to clients selling on open account terms. The seller may act as collector in order that the buyer need not to be informed.

Monetisation may reduce credit exposure and concentrations to certain counterparties to enable additional business flows.

Besides selling the assets, i.e. receivables, these may alternatively be used as collateral for a loan.

Technically, a *Receivables Purchase Agreement* RPA is stipulated between the seller and the finance provider, e.g. bank. A certified copy of the invoice is sent to the bank. Under the agreement, the seller provides the bank with an assignment of rights to the receivables being financed. Depending on the terms of the underlying agreement, a notice of assignment may be provided to the buyer.

Receivables discounting is structured as a *true sale*, and the rights and title to the receivables are transferred to the bank by means of an assignment, transfer of title, or by filing a security interest. The seller's expectation is that with deals without recourse the receivables are removed from the balance sheet.

Similar in mechanics, different in underlying payment obligation is *forfeiting*. The debt is usually embodied in some form of legal instrument distinct from the commercial transaction that gave rise to it.

These activities sail under the name of *supply chain finance*.

2.9.9   Considerations

Theorists (Stulz 2015) claim that a well-governed bank will have the processes to identify the optimal amount of risk that maximises bank value subject to regulatory and legal constraints and then to ensure that the actual risk of the bank is close to this optimal position.

Some decades ago the introduction of new products has massively changed banking through buying investment banks, the quest for very high profitability and several ensuing crisis. Therefore regulation has put strong emphasis on managing risk and having appropriate levels of capital. The scarce capital resource has lead internally to steer the business. Trade finance could not stay unscathed. Some banks have decided to become more of a risk trader than a risk taker as there are possibilities to contract risks and lay them off in the market or with partners.

Commercial bank's trade finance divisions have to compete not only with other external financial institutes but also with other internal service providers. The pressure to transfer risk is evident, and besides the market that is complicated to tap the most obvious choice is to transfer risk to credit insurers.

As we have seen from the previous trade finance is a very traditional paper or document based business. Commercial banks and associated players are not really famous for efficient systems and sophisticated processing. Therefore, such shortcomings lead to attempt to unload work to the credit insurer. Banks exert pressure on ECAs and credit insurers.

The *FinTech industry* has not yet got into a position to supplant older industries. But there is hope that things will be transformed into the direction of more efficiency. This means that credit insurers should get ready to become more digitised. But export credit agencies are often hampered by an arcane procurement regulation.

2.10   Credit Insurance: Post-shipment Products

The following description is rather short geared towards gaining enough understanding for pricing.

The credit insurance products are subdivided by phases of the export life cycle. Two phases are most often cited, i.e. pre-shipment and post-shipment. Reality is more complex than that (see Fig. 2.13), one ought to think of project finance, construction work or long-lead manufactured capital goods. Shipment may be

Fig. 2.13 The different phases of an export contract. The commercial contract extends beyond the post-shipment phase if we consider the warranty guarantee. The grace period is shown for infrastructure projects that cannot immediately after commissioning begin to repay the credit

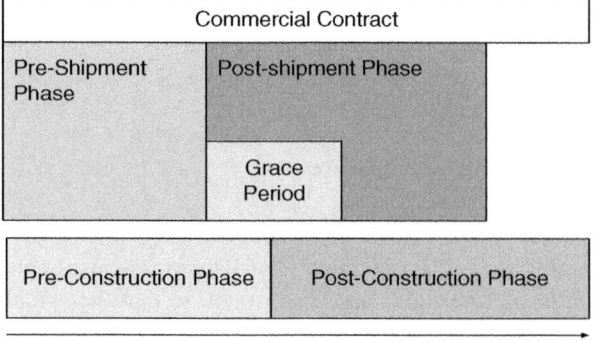

staged, and commissioning could be contractually more important than shipping. Manufacturing of custom-made artefacts may need a good portion of prepayment because the product may be valuable only for the one buyer.

Nonetheless, we stick to this terms. We invert the sequence because pre-shipment products depend on the receivables of the post-shipping credit.

In trade one will find banks involved in all situations, be only as remitting institution, as service provider, as party to a loan or as guarantor. Banks complement the credit situation between the supplier and buyer. Therefore, most credit insurance products see banks as involved parties. There is almost for every bank instrument a corresponding insurance product. The preeminent products are the *Supplier Credit* and the *Buyer Credit*. These two terms embed a fallacious logic, viz. the supplier credit is a credit *from* the supplier to the buyer and the buyer credit is a credit of the bank *to* the buyer.

In the following schematic depiction of the trade and its instruments we use lines with circled ends to symbolise agreements or contracts etc., and arrows denote a transport of the named item (see also Fig. 2.14). For those who want to know more than this brief description should consult the very good publication of Salcic (2014).

Fig. 2.14 Schematic illustration of the contract types. The three situations as depicted are used in the following exhibits of the products. Note that the beneficiary of a contract is not considered a party and that most often the assignment contract concerns the rights of one party of another contract. Not considered here is novation where rights and obligations are transferred, and one party is substituted by another

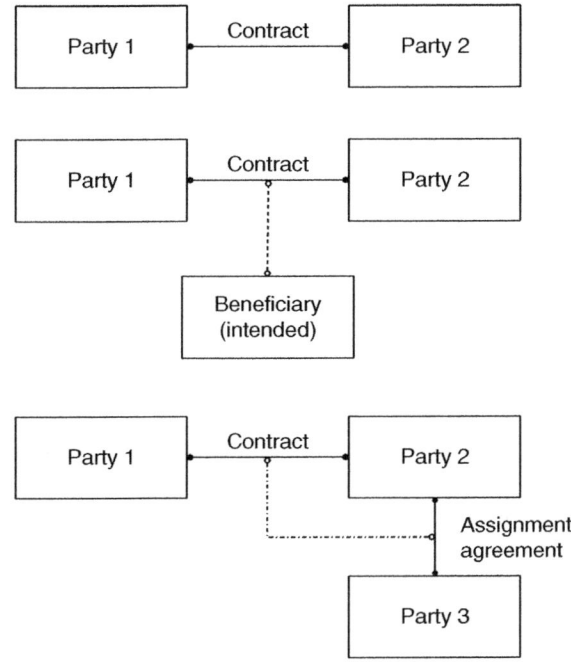

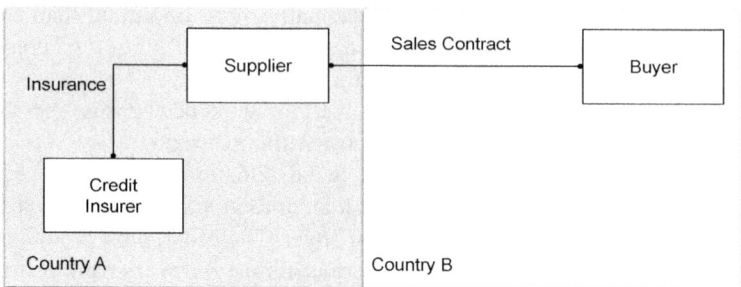

Fig. 2.15 Supplier credit insurance in its simplest form. The sales contracts contain both definition of goods and services and payment conditions

2.10.1 Supplier Credit

The basis for an export is the commercial contract between the supplier (or exporter) and buyer (see Fig. 2.15). The terms of the contract describe *inter alia* the goods or services to be delivered and the payment or credit terms. The credit is embedded in the sales contract.

The credit terms describe the payment terms. For credit insurance to be applied, by ECA for a longer term than 2 years, it is customary to have several instalment payments or receivables after delivery and acceptance of the goods or services. These payments are the subject matter of the credit insurance that can suffer from the defined credit events. By buying such a supplier credit insurance, the exporter transfers the risk of non-payment to the insurance company.

The credit insurance does not guarantee the existence, validity and enforceability of the creditor's rights. It is a general procedure of ECAs not to take any *documentary risk*. This remains the risk of the insured or involved bank.

The payments may be contingent on acceptance of deliveries or performance of the supplier and its goods. In supplier credit there is *performance risk*. There may be cases where the delivery or the completion of contractual obligations is disputed. If the buyer's objections are not manifestly groundless, the indemnification will not take place until the dispute has been resolved in the supplier's favour, either by court ruling or by an arbitration. When the debt is established so is the basis for indemnification. The debt is assigned or subrogated to the insurance company that retains a recourse possibility to the insured. This recourse is the theoretical security for the insurance company.

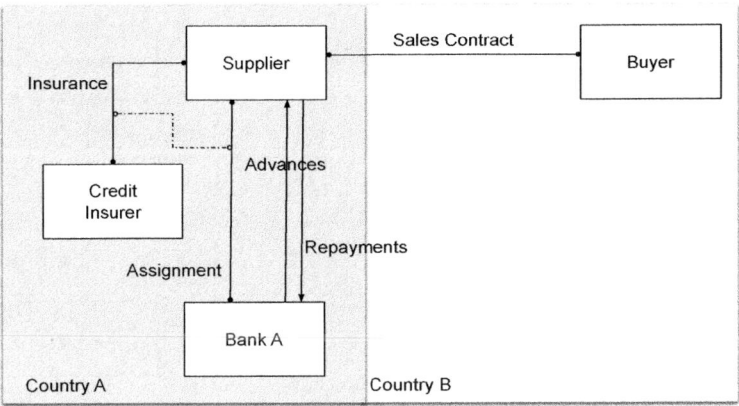

Fig. 2.16 Supplier credit insurance: Variant with assignment of the proceeds of the insurance to the domestic bank

2.10.1.1 Selling Claims to Bank

A product variation is to assign the receivables, that is selling the claims, and to assign the right of indemnification under the insurance to the bank which will advance the funds (see Fig. 2.16). Banks generally do not want to assume risks from the commercial contract and therefore prefer to be directly insured.

Assignments can be silent and thus not known to the buyer (but known to the insurer). This can be due to foreign regulation preventing banks to be involved in credit business. This has the effect that in the case of a credit event the assignment is reversed and the supplier has to pay the bank. The only effect is to create temporary liquidity to the supplier.

Assignment needs an assignment document, i.e. a legally valid contract or agreement.

2.10.1.2 Insuring the Bank

This paves the ground for another variant: The domestic bank A is insured directly in order to confirm the letters of credit of the buyer's bank B. Therefore the credit risk is shifted to the credit insurer. This general situation is depicted in Fig. 2.17, while Fig. 2.8 on page 35 is more granular on the letter of credit feature. One important effect of confirmation is the fact that the governing jurisdiction may change to the supplier's country and thus be helpful in the case of disputes (Figs. 2.18 and 2.19).

2.10.2 Buyer Credit

The buyer credit is the obvious choice for middle- to long-term credits. The credit takes the form of a loan or a credit facility agreement between the domestic bank and the buyer (Fig. 2.20) or the bank of the buyer (Fig. 2.21). In the latter case there will also be a separate security agreement between the buyer and its bank. The buyer

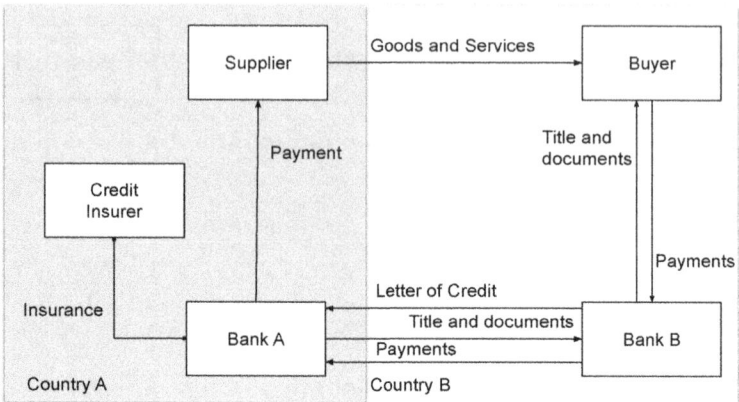

Fig. 2.17 Variant supplier credit insurance: Letter of credit confirmation insurance

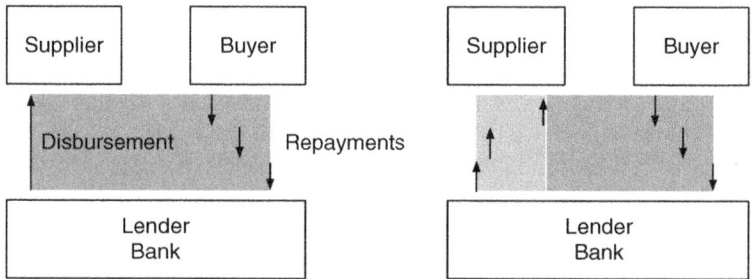

Fig. 2.18 Buyer credit with two disbursement patterns. The situation on left is the standard where the credit is established by crediting the supplier and debiting the buyer. The pattern on the right assumes several payments to the supplier typical for long-lead products and projects. As already discussed in Fig. 2.9 the situation on right can be understood as overdraft with term-out

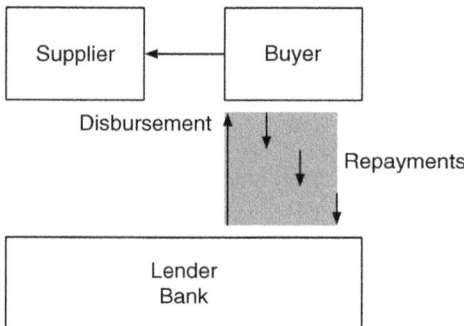

Fig. 2.19 Buyer credit with disbursement to the buyer. The bank must make sure that the disbursement to the supplier is carried out

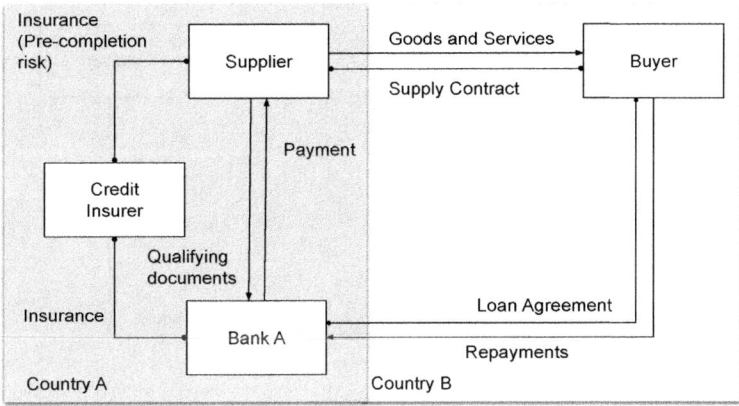

Fig. 2.20 Buyer's credit insurance

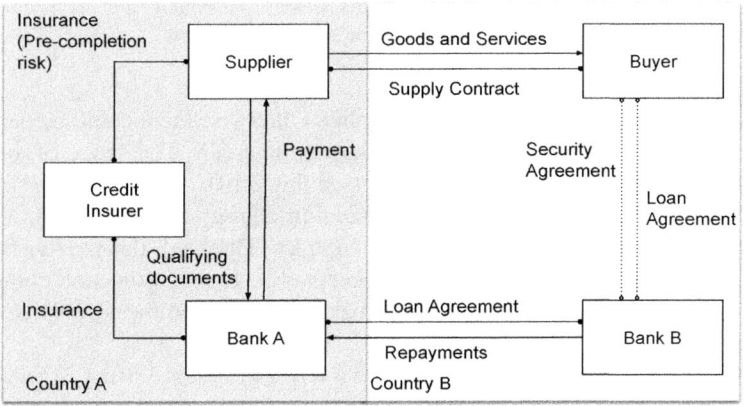

Fig. 2.21 Buyer's credit with foreign bank. The subject of the insurance is the loan agreement between the banks with the sole purpose to pay for the goods

now has two roles, viz. party in the commercial agreement and borrower to the bank (Fig. 2.22).

Figure 2.18 shows the mechanics of the buyer credit. It is established between the bank and the buyer by paying the credit sum to the supplier and agreeing on a regular repayment in equal instalments by the buyer of the goods. With long-lead products that are manufactured for the buyer there is also a possibility to draw down advance payments analogously to an overdraft by means of handing qualifying documents to the bank. Therefore, we have a situation of event-driven disbursements with regular repayment. From a pricing point of view it seems more appropriate to treat the many draw-downs as distinct from the term credit.

As a detail we mention the situation where a jurisdiction forbids the payout of the credit not to the borrower. Therefore, the bank must take precautions to make

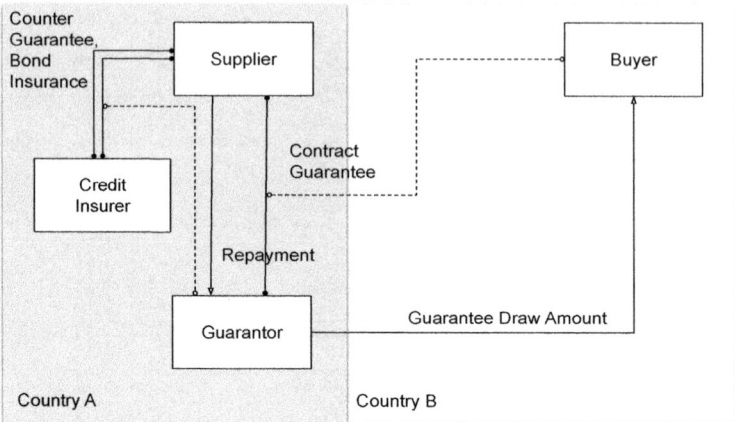

Fig. 2.22 Counter-guarantee with additional bond insurance. The dashed lines symbolise the beneficiaries to the guarantees, while it is stipulated between the supplier and credit insurer. The guarantee amount and repayment are only due if the guarantee is drawn

sure that the money is conveyed to the supplier. Otherwise there could be the risk of the buyer keeping the goods and not honouring the credit. The scope of the buyer credit is solely to pay for the export goods (see Fig. 2.19).

The loan agreement will feature a separation clause, called "Isabella clause", to cut any responsibility from the supply contract. The bank declines to take any risk from the export, e.g. disputes, non-acceptance, repudiation, non-compliance etc. Nonetheless, the security agreement makes reference to the receivables of the export contract.

Normally, the credit insurer has a keener interest in synchronising, standardising and influencing the loan agreement than in the export contract and its supplier credit where documentation risk is shun. The lender may want to agree not to seek recourse on the supplier upon a credit event in order to increase capacity and remove contingent liabilities from the financial reporting. The insurer must agree on this clause because it affects the risk of the cover. As it is an implicit performance guarantee it should be priced into the buyer credit insurance.

With a buyer credit the buyer loses some leverage on the supplier because the latter may have been paid. Here enter guarantees the picture. With the insured credit amounts becoming ever larger there are syndicates taking the role of a single lender. Two or more banks stipulate a single loan agreement between all parties. One bank is appointed as the *agent bank* that applies for the cover. It needs power of attorney in order to act for the syndicate with respect to the credit insurer.

2.11   Credit Insurance: Pre-shipment products

There is a commercial export contract defining delivery and payment. The bigger part of the payment is due after delivery of goods and services, acceptance or commissioning for a plant. Yet, the invoices are not presented and the receivables are not due. These are the prerequisites that the credit comes into existence. Therefore the question is what risks are to be covered before the credit?

2.11.1   Contract Guarantee and Counter-Guarantee

Contract guarantees as listed in Sect. 2.9.7 are issued by the supplier's bank to the benefit of the buyer. The supplier will be required to repay the bank in case that the guarantee is called by the buyer.

Now, credit insurer and supplier concord a counter-guarantee for the issuing bank as beneficiary. The supplier or exporter pays the fees for such a counter-guarantee in order not to keep cash collateral for the bank. These counter-guarantees are designed to create liquidity for the supplier.

The issuing bank has to pay unconditionally at the draw of the guarantee, always on behalf of the exporting supplier. The supplier is exposed to the risk of a so-called unjustified or unfair calling. This is an illegal, capricious demand although the supplier is in total compliance with the terms and conditions of the contract. Surprisingly, most causes for this are political risk. The supplier can be insured against this risk by a contract insurance. Thus the credit insurer is left with the difficulty to recover money from the supplier in the case of a fair calling not honoured by the supplier. But, the general purpose of contract guarantees is producing security and not payment.

2.11.2   Manufacturing Risk Insurance

It is the insurance cover that indemnifies the expenses undertaken by the exporter in order to fulfil its contractual requirements under the sales contract in the case that the actualisation of the order becomes impossible or production is discontinued due to:

- repudiation or unjustified cancellation of the contract,
- insolvency of the foreign buyer,
- embargo measures,
- political risk,
- Force Majeur etc.

The insured interests are the costs of the unfinished good minus work-in-progress that can be used otherwise or raw material. No profit margin can be covered. Some ECAs include pre-payment risk too that is a bundle of advance payment guarantees.

The cover is not primarily about the capabilities of manufacturing, which would qualify as performance risk, but about the buyer's duties and the buyer's country political situation.

2.11.3 Working Capital Guarantee

A loan guaranteed by the ECA has two effects on the supplier's liquidity: It creates the ability to include export-related assets into the borrowing base of the loan, e.g. foreign accounts receivable, export-related inventory, raw materials, work-in-progress and finished goods, and lifts the advance rates compared to conventional financing. The guarantee can cover both individual export contracts and multiple export transactions. The latter can be on a revolving basis.

Again, with the working capital credit facility we have a triangular situation, i.e. the exporter, the bank and the credit insurer (Fig. 2.23). Therefore, a guarantee is the better choice, because then the exporter is a contract party and the bank the beneficiary.

The lending institution creates a credit facility with the sole purpose to be used for one or several given export contracts. These are earmarked. The exporter may draw on the credit facility by presenting qualifying documents, e.g. for raw materials, supplies, labour cost etc., of the export goods in question.

With this guarantee the supplier is not covered for risks stemming from the buyer. Therefore, it is advisable to contract a manufacturing risk insurance and/or a supplier credit insurance.

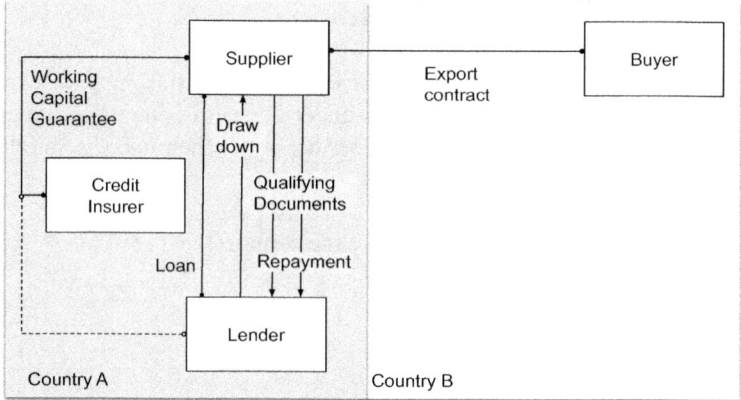

Fig. 2.23 Working capital guarantee scheme. The dotted line designates the beneficiary. The proceeds from the commercial contract should be assigned

The term of such credit guarantees is normally between 6 months and 2 years, either with an upfront premium with later correction for usage or on a running basis. The risk and therefore also the premium for working capital guarantees are higher than for the supplier or buyer credit insurances. The cover ratio is around 80%, often smaller than for post-shipment products. In case of bankruptcy of the supplier these export-related assets may be worthless.

Stephens (1999, 113) writes about this sensitive product: "However this is a difficult and high-risk area, especially if the exporter fails to perform its contractual duties and as a result is not paid by the importer. The export credit agency is then faced with the (usually politically sensitive) job of trying to recover from the exporter the money it has paid to the bank under it working capital facilities".

Another question arises spontaneously: Is this support fair towards small- and medium-sized enterprises that do not export?

2.11.4 Supply Chain Financing Guarantee

This guarantee complements obviously the receivable discounting of the bank (see Fig. 2.24). It is a product covering the domestic lender or bank against non-payment of the invoices by the buyer. In a true sale the lender has no recourse to the exporter. There is the potential to pool receivables of many buyers together what would lead to diversification and set up this operation as a programme.

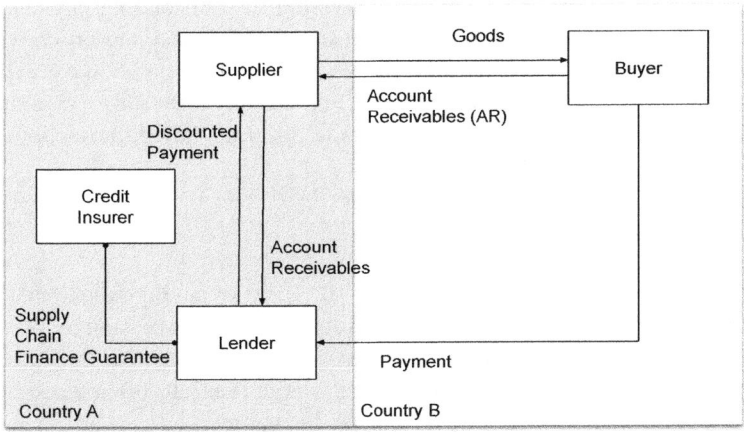

Fig. 2.24 Supply chain financing guarantee. Here applicant and beneficiary are both the lender

2.11.5 Advisory Services

Credit insurance products and export financing are rather complicated or even complex products that require extended experience. Credit insurer and ECAs especially offer a deep knowledge-based consulting with the exception of legal opinions. They can help structure an export transaction and mitigate some risks from the outset and optimise the combination of products.

They have a narrow knit network of banks and governmental offices where they can tap in for information. ECAs may be part of a whole governmental super-structure where several departments, special banks and agencies for import, trade, innovation, tourism, export and local promotion, start-up financing and the like and even economic departments of embassies abroad are managed. Export is also very close to governmental development financing. As an example we quote the mission of the US Trade and Development Agency:

> USTDA connects the US private sector to infrastructure projects in emerging markets. We achieve our mission by funding feasibility studies, technical assistance and pilot projects that integrate the innovation and expertise of American companies. We also connect overseas project sponsors with US partners through our reverse trade missions, industry conferences and expert workshops.

Many ECAs have begun to actively search for large projects abroad that may suit domestic suppliers (*business matching*). This can be a very competitive endeavour as it is an illusion and logical flaw that all ECAs are able to grow simultaneously despite their strategic mission.

Credit insurer also provides help in recovering the outstanding payments especially for small- and medium-sized enterprises that obviously are not very knowledgeable about foreign laws and procedures. Credit insurer may have experience with foreign attorneys that can be engaged. For very big issues also an ambassador may find his or her way to a foreign minister to discuss a failed transaction.

2.12   Last Resort

Doing business is risky and should stay so. Risk is an ingredient that fosters creativity and parsimony with scarce resources. Risk is a source of income. Therefore, a last resort should only bear risks that are beneficial to the economy as a whole but cannot be born otherwise. Very large risks are often passed to some risk taker of last resort. For ECA it is state or the market.

2.12.1 Government

From the banking crisis we know the term lender of last resort very well, designating the central banks. They have a pivotal role in keeping the economy and the related financial system afloat. But there is also an insurer of last resort. The UK Treasury writes in a very recent report, already aware of the Corona pandemic of 2020 (HM Treasury 2020, 5):

> The spread of democracy and the rise of the welfare state over the late 19th and 20th centuries saw the government's role guarding citizens against risk grow. As part of its responsibility to citizens the government now plays the role of insurer of last resort in a wide range of markets including flood risk, terrorism insurance, travel protection and supporting lending to small businesses. The insurer of last resort role creates liabilities that are uncertain but that may lead to future expenditure if specific conditions are met or specific events happen. Such liabilities are known as contingent liabilities.

These liabilities are an important policy tool to support economic growth and safeguard the economy in times of stress. What is the rationale for such contingencies:

1. to ensure markets work effectively,
2. to provide goods generally not provided by the market and
3. to achieve distributional objectives.

For credit insurers on state account the liabilities of the agency are also part of the government portfolio of contingencies that must be managed holistically. This can be achieved by an explicit guarantee to the ECA or by capital endowment or both.

2.12.2 Reinsurance

Reinsurance is both a long established method of risk sharing and an industry. The industry and its depth may be inferred from Table 2.3. We show the non-life premia as credit insurance is part of this category. The industry is highly concentrated between the two first companies and then follows a market and the rest.

Credit insurance does account only for a little more than 1% of the non-life premia worldwide in 2018. This is approximately 25 billion USD of a total of 2373 billion USD globally (SwissRe 2019, 11). Thus private credit insurance is a marginal business. Major reinsurance companies have a line of credit insurance where they cover *Bonding* or Surety, another name for guaranteeing contract bonds, commercial

Table 2.3 Major Reinsurance companies by non-life premium 2019 (Source: A.M. Best, by permission)

Rank	Entity	Net Non-life Premium [Mill. USD]
1	SwissRe	25,135
2	Munich Reinsurance	23,455
3	Hannover Rück	14,333
4	Berkshire Hathaway	11,112
5	Lloyd's	10,433
6	SCOR S.E.	6826
	Sub-total	91,294

credit and export credit insurance (SwissRe 1986, 205). For export credit it is in the form of facultative *quota share* and a limit per client base. Premium and potential loss are split according to an agreed percentage. In *facultative business* each risk accepted is an individual reinsurance contract.

2.12.3 Capital Market

The capital market is the place where issuance of capital is done. It consists of equity and debt instruments. Equity comprises common stock, from initial public offerings or secondary offerings, and convertibles. Global debt issuance comprises mainly notes and bonds. Syndicated loans do not really belong to the capital market as these loans are negotiated by syndicates of banks. But some standardised loans are securitised to the market.

Figure 2.25 shows the amounts raised in 2019 globally: Global equity and related amounts to 677.1 billion USD that are dwarfed by the debt instruments' 7687 billion USD, more than ten times the equity amount. Syndicated loans with its 3177 billion USD constitute quite big a share of the debt. Comparing the volume of officially supported credit volume (see Fig. 1.6) with either bond issuance or the volume of syndicated loans, we find that the supported portion is tiny. Suppose a volume of 80 billion USD, as in the year 2010 or 2013, then it accounts for 2.5% of syndicated loans. Table 2.4 puts the figure also in some perspective. The statistics lead to an average upfront fee of approximately 75 bp.

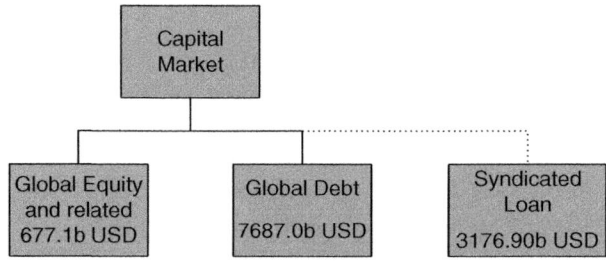

Fig. 2.25 Size of the capital market by issuance for the year 2019 (Source: Refinitiv)

Table 2.4 Top global syndicated loans for general corporate purposes 2019 and Q1 2020 (Source: Refinitiv)

Date	Borrower	Amount [Mill. USD]
23.04.2019	Ford Motor Co	16,900
14.05.2019	WalMart	16,810
31.03.2020	Airbus SE	16,543
24.10.2019	Charter Communication Inc	15,250
25.01.2019	Altira Grp Inc	14,600
6.02.2020	Boeing Co	13,825

Other purposes for large syndicated loans are inter alia M&A

Therefore, the capital market could easily absorb the supported middle- to long-term credit. Supported short-term insurance or guarantees are not included in the 80 billion USD.

If there were a steady flow of credit insurance policies, they could be taken as reference to a synthetic non-amortising securitisation. Thus are *credit-linked notes* issued. Unfortunately such vehicles are very expensive to set up. Other products are so-called insurance-linked securities where the interest rate and/or the principal repayment is contingent on some insured credit events. This is a highly specialised market. Credit insurance though is more difficult to explain than natural catastrophes (Cat bonds).

2.13 Credit Events

Credit events, also called default events in loan language, are the risks covered. Their definition is of utmost importance. Where a credit insurer covers a loan or a bond, it is important to synchronise the events of the covers with the underlying credit instrument (Tables 2.5 and 2.6).

For credit derivatives the International Swaps and Derivatives Association (ISDA) has seven standard credit events:

1. bankruptcy,
2. obligation acceleration,
3. obligation default,
4. payment default,
5. repudiation/moratorium,
6. debt restructuring and
7. governmental intervention.

The last item was added in 2014, because 1 year prior the Dutch government expropriated subordinated bonds for SNS Bank NV. This needed amendment. Consequently we find this trigger also in the general conditions of the Dutch ECA, see Table 2.7.

Table 2.5 Tentative list of credit events

Political	Economical	Political and Economical
Sanctions of payments	Bankruptcy	Force majeure
Sovereign default	Obligation default	Third party sanctions
Moratorium	Failure to pay	Political Violence
Convertibility	Repudiation	Terrorism
Transferability	Restructuring	
Confiscation	Fraud	

Table 2.6 Table of content of Single Currency Term Facility Agreement for Use in Export Finance Buyer Credit Transactions of the Loan Market Association LMA, by permission

Nr	Title	Nr	Title
1	Definitions and Interpretation	22	**Events of Default**
2	The Facilities	23	[Subrogation]
3	Purpose	24	Changes to the Lenders
4	Conditions of Utilisation	25	Changes to the Obligors
5	Utilisation	26	The role of the Agent and the Arranger
6	Repayment	27	**Role of the ECA Agent**
7	Prepayment and cancellation	28	Conduct of business by the Finance Parties
8	Interest	29	Sharing among the Finance Parties
9	Interest Periods	30	Payment mechanics
10	Changes to the calculation of Interest	31	Set-off
11	Fees	32	Notices
12	Tax Gross up and Indemnities	33	Calculations and certificates
13	Increased Costs	34	Partial Invalidity
14	Other Indemnities	35	Remedies and waivers
15	Mitigation by the Lenders	36	Amendments and waivers
16	Costs and expenses	37	Confidential Information
17	Guarantee and indemnity	38	Confidentiality of Funding Rates
18	Representations	39	Counterparts
19	Information undertakings	40	Governing law
20	**Financial covenants**	41	[Enforcement, Arbitration]
21	**General undertakings**	42	Waiver of Immunity

Buyer's credit, i.e. a bank loan agreements, must integrate the ECA specific requirements. The *Loan Market Association* LMA has developed in 2018 a template for a single currency export finance buyer credit agreement (see Table 2.6).

Accordingly, the loan or facility agreement will need to be amended, and consideration should be given to ensure that the contractual relationship between the lenders, the borrower and the exporter operates as intended. Typically lenders seek to include a number of additional mandatory prepayments or automatic cancellation events, such as:

(a) events relating to the export contract, e.g. termination, invalidity, illegality or material litigation or
(b) automatic cancellation of a proportion of available commitment where the export contract value is reduced, e.g. mandatory advance payments.

Certain ECAs require the inclusion of specific events of default where the ECA cover document lapses, terminates or otherwise ceases to be in full force and effect, in addition to, or instead of, an ECA mandatory prepayment event.

Table 2.7 Credit events as defined by the Dutch ECA (Atradius 2013) as an illustration, by permission

Credit event	Specification
1. Insolvency	1. the Borrower is declared bankrupt; 2. the Borrower is granted temporary or permanent suspension of payment; 3. a settlement out of court offered by the Borrower is accepted with the agreement of Insurer; 4. enforcement of a judgement that has or not fully resulted in payment of the Insured Receivables; 5. a judicial debt-repayment arrangement has been imposed on the Borrower; as well as procedures or situations abroad whose effect is comparable with bankruptcy, suspension of payments or a judicial debt-repayment arrangement.
2. Moratorium	General suspension of debt repayment announced by the government of the country of the Borrower or by the government of another country through which the payment of an Insured Receivable has to be made.
3. Transfer Problems	Statutory or administrative measures outside the Netherlands which prohibit local deposits, or a situation in which the transfer of amounts deposited by the Borrower or its guarantor is prevented or delayed as a result of political events, economic difficulties, shortages of foreign currency or statutory or administrative measures outside the Netherlands.
4. Conversion Problems	A generally applicable measure taken in the country of the Borrower or its guarantor whereby a deposit problem made by the Borrower or its guarantor would discharge him, but at the time of transfer generates less than the amount receivable when converted into the currency of the Loan Agreement as a result of a change in exchange rate, or the application by the government of the country of the Borrower or its guarantor of a conversion rate which is less favourable than the generally used reference rate for converting local currency into a convertible currency
5. Force Majeure	An impediment to the repayment of the Insured Receivables as a result of the occurrence outside the Netherlands of, for example, a. international measures: resolutions by international organisations that the Netherlands is obliged to implement; b. war: war, civil war, revolution, civil disturbance, terrorism and sabotage; c. general strike; d. catastrophe: hurricane, earthquake, volcanic eruption, flood or other type of natural disaster; e. nuclear disaster: nuclear fusion, nuclear fission or radioactive contamination; f. epidemic.
6. Government Intervention	An impediment not attributable to the Insured and/or the Borrower of the repayment of the Insured Intervention Receivables as a result of measures, actions, decisions or default of a foreign government, other than Moratorium, Transfer Problems, Conversion Problems or Force Majeure.
7. Protracted Default	The fact that the Borrower has not paid an Insured Receivable by the date of the expiry of the Waiting Period to the extent that the non-payment is not a consequence of Insolvency, Moratorium, Transfer Problems, Conversion Problems, Force Majeure or Government Intervention.

The following usual clauses for ECAs are *inter alia* included:

1. an "Isabella clause": This separates the obligations and rights under the underlying export contract from the financing, preserving the borrower's obligation to repay the loan in the event of a dispute in connection with the export contract;

2. an "ECA override": This is a commonly incorporated clause to help ensure that the terms of the financing do not conflict with ECA's requirements or policy documents.

The OECD Arrangement requires a mandatory prepayment of 15% before the start of the credit. Therefore either it is stipulated as a *condition precedent* or an express covenant is included requiring the borrower to provide evidence of the payment.

An unfettered right for the lender to assign its rights or transfers its rights and obligations to the ECA could also be envisaged.

In the case of a guarantee to an issue of bonds or notes, there needs to be an additional provision in the wording, because there is not a designated lender but a virtual community of bondholders that cannot act and fulfil the responsibilities of the beneficiary. These responsibilities must be transferred to some kind of proxy or agent who can act on behalf of the bondholders.

These non-exhaustive arguments are just mentioned to make clear how intertwined loan agreement and credit insurance can be. For transparency reasons and to abide to the OECD's aim to create a level playing field in support for exports, it is of course necessary to set premia also in respect to the credit events covered. Table 2.5 gives an illustration showing the entanglement between political and economical risks.

Force majeure may embrace the following, non-exhaustively: war, riots, terrorism, fire, flood, hurricane, typhoon, earthquake, lightning, explosion, strikes, lockouts, slowdowns, prolonged shortage of energy supplies and acts of state or governmental action prohibiting or impeding any party from performing its respective obligations under the contract. The latter may also be political risk.

The argument is thus whether these events are part of Force Majeure or not. *Third party sanctions* are contended as political risk or even as insurable events.

2.14   Indemnification

Indemnification shall be the same as payment of claims, both terms used for honouring the policy.

The insured has to prevent the loss causing event as if he or she were not insured, must promptly respond to new circumstances, take practical and sensible measures to prevent loss and thus has to inform the insurance company of such problems (Jus 2013, 94). But obviously the loss cannot always be prevented.

The insured, bank or supplier, has to notify the insurer of a non-payment event by the buyer within the period stated in the terms of the policy and request indemnification. Insurers, especially ECAs, do not monitor the credit. Insurers will not pay immediately but apply a waiting period of 90–180 days to allow for technical difficulties to be resolved and also to assess whether a covered credit event has really happened. In obvious cases of bankruptcy or on-going juridical proceedings the waiting period can be shortened. Often follows a handling period before the money is transferred.

Normally, as a condition for indemnification, the supplier or bank has to transfer the right to the outstanding payments to the insurer. In situations where an assignment complicates the procedure, e.g. due to requiring a license for money transfer, or the debilitating awareness of the buyer that the supplier has been indemnified and suffers only a small loss, ECAs require the supplier to enforce payment. Some commercial contracts prohibit the assignment of claims. The insurer needs to know before issuing a policy. An alternative transfer of rights can be effected by *subrogation* by indemnifying without further provisions if the governing law of the contract allows.

If security has been provided, the question about enforcing it arises, in principle and whether before indemnification. Enforcing security may be easy, e.g. calling a guarantee, or complex and time consuming, e.g. retention of title, involving selling goods, machinery, land etc. Insured supplier or banks prefer to assign the securities to the insurance company, and the insurer will not have the insured exhaust all possibilities before indemnifying. Costs for enforcement can be shared proportionally.

ECAs must ascertain the claim. This comprises *inter alia*:

- check representations and exclusions,
- establish that the payments are not disputed,
- payments are assigned to the ECA,
- the claim amount is less or equal to the covered maximum amount,
- the claim is within time limit etc.

The indemnification comprises mainly principal and contractual interest outstanding payable when due. Loan agreements and also commercial contracts may contain acceleration clauses which entitle the creditor in a credit event to declare due and payable the whole amount. ECAs may decide whether to instruct to accelerate irrespective of the indemnification. Banks prefer to be indemnified according to the original schedule in order not to incur potential breakage costs. In the rare event of a one off payment the outstanding receivables are discounted. If there is reinsurance cover, the reinsurer should be notified.

For large claim amounts the decision-making of an ECA foresees the board of directors to approve the indemnification. For more details see Salcic (2014, 166–178).

It is universally true that the speed of indemnification hinges upon the quality of documentation of the credit event and the loss incurred (Jus 2013, 146).

2.15   Work-Out

2.15.1 Rescheduling

The request of rescheduling the payments is most often the first request of a foreign buyer to the supplier or bank when financial difficulties arise. The insured must notify the insurer of such requests. If the distress is such that otherwise bankruptcy will ensue, it is economically wise to consent. But the buyer must have a reasonable chance to continuing in business. This consent does not automatically amend the policy. The insured has bought cover in the expectation to secure the original payment schedule and not a rescheduled one. The insured must agree to amendments.

The rescheduling and amendment thus rest on the relationship between creditor and buyer.

In case that the rescheduled payment stream is not honoured and there is another credit event, the original pattern has to be considered unless the policy has also been amended.

2.15.2 Recovery

For some time the accounting of loans or guarantees followed the philosophy of *loss incurred*. Only after a default was reported or known the institution was allowed to make provisions for the impairment.

Since a couple of years the International Accounting Standards Board (IASB) made changes to the IFRS-9 reporting standard that introduced the *expected credit loss* (ECL) framework. Financial institutions are required to recognise expected credit loss at all times, i.e. considering past events, current conditions and forecast information, and to update the amount of ECLs recognised at each reporting date to reflect changes in an asset's credit risk. It is a more forward-looking approach than its predecessor and will result in more timely recognition of credit losses.

This introductory remark is to show that defaults and credit events mean more than just the realisation of the fact. Credit quality is a continuum.

There are at least three types of buyers, i.e. sovereign, public and private. For sovereigns there is obviously no bankruptcy procedure. A public company is a hybrid being subject to bankruptcy and at the same time backed by the government. Private companies, limited by their capital, are subject to formal bankruptcy legislation.

In the following we account for public buyer in the sovereign category. Sovereign default and private default are quite different things.

What are the main differences between recovery from a sovereign and a private company? Privates are bound to legal bankruptcy laws where in the end a judge can award the different stakeholders with portions of the financial remains of the debtor when a restructuring has failed. Such laws foresee priorities in allocating funds. They prevent also vexatious and frivolous invocation but organise the collective action. There is no bankruptcy law for sovereigns, and the priority is only informal but unchallenged: IMF, World Bank and some other multilateral development banks are the most senior debtors. This is due to the fact that their role is not to invest for economic purposes but to help international finance. Then there is the question of whether to treat all creditors, e.g. domestic and foreign, equally. Domestic creditors suffer not only direct financial distress but also by reduced income from tax increases, cuts in public spending and services, e.g. defence, police, education, reduction in public salaries and public pensions etc. (Roubini and Setser 2004, 266). With sovereign there is also the absence of a mechanism that provides for majority action among a diverse set of creditors.

2.15.3   Sovereign Default

The definition of sovereign default is in reality quite a challenge. The starting point is of course the breach of some promises embodied in a debt agreement that leads back to the famous events of credit. A breach may differ in severity. The sovereign debt can be domestic, foreign or official, i.e. debt to multilateral or bilateral financial institutions.

Ams et al. (2018, 3) propose three kinds of default with different implications:

- technical default,
- contractual default and
- substantive default.

Technical default includes any contractual event of default occurrence for domestic and official debt "that does not also constitute default under third-party definitions, such as those used by rating agencies and in standardized derivatives contracts. Administrative errors and some covenant defaults viewed as minor by market participants would fit under this heading".

Contractual defaults on the other hand are breaches in accordance with reputable third party definitions. At least missed payments and *payment shortfalls* that persist for longer than the typical grace period would fit. But restructurings that follow contractual modification provisions would not fall into this class.

And substantive default would materialise when none of the above happens but *distressed restructuring* of the debt with *haircuts* would be implemented by the debtor.

Credit default swaps for sovereign typically stipulate, for a country like the USA:

1. failure to pay,
2. repudiation/moratorium and
3. restructuring.

In certain contracts, the occurrence of a credit event has to be coupled with a significant price deterioration in a specified reference obligation. This requirement, known as a *materiality clause*, is designed to ensure that a credit event is not triggered by a technical default.

2.15.3.1 Bilateral Negotiation

In a first step trying to recover a single debt it is most promising to negotiate bilaterally if the debtor has still a certain ability to pay its debt. Other outcomes are

- rescheduling of payments,
- reduction of interest rates,
- reduction of debt,
- a combination of the three or
- multilateral negotiations.

As the example from the vulture fund below will show, judiciary action for big private creditors has become feasible. Multilateral negotiations take place in the Paris Club.

2.15.3.2 IMF Restructuring

The *sovereign debt restructuring mechanism* SDRM should be invoked "where there is no feasible set of sustainable macroeconomic policies that would enable the debtor to resolve the immediate crisis and restore medium-term viability unless they were accompanied by a significant reduction in the net present value of the sovereign's debt" (Krueger 2002, 4).

There has been a marked shift from syndicated bank loans towards traded securities on the international capital markets. As a consequence the investor base for financing emerging market sovereigns is much broader. It includes also vulture funds that try to gain from sovereign distress. In the case of Argentina in 2002 the government agreed to a settlement that would allow Paul Singer's fund Elliott Capital to walk away with USD 2.4 billion for bonds that had been purchased for about USD 117 million, a return of 2,050%.

An IMF programme is a prerequisite for multilateral negotiations in the Paris Club.

2.15.3.3 Paris Club

The so-called Paris Club is an ad hoc organisation of creditor states and their export credit agencies. It is hosted by the French government. Debtor states need to be invited to negotiations when they have concluded an *appropriate programme* with the IMF. This link is intended to restore a sound economic framework in order to lower the future probability of financial difficulties.

Negotiation decisions are taken unanimously by the creditor states and documented as "Agreed Minutes" that are mere recommendations to the creditors. Then bilateral agreements implement the decisions taken and documented. In summary it is a three-step approach:

1. adherence to IMF programme,
2. Paris Club negotiations and
3. bilateral agreement.

The restructuring by the Paris Club members, that are by the way also the biggest stakeholders in the IMF, is described as arcane. It assumes that its restructuring precedes the private one and tries to decide what share of near-term cashflow it should take leaving the remainder for other creditors (Roubini and Setser 2004, 261).

The Paris Club restructures only those payments coming due in the so-called consolidation period, in the PC parlance the term of the IMF programme. This is a "flow" restructuring in contrast to a more comprehensive "stock"-based action where the whole outstanding debt is considered. This is the approach of the privates. The discrepancy causes some problems to reach a "comparable" restructuring for states and private creditors.

For budgetary reasons in the creditor's national accounts there is a preference for not reducing the par value of the debt but rather to allow debtors to roll-over principal and capitalised interest at their own discretion. Debtors know that going into arrears with bilateral creditors has few consequences. As Roubini and Setser (2004, 259) write: "Paris Club creditors do not litigate and never panic". Table 2.8 shows Paris Club claims as of end of 2018. The total amounts to USD 315 billion. Figure 2.26 shows a typical repayment pattern with implicit priority.

This mechanism makes it very difficult for ECAs to establish the *ultimate loss* from insuring sovereigns. In their accounts the value of defaulted sovereign credit must be established by own principles.

2.15.3.4 Private Creditors

The two major classes of private creditors are traditionally banks that operate in syndicated loans and bondholders, which can be quite atomised.

Lately the bond volume to emerging sovereigns has increased, while the involvement of banks has decreased. Banks are organised even more informal in the *London Club* that holds its meetings in New York. Bondholders are not organised at all. In theory, they should profit from the restructuring in the Paris Club which promotes

Table 2.8 Top 10 Paris Club's claims as of 31 December 2018 in USD million (Source: Paris Club)

Country	ODA	NODA	Total
Greece	–	58,790	58,790
India	22,010	2986	24,996
Vietnam	17,404	2138	19,542
China	13,155	939	14,094
Egypt	7333	5171	12,504
Iraq	3789	8276	12,066
Pakistan	8416	2375	10,791
Philippines	7565	138	7704
Belarus	19	7522	7541
Bangladesh	5694	1768	7462
Grand Total	164,511	150,144	314,655

ODA stands for Official Development Assistance and NODA for Non-Official DA

Fig. 2.26 Waterfall or
Roman fountain model of
debt repayments

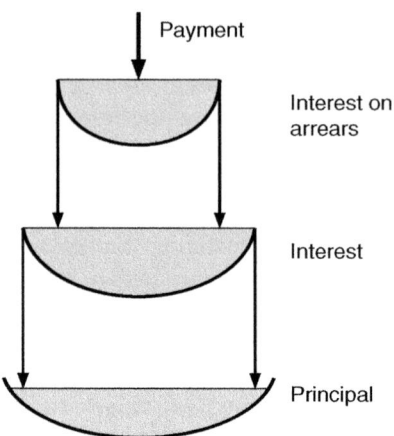

comparable treatment for the non-members of the club. But privates have another attitude towards recovery. First a stock restructuring seems more natural and hold-out, i.e. insistence on full payment, cannot be ruled out by some super majority as in corporate recovery.

Litigation in sovereign debt defaults has become quite common beyond the general perception. Schumacher et al. (2018, 6) write: "The first wave of sovereign debt litigation was triggered by the 1980s debt crisis in Latin America and beyond. Lawsuits were mostly filed by banks and other buy-and-hold investors who aimed at enforcing better terms than those negotiated in the London Club process". In recent times half of debt crises involved legal disputes affecting two dozen countries. As we have said above, hold-out creditors like distressed debt funds aka vulture funds are most often involved. The slow pace in restructuring gives opportunities to massively buy distressed bonds. Argentina defaulted on 22nd May 2020 on a bond of USD 66 Billion by missing overdue interest payments. Argentina has technically entered default for the ninth time in its history. As of 4th August 2020 according to a Bloomberg dispatch, the breakthrough came with a call between Argentine Economy Minister Martin Guzman and BlackRock Inc. managing director Jennifer O'Neil. The agreement between three main bondholder committees and more investors should grant Argentina significant debt relief. Creditors would receive about 55 cents on the dollar.

2.15.4 Corporate Work-Out

This is a vast topic involving varying situations and differing judicial systems. At least four elements are involved, viz. the debtor, the creditor, other creditors and stakeholders, and the legal system. A much deeper insight than the following is proposed by Garrido (2012).

The fundamental prerequisite for restructuring is the persuasion of the viability of the debtor's business. Otherwise, the demise and liquidation is the only alternative.

2.15.4.1 Bilateral Negotiation and Enforcement

When financial difficulties of the buyer in the export contract or a credit event are notified to the credit insurer the first reaction is to analyse whether this is only a temporary or technical situation that can be overcome by rescheduling the payments, amending the credit terms etc., or by actions that to a certain extent are already foreseen in the commercial contract or loan agreement. It has also to be established whether fraud or misconduct of the debtor may be involved. Is the non-payment due to disputes concerning the performance of the supplier, the insurer would most probably wait for a judgement of court or an arbitration award proving the supplier's right to claim payment.

There is then the possibility to seek individual enforcement of the debt by going to court. Obviously deep enough an analysis must have concluded that there are reasonable chances to recovery a substantial part of the debt.

Individual contractual negotiations and agreements must leave other debtors unchanged in their financial situations and not granting special favourable treatment to the detriment of the remaining creditors. In a later formal procedure this avoidance action could be voided.

2.15.4.2 Collective Negotiation

A general financial difficulty, mainly in the form of liquidity problems, of a debtor may concern all creditors that are interconnected by a *cross-default clause* in financial agreements. This is always the case with bonds issued by the debtor.

As depicted in Fig. 2.27 there is the contractual negotiation outside the court, and there is the formal proceeding. There is also some middle-ground that we could call "under the auspices" of a financial supervisor or the law.

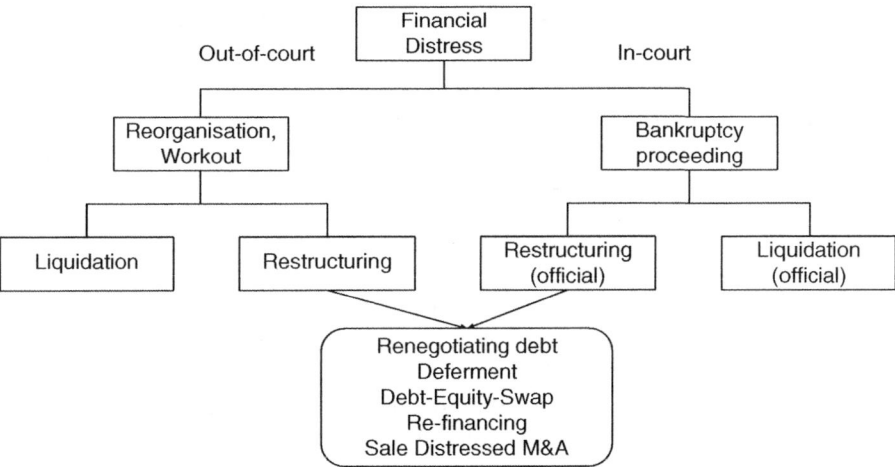

Fig. 2.27 Synopsis of financial distress resolution, adapted from Iannotta (2010, 176)

The result is always the same, viz. a restructuring or the liquidation of the debtor. There are two types of restructuring, i.e.

- operational restructuring and
- financial (or debt) restructuring.

With operational restructuring the business of the debtor will be altered by *inter alia*:

- – asset sale,
- – sale of business units,
- – downsizing of the continuing business,
- – carve-out of profitable units,
- – distressed M&A etc.

We concentrate on the financial restructuring.

A collective contractual debt negotiation needs the participation of the major creditors and the banks that must have a constructive attitude towards such a negotiation. As in contract law, an agreement must not touch the rights of third parties not taking part in the agreement. Some stakeholders should be excluded from the negotiations out of practicality. These are non-financial parties like workers, consumers and even non-financial trade creditors because they have largely divergent interests and legal positions. Then there are those hold-out creditors that hope to reap advantages from the negotiation without diminishing their asset value ("free riders"). There are also stakeholders that are not allowed by law to participate, e.g. tax authorities.

The debtor must also have a constructive attitude towards the negotiation that must promise better outcomes than a formal proceeding. With such an agreement the management stays in place and is not under special threat of liability for fraud or mismanagement.

The negotiations begins by the main financial creditors taking the lead and organise the representation of the other participating creditors often by a creditors' steering committee. Thus there are two negotiations taking place, viz. between creditors and debtor as well as between the creditors. The latter discussion is eased by a small number of participants and a common aggregate position and aggravated by differing interests. Suppose a substantial creditor is insured by credit default swaps against default and may have an interest to enforce the credit event or a distressed fund, aka "vulture fund", has bought a big stake of the debt at a big discount. Then discussions will fail.

The parties will define a negotiation period that is accomplished by entering into a standstill agreement to suspend adverse actions by both the debtor and the creditors.

Very often external independent advisers are hired to help with the negotiations and try to alleviate the mutual distrust. It is of utmost importance that the financial situations of both debtor and creditors are transparent.

In the best of cases negotiations terminate with a contractual agreement to restructure the debtor's finances. The biggest stumbling block will be the required unanimity of creditors.

The agreement may contain provisions of the following kind:

- rescheduling of payments and extension of maturity
- conversion of currency,
- alteration of interest rates,
- forbearance of penalties,
- alteration and waiver of covenants,
- debt-equity swaps,
- restructuring of security,
- interest forgiveness and
- debt write-off.

These actions are important but often do not suffice to remove the financial difficulty. *New loan facilities* must be provided with an additional security or provisions for those who provide new financing.

2.15.4.3 Legal Action

Some codes of obligation foresee the necessity to inform the court or some authority about illiquidity and insolvency. In this case a contractual restructuring may not even be possible.

Under the auspices of an authority, e.g. finical supervisor or court, there are tools for hybrid restructurings. An example are pre-packaged insolvency plans that rest on some social norms. There is the so-called London approach fostered by the Bank of England (Garrido 2012, 41).

Resorting to insolvency proceedings has some disadvantages but also advantages. Low speed and higher cost are just some of the negative sides. On the other hand formal proceedings come always to an end, create higher transparency and better analysis of the financial situation, remove the hold-out problem etc.

As shown in Fig. 2.27 there are two major options, i.e. restructuring if the business is still viable or liquidation. The proceeding is opened with a preliminary procedure to secure the situation and to allow for the analysis for later decision.

The bankruptcy proceedings differ widely from country to country and by legal system. Some codes favour the protection of the company, e.g. the USA, or of the creditors, e.g. Germany. Most often the jurisdiction of the debtor's domicile is relevant, but there may be cases where the so-called centre of main interest is decisive.

For ECAs and their proverbial patience and long view they prefer a higher recovery above a quick resolution. Liquidity is not their problem.

References

Agarwal, N., & Wang, Z. (2017). Does the US EXIM Bank really promote US exports? *The World Economy, 41*(5), 1378–1414.

Ams, J., Baqir, R., Gelpern, A., & Trebesch, C. (2018). Sovereign default. In IMF (Ed.), *Sovereign Debt: A Guide for Economists and Practitioners*. Washington DC: IMF. https://www.imf.org/~/media/Files/News/Seminars/2018/091318SovDebt-conference/chapter-7-sovereign-default.ashx?la=en.

Atradius (2013). *General Conditions: Buyer Credit, GC 370/13, Abroad* . Publication, Atradius Dutch State Business NV, Amsterdam. https://atradiusdutchstatebusiness.nl/nl/documenten/370---44.314.02.e--buyercredit-370-13.pdf.

Bate, J., & Earle, W. (1820). In J. Bate & W. Earle (Eds.), *A plan for the establishment of a British commercial insurance company, for the protection of trade*. London: G. Sydney.

BCBS (2018). The treatment of large exposures in the Basel capital standards—Executive Summary. In *Executive summary, bank for international settlements: Basel committee on banking supervision*. Basel: Financial Stability Institute. https://www.bis.org/fsi/fsisummaries/largeexpos.pdf.

Britannica (2020). Bottomry—The Editors of Encyclopaedia Britannica. https://www.britannica.com/topic/bottomry. [Online; accessed 18-August-2020].

CGAP (2006). Commercial loan agreements. In *A technical guide for microfinance institutions*. Washington, DC: Consultative Group to Assist the Poor/The World Bank.

Czarnocki, C., Champion, R., & Apeadu-Siaw, J. (2020). *International trade finance: Commercial letters of credit and independent payment undertakings, Thomson Reuters Practical Law*. https://ca.practicallaw.thomsonreuters.com/5-517-9373?transitionType=Default&contextData=(sc.Default)&firstPage=true#co_anchor_a346259.

Freund, C. (2016). *The US export-import bank stimulates exports*. Washington, DC: Policy brief, Peterson Institute for International Economics. https://www.piie.com/system/files/documents/pb16-23.pdf.

Garrido, J. (2012). *Out-of-court debt restructuring*. Washington, D.C.: World Bank

Gianturco, D. (2001). *Export credit agencies : the unsung giants of international trade and finance*. Westport, CT: Quorum Books

Gigerenzer, G., Swijtink, Z., Porter, L., Beatty, J., & Krüger, L. (1989). *The Empire of chance: How probability changed science and everyday life*. Cambridge, England, New York: Cambridge University Press.

Hamann, K., & Habicht, H. (1966). Zur Geschichte der deutschen Exportkreditvresicherung. In C. Claussen, H. Schäffer, & H. Abs (Eds.), *Neue Perspektiven aus Wirtschaft und Recht: Festschrift für Hans Schäffer zum 80. Geburtstag am 11. April 1966*, (pp. 197–207). Homblot: Duncker u. https://books.google.ch/books?id=8Qh0hsRiJpcC.

HM Treasury (2020). *Government as insurer of last resort: Managing contingent liabilities in the public sector*. London: UK Government. https://assets.publishing.service.gov.uk/government/uploads/system/uploads/attachment_data/file/871660/06022020_Government_as_Insurer_of_Last_Resort_report__Final_clean_.pdf.

Iannotta, G. (2010). *Investment banking: A guide to underwriting and advisory services*. Berlin, London: Springer.

Julius, H. (Ed.) (1905). *Meyers Konversations-Lexikon, Ein Nachschlagewerk des allgemeinen Wissens 1893–1901* (5th edn.). Leipzig, Germany: Bibliographisches Institut.

Jus, M. (2013). *Credit Insurance*. San Diego, CA: Elsevier Science.

Kagan, J. (2020). *What is an aleatory contract?* https://www.investopedia.com/terms/a/aleatory-contract.asp.

Krueger, A. (2002). *A new approach to sovereign debt restructuring*. Washington, D.C.: International Monetary Fund.

Luk, K. (2011). *International trade finance: A practical guide* (2nd edn.). Kowloon, Hong Kong: University of Hong Kong Press.

Pozzolo, A. F. (2002). Secured lending and borrowers' riskiness. *SSRN Electronic Journal*. https://www.bis.org/publ/cgfs19bdi1.pdf.

Roubini, N., & Setser, B. (2004). *Bailouts or bail-ins?: responding to financial crises in emerging economies*. Washington, D.C.: Institute for International Economics

Salcic, Z. (2014). *Export credit insurance and guarantees: A practitioner's guide*. Basingstoke: Palgrave Macmillan.

Schumacher, J., Trebesch, C., & Enderlein, H. (2018). Sovereign defaults in court. In *CESifo Working Paper Series 6931*, CESifo.

Stephens, M. (1999). *The changing role of export credit agencies*. Washington D.C.: International Monetary Fund.

Stiglitz, J. E., & Weiss, A. (1981). Credit rationing in markets with imperfect information. *The American Economic Review, 71*(3), 393–410.

Stulz, R. (2015). Risk-taking and risk management by banks. *Journal of Applied Corporate Finance, 27*(1), 8–18.

SwissRe (1986). *A reinsurance manual of the non-life branches* (4th edn.). Zurich: Swiss Reinsurance Company.

SwissRe (2017). La storia delle assicurazioni in Italia. Zurich: Brochure, Schweizerische Rückversicherungsgesellschaft. https://www.swissre.com/dam/jcr:1a10f44c-0996-4ba4-9cc5-42ba0df7de3a/150Y_Markt_Broschuere_Italy_webN.pdf.

SwissRe (2019). World insurance: The great pivot east continues. *Sigma, 3*, 2019. https://www.swissre.com/dam/jcr:b8010432-3697-4a97-ad8b-6cb6c0aece33/sigma3_2019_en.pdf.

Tirole, J. (2009). *The Theory of Corporate Finance*. Princeton: Princeton University Press.

Wikipedia contributors (2019). Loan agreement—Wikipedia, The Free Encyclopedia. https://en.wikipedia.org/w/index.php?title=Loan_agreement&oldid=889582446. [Online; accessed 28-April-2020].

Wikipedia contributors (2020). Insurance—Wikipedia, The Free Encyclopedia. https://en.wikipedia.org/w/index.php?title=Insurance&oldid=954393600. [Online; accessed 2-May-2020].

Insurance Background

3

Insurance as a tool rests upon two pillars, a *juristic* and a *statistic*. Jurist has developed over the centuries a heavy body of rules and philosophies. *Utmost good faith* is such a stronghold. It requires all parties to reveal any information that could feasibly influence their decision to enter into a contract. Applicants for cover are legally obliged to present all material and known facts truthfully. Material *misrepresentation* can void the contract, i.e. the insurance policy.

But we do not want to dwell on this pillar. In the following we present statistical and mathematical background of insurance, especially credit insurance.

3.1 The Central Limit

In the time of Enlightenment the classical probabilists took over the aleatory contracts, e.g. insurance, from the jurists (Gigerenzer et al. 1989, 26). This is especially true for life insurance where the first life tables were compiled.

The first recognition that the *variation* of sums, or the mean of sums, does not increase linearly with the addition of terms dates back to the eighteenth century. Pierre Simon Laplace described this phenomenon quite generally in 1810 (Stigler 2016, 51ff) that became known as the *central limit theorem*. For a very simplified version one could think that the variation of a sum – or its mean, that is the sum divided by the number N – of terms added, increases proportionate to $\sqrt{N}$, provided that the terms to the sum have some similarity but are independent from each other. Taking the sum of the weight of a thousand ants plus one elephant would not fit into this theory (see Fig. 3.1).

This implies that the sum of many single items, e.g. rather a homogeneous insurance portfolio, experiences a lesser variation of claims. This is the diversification effect for large enough a portfolio. This also means that one has to provision less than the sum of the portfolio exposures.

C. Franzetti, *Pricing Export Credit*, Management for Professionals,
https://doi.org/10.1007/978-3-030-70285-4_3

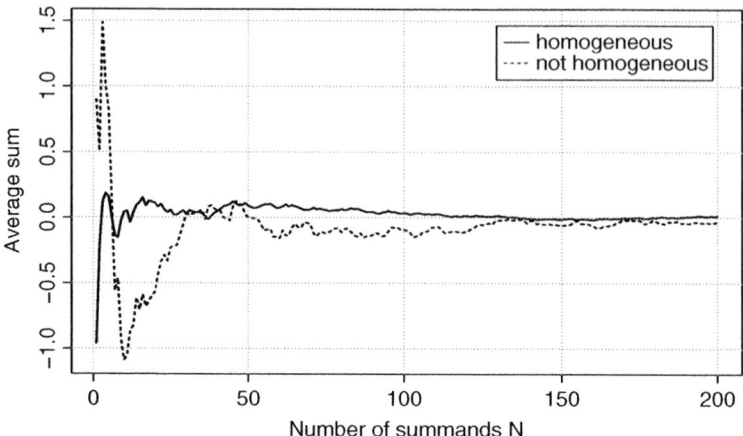

Fig. 3.1 A random run of sums. The more random terms are added the closer converges the curve to zero and the more homogeneous the summands the smaller the variation. The sum can be the annual loss of an insurance

Embedded in this phenomenon is the notion of *insurability* that requires a rather large number of policies of rather uniform and little correlated covers. This is called a homogeneous portfolio. For quantification we need to introduce the expectation $E()$ (see page 77) and the variance $Var()$. The expectation can be thought as mean or average and the variance as the dispersion or average deviation in an experiment where a random variable L is drawn many times.

Quantitatively this homogeneity is estimated by the *Lindeberg condition* (see Bronstejn and Semendjajew 1985, 677) that states that an insured risk with cover L_i should comply with

$$\frac{L_i - \mathrm{E}(L_i)}{Var(L)} < \epsilon, \tag{3.1}$$

or with risk capital RC as proxy for the variance of the portfolio and the pure premium $\pi^* = \mathrm{E}(L_i)$:

$$L_i - \pi_i^* < \epsilon \cdot \mathrm{RC}. \tag{3.2}$$

Regulators, both in banking and insurance, set for ϵ a maximal value of 15–25%.

In simple words: every single cover minus premium must stay below a given rather low threshold defined as a relation to the risk capacity of an insurance company.

In lines of insurance, e.g. hail or credit and surety, the potential damage is variable within limits. Single large losses above a certain threshold are classically modelled by Pareto I distributions with typical parameters. For credit and surety above one million CHF the Swiss regulators assume a value of 0.75, for liability 1.8

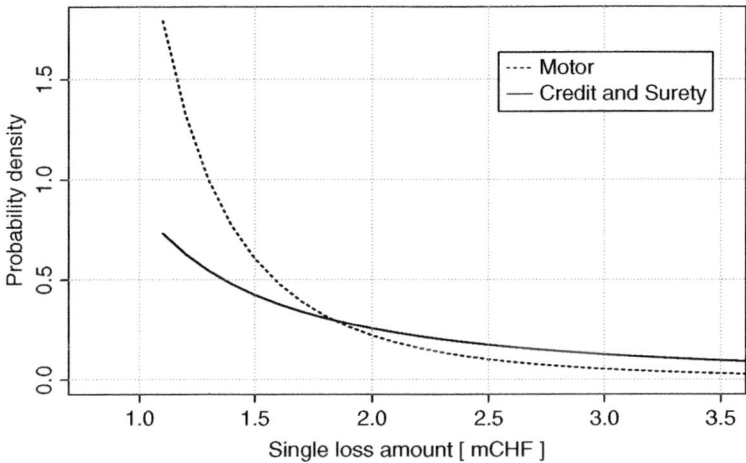

Fig. 3.2 Severity of insurance lines. Comparison of typical motor liability insurance and credit and surety single loss amount beyond threshold. These are the large losses. C&S is more risky and more inhomogeneous than motor

and for motor 2.5. Figure 3.2 shows the distributions. The function was originally conceived for the distribution of income.

3.1.1   Probability

Probability is a very difficult philosophical subject. Modern textbooks on the subject treat it axiomatically, "a real number assigned to an event A following the three axioms ..." (Wasserman 2004, 5). This means there is a set of rules to which "probability" abides and we will not dwell too long on the matter. For a deeper exploration see for example (Franzetti 2011, 62–67).

Subjective Bayesians advertise probability as a degree of belief, confidence or credence of suitable agents. For (Keynes 1921, 5) the probability concerns propositions, i.e. statements that can be either true or false, and not "events" or "occurrences". Thus he states:

> Let our premises consist of any set of propositions h, and our conclusion consist of any set of propositions a, then, if a knowledge of h justifies a rational belief in a of degree α, we say that there is a probability relation of degree α between a and h.

Similarly, Bruno de Finetti posits that probability exists only subjectively within the minds of individuals. He defined subjective probabilities in terms of the rates at which individuals are willing to bet money on events, even though, in principle, such *betting rates* could depend on state-dependent marginal utility for money as well as on beliefs. Probabilities exist as "the degree of belief in the occurrence of an event attributed by a given person at a given instant and with a given set of information" (de Finetti 1974, 3).

For Richard von Mises, the subject of probability theory are long sequences of experiments or observations repeated very often and under a set of invariable conditions. Thus, probability can be thought as a *limit of frequency*. This is the frequentist approach. With this concept there exists no probability for a single event, e.g. probability of rain tomorrow. Finance and actuarial science base many calculations on such time series. But subjective probabilities are also considered in an aspect called *credibility theory*. Actuaries are rather practical theorists.

Now, the subjectivist's view is broader than the frequentist's. The frequencies can be the basis of knowledge or information upon the subjective probability is founded. In the subjective approach the argument, we do not have enough data, is not valid. It equates to "we don't have enough fantasy".

3.1.2 Random Walk and Diffusion

The concept of random walk has been elaborated at the very beginning of the twentieth century, separately and simultaneously, in different fields. In 1905, the statistician Karl Pearson asked for a distribution of mosquitoes infestating a forest. At each time step, a single mosquito moves a fixed length a, at a randomly chosen angle. He coined the term "random walk", although mosquitoes fly. The same year Albert Einstein also published his seminal paper on Brownian motion that he modelled as a random walk, driven by collisions with gas molecules.

A couple of years earlier, the theory of random processes was also developed by Louis Bachelier in his truly remarkable doctoral thesis, *La Théorie de la Spéculation*, published in 1900 (Bachelier 1900). He proposed the random process or random walk as the fundamental model for financial time series, e.g. stock prices, many decades before this idea became the basis for modern theoretical finance, e.g. Black–Scholes formula for options.

The term became famous again with the book of Malkiel (1981) "A random walk down Wall Street" wherein he states: "the market prices stocks so efficiently that a blindfolded chimpanzee throwing darts at the Wall Street Journal can select a portfolio that performs as well as those managed by the experts". Nowadays, the animal has to throw something else at a screen.

In diffusion from a point source, i.e. the mosquitoes are released in the middle of the forest or a pollutant is thrown in the middle of a pond, each particle can move right or left by a distance a with equal probability (in a one-dimensional forest). After some big number of moves N the location of the particle is distributed according to a normal distribution as a consequence of the *central limit theorem*. Thus graphically we start with a very narrow distribution that flattens out over time (see Fig. 3.3). The curve is symmetric implying the mean to be zero. But the deviation s is proportionate to $\sqrt{N}$.

Suppose we observe a credit rating of ρ at time $t_0 = 0$. If the rating follows something similar to a diffusion process, then over time there will be an increasing likelihood that the rating has drifted away from ρ. This can be observed in the rating migration tables of the rating agencies.

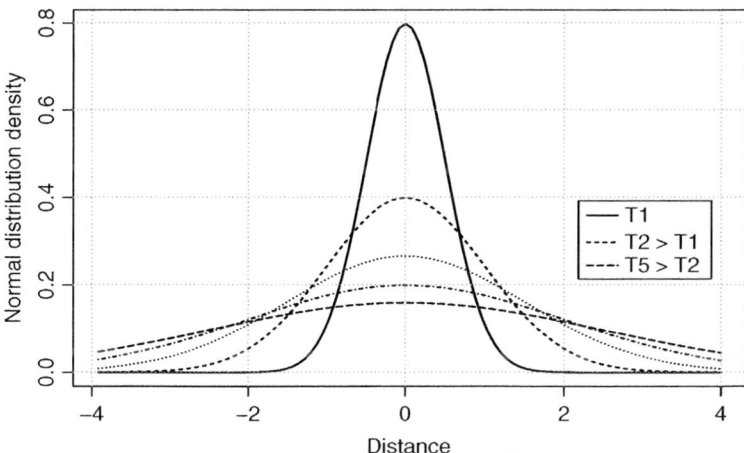

Fig. 3.3 A diffusion process, schematically. The normal distribution density in a diffusion setting becomes wider with the passage of time

3.1.3 Expected Value and Utility

We have discussed probability that is closely related to expected value. In the seventeenth century the *expected value* or expectation was easier to grasp than probability because it is observable as fair price of an aleatory contract or even more as fair price in gambling. The fair price is the average payoff in a long run of similar gambles (Hacking 2006, 91). Later on the expectation $E()$ was understood as the probability of an event $p(a)$ times the outcome of the event v,

$$E(a) = p(a) \cdot v, \tag{3.3}$$

or for multiple events a_i analogously

$$E(a) = p(a_1)v_1 + p(a_2)v_2 + \ldots + p(a_n)v_n. \tag{3.4}$$

For a simple insurance with loss probability $p(a)$ and loss L there are two states, i.e. loss happens with loss L, or loss does not happen with zero loss. Thus

$$E(L) = p(a) \cdot L + (1 - p(a)) \cdot 0. \tag{3.5}$$

Implicitly we have made usage of the facts (or settings or axioms) that the probability of all possible events sums to 1, the sure event has probability 1 and there are no negative probabilities. Therefore, probabilities are in the range of 0–1.

Example 3.1 (Dice Rolling). What is the fair price of a gamble consisting in rolling a fair dye and paying out the numbers thrown? The probabilities are all 1/6 for each face. The expected value is

$$E(v) = \frac{1}{6} \cdot (1 + 2 + 3 + 4 + 5 + 6) = 3.5.$$

The player pays 3.5 and has the chance of a payout between 1 and 6. In the long run there should be no winner or loser. Luck is ephemeral. The variance is also an expectation but not of v but $(v - \mu)^2$. For the dice this yields

$$Var(v) = E[(v - E(v))^2] = \frac{1}{6} \cdot (2.5^2 + 1.5^2 + 0.5^2 + 0.5^2 + 1.5^2 + 2.5^2) = 2.91.$$

The standard deviation is the square root of the variance, thus sd $= 1.71$.   △

Example 3.2 (Insurance Premium). A very simple insurance contract would stipulate: an event triggers a loss L of 100. The probability p for the event occurring is 25%. What is a "fair price" π? According to the discussion so far it is simply:

$$\pi = E(L) = p \cdot L = 0.25 \cdot 100 = 25.$$

Suppose we have just insured a launch of a satellite.   △

The concept of *utility* was introduced by Jeremy Bentham in 1780. His book begins with the following words (Bentham 1789, i):

> Nature has placed mankind under the government of two sovereign masters: *pain* and *pleasure*. (…) The principle of utility recognizes this subjection. (…) By the *principle of utility* is meant that principle which approves or disapproves of every action whatsoever, according to the tendency which it appears to have to augment or diminish the happiness of the party whose interest is in question.

Maximising utility means that human beings avoid pain and try to maximise pleasure.

The definition of utility is as follows:

> By utility is meant that property in any object, whereby it tends to produce benefit, advantage, pleasure, good, or happiness, (all this in the present case comes to the same thing) or (what comes again to the same thing) to prevent the happening of mischief, pain, evil, or unhappiness to the party whose interest is considered: if that party be the community in general, then the happiness of the community: if a particular individual, then the happiness of that individual.

Nowadays, economists discuss utility much more soberly, understanding it to be a variable whose relative magnitude indicates the direction of preference for some good (Hirshleifer 1988, 89). Moreover, they nearly always invoke the so-called rule of diminishing marginal utility, that is $u'' \leq 0$. On utility functions see for example Haugen (2001, 132). In this context we are much more concerned with losses than

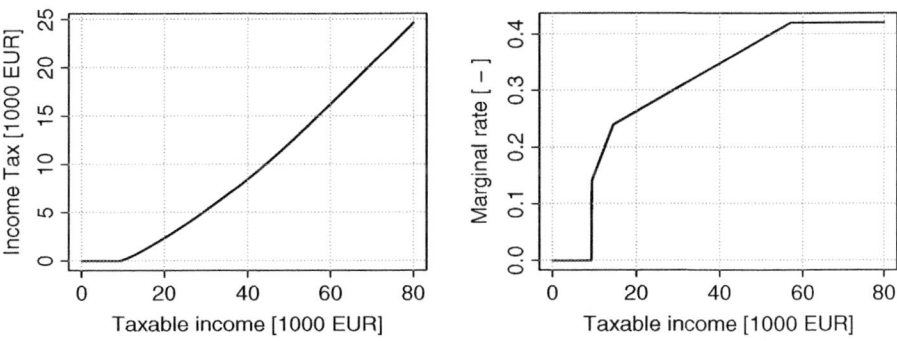

Fig. 3.4 German income tax system. Left the absolute amount of the tax, right the marginal increasing rate. Thus the "harm" to the tax payer increases

with gains. So the analogy would be that aversion increases with the potential degree of loss. Insurance actuaries' corresponding notion is called harm function $h(x_i)$ with the general property $h'' \leq 0$ (Daykin et al. 1994, 190). So, instead of using the loss L we could take $h(L)$ for incorporating our risk attitude.

Risk attitude or tolerance can be modelled by utility functions. They would be applied for example on risk-neutral premia to incorporate a risk surcharge.

Example 3.3 (Utility/harm of Income). Most income tax systems embody the principle of diminishing utility as a means of attaining some distributional effect within society. This is a feature of liberal policies as promoted by John Stuart Mill. This means that with increasing income the tax rate increases. Figure 3.4 shows an implementation of this increasing rate in the German tax system, the only to the author's knowledge to use a mathematical formula and not a table. △

3.1.4 Diversification, Compensation

A definition of insurance from Alfred Manes is (Wikipedia 2020):

> The essence of insurance lies in the elimination of the uncertain risk of loss for the individual through the combination of a large number similarly exposed individuals who each contribute to a common fund of premiums sufficient to make good the loss caused any one individual.

This is a hidden description – "large number similarly exposed" – of the central limit theorem above, the corner stone of insurability.

3.1.4.1 Diversification in the Collective
The diversification in the collective, i.e. the pool or portfolio of insured risks, is a profane description of the mathematical limit theorem. The ideal of equal potential

loss amounts from independent risks can hardly be attained. This situation may be alleviated by using reinsurance to level the peaks and to increase homogeneity. A second precaution involves provisioning for this situation, because the less homogeneous the portfolio the higher the technical provision.

Having a very little diversified pool of risks brings insurance close to betting, as in insuring a lonely satellite launch.

3.1.4.2 Compensation in Time

Insurance companies that are not in the run-off must accumulate reserves in times of prosperity. Enough high a capital endowment secures the business. It is often cited the "gambler's ruin" situation. The more money he brings to the roulette table the longer he will be playing.

We expand on the example with an insurance cover for a satellite launch. As they are rather rare it might be impossible to have several covers in the same year and producing some diversification. But insuring the launches over several periods may deliver a positive equalising effect. Compensation in time could be dubbed longitudinal versus latitudinal for the diversification in the collective.

Higher capital is often seen as costly. But there is still the *Modigliani–Miller theorem* of indifference saying that the capital structure is not relevant for the cost of capital.

3.2   Conservation of Risk

In physics you have the classical conservation laws, that is of mass, energy, momentum and angular momentum. In business there is the conservation of risk as potential harm. The probability of the risk materialising may be reduced but not the potential. The risk comes into existence through contracts, duties and rights with promises. In an inner circle of participants to export you may find the supplier, the buyer, the insurer and a bank. So the risk from the commercial export contract can be allocated between these four participants. Every party is bound by contracts – maybe by law or some other form of agreement – to other stakeholders. From this second circle the whole economy is tied in (see Fig. 3.5).

With insurance type of contracts one party decides to take a specific risk for a premium. If there was no insurance either the undertaking would not take place or someone else would have to take the risk. In our context there are risks, or at least one class of risks, that are out of scope. The breach of the commercial contract, let us call it *performance risk*, is in theory not insurable because it may not be fortuitous. If it materialises there is at best a *recourse provision* to cure the effects of this risk. But if the supplier goes into bankruptcy there may be nothing left.

Because there are no effective remedies the ECA implicitly assumes this risk. Nobody else will. Banks devise mechanisms to steer clear of this risk. The same is true for breach of the insurance contract by the exporter when the proceeds have been assigned. Banks shun this situation.

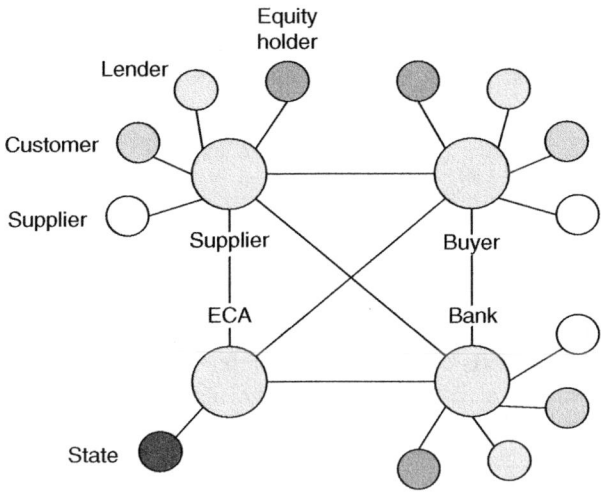

Fig. 3.5 Risk and the contractual network

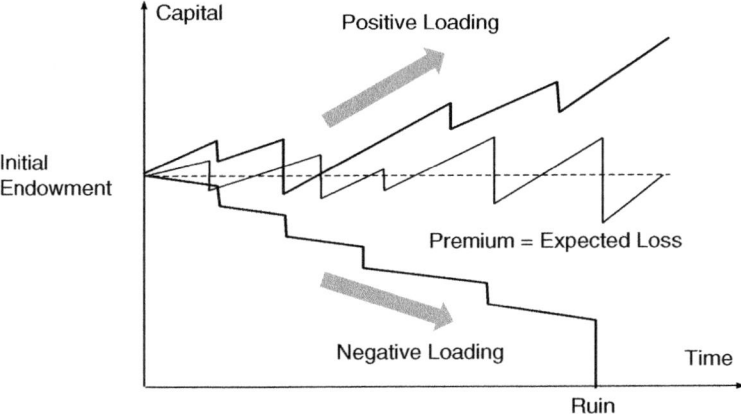

Fig. 3.6 Ruin process. Regular premium payments accrue the capital, while claims reduce it. Charging less than the expected loss will lead almost certainly to ruin

3.3   Ruin Process

Figure 3.6 depicts in a very synthetic way the fundamental situation of an insurance company. It is the *Lundberg Process* (Lundberg 1909). While premium arrives quite regularly, claims happen randomly but according to some probability distribution and with sizes of another distribution. As with the gambler's ruin the company stays the longer in business the higher the initial endowment. This is a necessary but not sufficient condition for survival. The insurance company should impose premia that are higher than the expected loss. For two reasons: first the company can err on the distribution (model risk) and secondly must prevent extremely high random losses. Now a company, an ECA backed by the government, may have extremely deep pockets. Then the insurer could argue for a premium equalling the expected loss plus margin for administrative cost in the limit.

The endowment or risk capital is similar to the concept of distance to default that is also used outside the insurance industry.

3.4   Pricing Strategies

We describe both pricing strategies of insurance companies and of commercial lender for loans. For ECAs as direct lenders both aspects are relevant.

Pricing strategies to a vast extend are meant to steer risks. Setting the price also means, at least as a control, to calculate the cost. Accountants speak then of costing. Pricing of credit is done by the market maker for bonds or by bid and asks requests of investors on exchanges.

3.4.1 Insurance Companies

Since the seventeenth century the fair price in aleatory contracts and especially in insurance is the expected loss in an insured interest. The operational cost differs by insurance type. In natural disaster cover the expected loss shadows the operational cost, whereas in motor liability the efficiency and control of operational cost are essential. In state backed middle to long-term credit insurance the expected loss component is preponderant.

Therefore, the pricing, pardon costing, is done according to the following scheme:

$$
\begin{aligned}
\text{Premium} = \ & \text{Expected Loss} \\
& + \text{Loading for risk} \\
& + \text{Margin for operational cost} \\
& + \text{Margin for capital and profit.}
\end{aligned} \tag{3.6}
$$

The expectation can be based on empirical "experience", on subjective probabilities or a mix of both. The lack of reliable time series does not suffice to not get to an opinion.

3.4.2 Banks

For many borrowers, the factors that determine a bank's interest rate are a mystery. And for credit insurers also. Commercial banks have the treasury department as internal bank. It decides with the *Asset and Liability Committee* ALCO, i.e. with the business divisions, treasury and risk management, how to steer the bank and its balance sheet by means of internal risk-adjusted prices (see Fig. 3.7). Incentives and disincentives are used to steer the bank. Therefore, the funding cost for the treasury need not be the funding cost allocated internally.

A very simple loan-pricing model – actually it is a costing model – assumes that the rate of interest charged on any loan includes four components (Diette 2000):

1. the funding cost incurred by the bank to raise funds to lend, whether such funds are obtained through customer deposits or through various money markets;
2. the, internal or outsourced, operating costs of servicing the loan, which include application and payment processing, and the bank's wages, salaries and occupancy expense;
3. a risk premium to compensate the bank for the degree of default risk inherent in the loan request; and
4. a profit margin on each loan that provides the bank with an adequate return on its capital.

This is to show that banks are not more sophisticated than insurance companies in assessing the price of risk.

Many investment banks have for trading purposes a so-called credit value adjustment CVA desk where credit deals have to be "insured". The adjustment, which can be thought as a premium, is levied for risk management purposes and to allocate funds efficiently. The methods applied are much more sophisticated than in trade finance.

Fig. 3.7 The treasury as internal bank (Franzetti 1995, 212). It is responsible for the overall asset and liability management and steering with internal funding cost

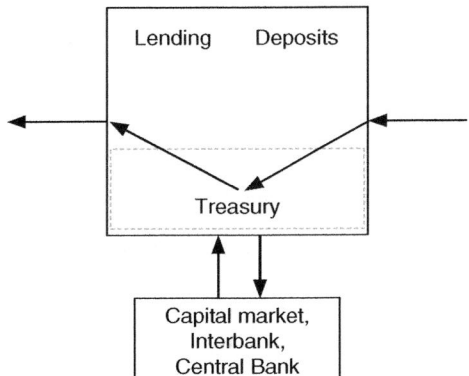

3.4.3   Credit Market

The credit market is constituted mainly by bond trading and credit derivatives trading. The first is very illiquid for corporate bonds and effected through dealers. Bond dealers post bid/ask prices when solicited to do so. Most quoted prices are only indicative.

The dealer does not know whether the customer wants to buy or to sell and therefore he or she incorporates in the quotes his or her risk surcharge beyond expected default, if ever he or she uses this notion. Bond yields may be taxable and such arguments find their way into the price.

Credit derivatives are very clean instruments that do not consider the many features of a bond, e.g. callability etc., and may have a different scope, e.g. restructuring is not a credit event. But the drawback here is that this market does not cover the same breadth as corporate bonds.

3.4.4   Direct Lender

Direct lenders have to do both pricing of credit risk and pricing a loan. They must consider the banking industry in order not to undercut their interest rate.

As a governmental agency the funding cost of a highly rated country may be lower than those of the domestic banks. Even the cost for an issuance is much lower for governments. Therefore some provisions are taken to set minimum interest rates and have a "level playing field".

Banks are supposed to be able to borrow at interbank-lending rates that are actually not true. Nonetheless, it is logical to use such benchmarks and to add arranging or underwriting fees. Very good banks borrow on average 55 bp above treasury rates, and fees are about 77 bp. Level playing fields mean here that the agency must make necessarily some profit.

References

Bachelier, L. (1900). *Théorie de la spéculation*. Paris: Gauthier-Villars.
Bentham, J. (1789). *An introduction to the principles of morals and legislation: Printed in the year 1780, and now first published*. Goldsmiths'-Kress library of economic literature 1450–1850. London: T. Payne. https://books.google.ch/books?id=vCI0AQAAMAAJ.
Bronstejn, I. N., & Semendjajew, K. A. (1985). *Taschenbuch der Mathematik* (23rd edn.). Thun: Deutsch.
Daykin, C., Pentikainen, T., & Pesonen, M. (1994). *Practical risk theory for actuaries*. London: Chapman & Hall.
de Finetti, B. (1974). *Theory of probability* (Vol. 1). New York: John Wiley & Sons.
Diette, M. D. (2000). *How do lenders set interest rates on loans? A discussion of the concepts lenders use to determine interest rates*. https://www.minneapolisfed.org/article/2000/how-do-lenders-set-interest-rates-on-loans.
Franzetti, C. (1995). Riskmanagement von Finanzinstituten. In H. Siegwart (ed.), *Jahrbuch zum Finanz- und Rechnungswesen* (pp. 195–214). Zürich: WEKA-Verlag.

Franzetti, C. (2011). *Operational risk modelling and management*. Boca Raton: CRC Press.

Gigerenzer, G., Swijtink, Z., Porter, L., Beatty, J., & Krüger, L. (1989). *The Empire of chance: How probability changed science and everyday life*. Cambridge, England, New York: Cambridge University Press.

Hacking, I. (2006). *The emergence of probability : a philosophical study of early ideas about probability, induction and statistical inference*. Cambridge, New York: Cambridge University Press.

Haugen, R. (2001). *Modern investment theory* (5th edn.). Upper Saddle River, N. J.: Prentice Hall.

Hirshleifer, J. (1988). *Price Theory and Applications* (4th edn.). Englewood Cliffs: Prentice-Hall.

Keynes, J. M. (1921). *A Treatise on Probability*. London: MacMillan.

Lundberg, F. (1909). Über die Theorie der Rückversicherung. *Transactions of the International Congress of Actuaries, 1*(2), 877–955.

Malkiel, B. (1981). *A random walk down Wall Street : the time-tested strategy for successful investing*. New York: W.W. Norton & Company.

Stigler, S. (2016). *The seven pillars of statistical wisdom*. Cambridge, Massachusetts: Harvard University Press.

Wasserman, L. (2004). *All of statistics : a concise course in statistical inference*. New York: Springer.

Wikipedia (2020). Versicherung (Kollektiv)—Wikipedia, Die freie Enzyklopädie. [Online; Stand 29. April 2020].

Finance Fundamentals

4

We would like to be as brief as possible, nonetheless laying the groundwork for later use in the pricing section or other calculations. We touch credit risk, interest rates, yields, risk-neutral probabilities and the Merton model in addition to default rates and recovery as well as risk assessment.

4.1 Credit Risk

Credit risk can be seen at least in two very different ways: as an analogy to life insurance where a subject may have a given survival rate given specific features like sex, age, health conditions etc. Such survival rates are established from actuarial procedures based on historical data collections. In this frame the survival of a debt depends on features like rating, maturity, economic conditions and so forth.

The second framework treats credit as a market good that is traded through risky fixed-income products. The products are mainly corporate bonds. Bonds are complex derivatives from interest rates and credit. The most disentangled products are credit default swaps, because both interest rates and term to maturity are distilled out.

In a division Sales & Trade of an investment bank there is the clear traditional distinction between operational trading desks named "Rates", "Credit" and "Equity", see Fig. 4.1 (Kuznetsov 2007, 321). Interest rates and credit risk can be treated separately.

These two different views of the same subject, i.e. market and life table, imply also two distinct pricing mechanisms. The actuarial is grounded on historical time series of credit event recordings and thus is smooth and stable over time. Market data of credit is high frequency data that incorporates almost immediately relevant economic news. Export credit agencies need to choose or to blend the two data sets for their pricing.

We will return to this subject while considering different notions of probability.

© The Author(s), under exclusive license to Springer Nature Switzerland AG 2021   87
C. Franzetti, *Pricing Export Credit*, Management for Professionals,
https://doi.org/10.1007/978-3-030-70285-4_4

Fig. 4.1 Trading desks in an
investment bank. Fixed
income is split into rates and
credit. The main driver for
corporate bond prices is
"credit". Convertible bonds
on the other hand are with
equity

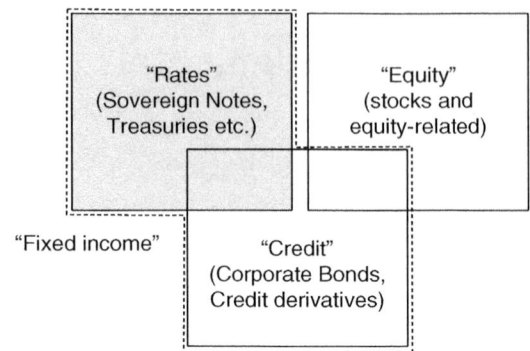

4.2   Interest Rates and Term Structure

Interest is payment from a borrower to a lender of an amount above repayment of the amount borrowed, that is the principal sum. Expressed as a fraction of the principal it becomes the *interest rate*.

The interest rate is a function of many independent variables, inter alia:

- opportunity cost,
- inflation,
- default risk,
- term to maturity,
- policy action of central banks etc.

There are several hypotheses for the shape of the term structure, see also Fabozzi and Modigliani (2009, 380–389).

The *liquidity preference theory* states that investors are risk-averse and therefore demand a premium for holding securities with longer maturities than preferred. Investors prefer to have cash available today rather than later. Therefore it is expected that the yield curve as premium for liquidity should have a rising slope.

According to the *pure expectations hypothesis* the forward rates determine the curve as expectations of future spot rates. Instead of buying a long-term bond, an investor could roll-over short-term bonds. Arbitrage equalises the fixed term and the roll-over strategy. Thus, upward sloping would imply an expected increase in short-term rates. Evidence supposes that there is nonetheless an unexplained risk premium.

Segmented markets hypothesis assumes distinct segments with their own preference that can be shifted by higher premia in other segments. This shift is associated with the so-called preferred habitat theory. The resulting yield curve is therefore shaped by the factors of supply and demand at each maturity length.

Interest rates are used to determine the time-value of money. Since some years the interest rates have become so low or even are below zero that it seems obvious that central banks with their huge programmes drive the rates and not the markets.

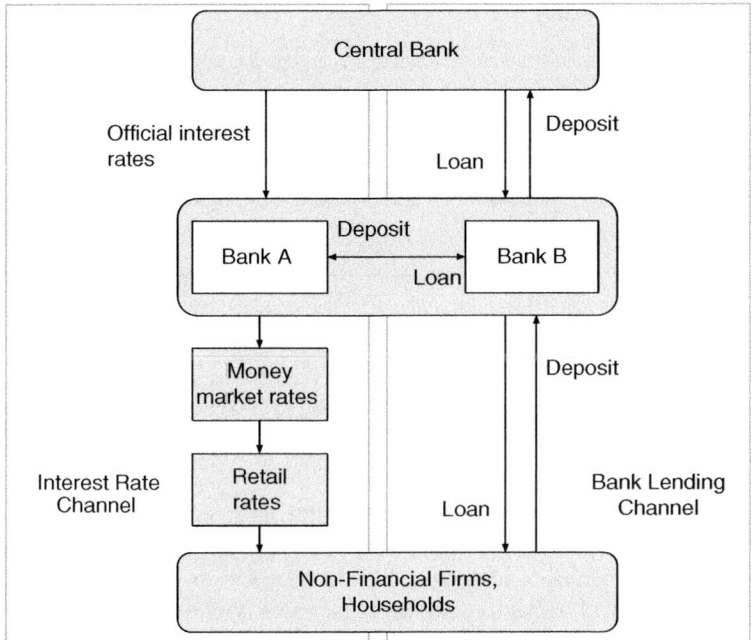

Fig. 4.2 The two interest rate channels (Source: Nomura Global Economics)

Or there is so much surplus of money that cannot be invested sensibly. Central banks use two channels as shown in Fig. 4.2. The focus is on price stability, i.e. inflation. For some calculations with interest rates negative values may pose a problem.

4.3   Time-Value of Money

The concept of time-value of money, i.e. the present value and the future value, rests on the idea of opportunity cost. If I have one monetary unit MU today, I could spend it or consume it later. In the second case I could lend it to somebody who needs it today and would repay later. What is the price for lending or the price of postponing consumption?

There are reference rates for interest with respect to the credit quality of the borrower. The most used methodology is to extract a nearly risk-free rate from the best borrowers and then to add some additional margin, viz. the *credit spread*, for the borrower in question.

The actual value of money today is the so-called (net) present value PV (or v_0) as opposed to the future value FV (or v_1 and v_2 in Fig. 4.3). Calculating the present value of a future value is called discounting. Inferring the future value from a prior value is dubbed accruing. The link between the two is given by the interest rate (Fig. 4.5) that is identified as yield of government bonds and notes with their respective maturity. Thus the name yield curve.

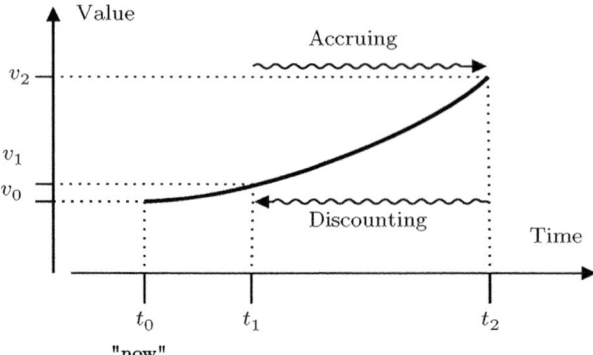

Fig. 4.3 Time-value of money. Earning interest from t_1 to t_2 is called accruing; the opposite time travel is called discounting

There are many ways to define interest rates as it is done for many specific instruments and situations, e.g. short-term lending, repos, notes and bonds with coupons, rates for bank accounts etc., having all their special features. Now it is the duty of the central banks to distil all these rates, yields or prices into the most basic interest term.

The calculation between the present and future values can be made according to the following formulae:

$$\text{PV} = v_0 = df(t_0, t_1) \cdot v_1 = df(t_0, t_2) \cdot v_2 \tag{4.1}$$

$$\text{FV} = v_2 = a(t_0, t_1) \cdot v_0 = a(t_1, t_2) \cdot v_1, \tag{4.2}$$

with $a(t_0, t_1) = 1/df(t_0, t_1)$. From this it follows, some kind of arbitrage free condition ("telescoping"):

$$df(t_0, t_2) = df(t_0, t_1) \cdot df(t_1, t_2) \tag{4.3}$$

$$a(t_0, t_2) = a(t_0, t_1) \cdot a(t_1, t_2). \tag{4.4}$$

This means that the discounting and accruing can also be done piece wise.

We can call the term $df(t_1, t_2)$ a "forward discount function", defined as

$$df(t_1, t_2) = \frac{df(t_0, t_2)}{df(t_0, t_1)}. \tag{4.5}$$

Discounting is additive, i.e. you can calculate the present value of a collection of future values. Assume three future payments c_1, c_2 and c_3 at the dates t_1, t_2 and t_3, and then the present value of the sum PV equals

$$PV(t_0) = df(t_0, t_1) \cdot c_1 + df(t_0, t_2) \cdot c_2 + df(t_0, t_3) \cdot c_3, \tag{4.6}$$

or more general with a more parsimonious writing, i.e. df_i for $df(t_0, t_i)$:

$$PV(t_0) = \sum_{i=1}^{N} c_i \cdot df_i. \tag{4.7}$$

Now we have to relate the discount factors to the interest rates. We skip here the money-market treatment of interest and show the ISMA and the continuous compounding method that is cherished by mathematicians. ISMA calculates as follows with $t = t_1 - t_0$ and the interest rate r_t:

$$df(t_0, t_1) = \frac{1}{(1 + r_t)^t}, \tag{4.8}$$

while continuous means

$$df(t_0, t_1) = \exp(-\hat{r}t) = e^{-\hat{r}t}. \tag{4.9}$$

There is a very slight difference in the interest rates, i.e. $r \neq \hat{r}$. E.g. $r = 0.05$ p.a., then $\hat{r} = 0.04879 = \log(1 + r)$.

There is another skew to be corrected, viz. the payment frequency. An annual interest of R is paid semi-annually as $R/2$. Therefore this pattern accrues as the first term and equals a single accrual as follows:

$$\left(1 + \frac{R}{2}\right)^2 = (1 + r), \tag{4.10}$$

or generally

$$\left(1 + \frac{R}{h}\right)^h = (1 + r), \tag{4.11}$$

with h the frequency of annual payments.

The discount factors are derived from the so-called yield curve that is constructed from money-market rates in the short term and bond and note yields in middle and long term. Bonds typically pay regular coupons $g_i = g$ and principal C at maturity.

Their price B is calculated from

$$B = \sum_{i=1}^{N} \frac{g_i}{(1 + r_i)^{t_i}} + \frac{C}{(1 + r_N)^{t_N}}. \tag{4.12}$$

For each payment date there is an appropriate interest rate r_i. The procedure to extract the r_i form bond prices is called "bootstrapping" by which the *yield to maturity* y is calculated as an average; thus, *yield curve* or *spot rate* is

$$B = \sum_{i=1}^{N} \frac{g_i}{(1 + y)^{t_i}} + \frac{C}{(1 + y)^{t_N}}. \tag{4.13}$$

We will use the bond spread later on, here the so-called Z-spread z as follows:

$$B = \sum_{i=1}^{N} \frac{g_i}{(1 + r_i + z)^{t_i}} + \frac{C}{(1 + r_N + z)^{t_N}}. \tag{4.14}$$

In some instances it can be useful to use the following approximation for small values $r_f \ll 1$ and $z \ll 1$:

$$1 + r_f + z \approx (1 + r_f)(1 + z) \tag{4.15}$$

and the discount function:

$$(1 + r_f + z)^{-t} \approx (1 + r_f)^{-t}(1 + z)^{-t}. \tag{4.16}$$

With this transformation Eq. (4.14) can be interpreted as a double discounting, with the risk-free rate and with the spread.

An other curve describes the *par yield*, i.e. the coupon rate g^* that values the bond at par:

$$1 = \sum_{i=1}^{N} \frac{g^*}{(1 + r_i)^{t_i}} + \frac{1}{(1 + r_N)^{t_N}}. \tag{4.17}$$

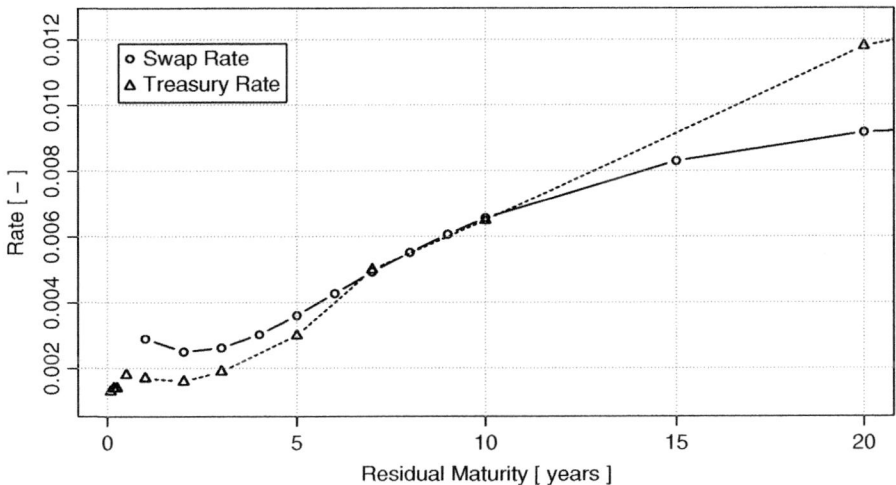

Fig. 4.4 Comparing swap and treasury rates as of 29th May 2020 (Source: US Treasury, St. Louis Fed, ICE). This snapshot in time contradicts the simple assumption that the swap rate due to its higher risk is just a shift of the treasury rate

Just for the sake of completeness we give the definitions of the most used "spreads":

- Z-spread, "zero-volatility spread" z, Eq. (4.14),
- I-spread: difference bond's yield y and the swap rate s,
- G-spread: difference between treasury bond yields r and corporate bond yield y,
- option-adjusted spread: zero-volatility spread z minus the call option's value.

For comparing CDS spreads with bonds we will use the Z-spread. Figure 4.4 shows actual swap and treasury rates. The curves intersect and do not show the typical relationship.

In order to get a smooth curve the yields are fitted to special functions. The ECB uses the following formula with six parameters (Nymand-Andersen 2018, 16), known as *Svensson's model*:

$$y(t) = -\beta_0 + \beta_1 \cdot \exp(-t/\tau_1) + \beta_2 \cdot \exp(-t/\tau_1) \cdot t/\tau_1 + \beta_3 \cdot \exp(-t/\tau_2) \cdot t/\tau_2. \tag{4.18}$$

Actual parameter values are given in Table 4.1. A simple alternative is the following from Haugen (2001, 347) with 4 parameters:

$$y(t) = (a_1 + a_2 \cdot t) \cdot \exp(-a_3 \cdot t) + a_4, \tag{4.19}$$

Table 4.1 The parameters
of the ECB for the yield curve
model (Eq. (4.18)) (Source:
ECB)

Parameter	2010-04-10	2020-04-12
β_0	3.330111	0.342924
β_1	−3.090130	−0.928774
β_2	7.162508	12.315088
β_3	−1.567309	−14.061122
τ_0	6.786207	2.125900
τ_1	1.965349	2.217366

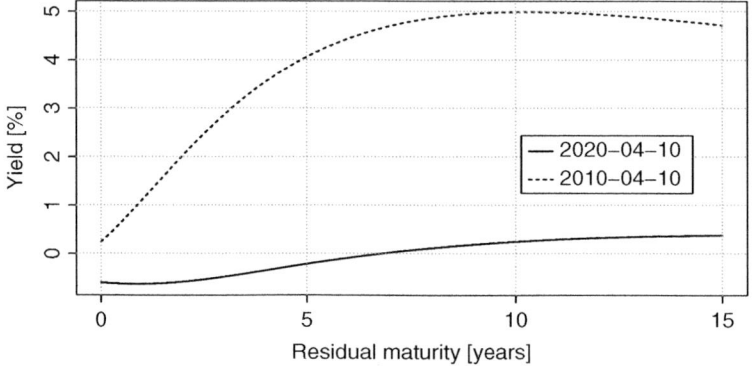

Fig. 4.5 Yield curves from the European Central Bank for EUR. The two curves are 10 years and one crisis apart. Negative interest rates are becoming customary. Negative rates lead to accruing discounts and vice versa

or Nelson–Siegel formula (Elton et al. 2001, 274):

$$y(t) = a_0 + (a_1 + a_2) \left[\frac{1 - e^{-a_3 t}}{a_3 t} \right] - a_2 e^{-a_3 t} \tag{4.20}$$

also with four parameters.

With the yield curve we are able to establish the time-value of future payments. The curve is fictionally "risk-free", in reality the yields of the best available qualities.

In Fig. 4.5 we see two yield curves for EUR implying the discount factors of Fig. 4.6. The two are just 10 years apart. While in 2020 we have the well known situation of massive liquidity pumped into the economy, thus showing negative yields, in 2010 we had quite a normal shape of the curve. Discounting with negative yields leads to an accrual. For practical purposes it is often assumed that yields are at minimum zero.

The US Treasury publishes daily a yield curve as series for given maturities. The FED argues against a parametric model. Thus users may interpolate the yields they need.

The credit quality relative to the best qualities, either sovereign or AAA rated, is often taken into consideration by adding a *credit margin* or *credit spread* to the risk-free yield.

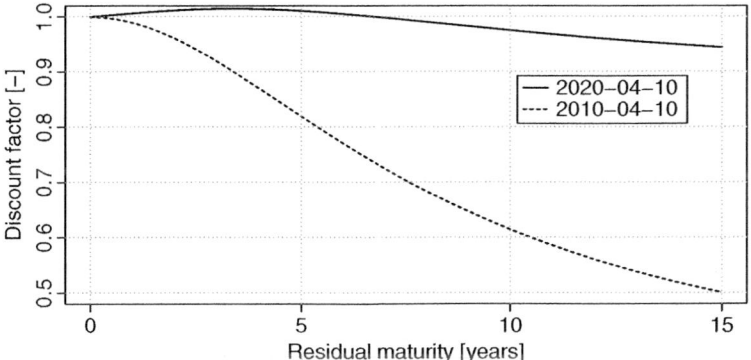

Fig. 4.6 Discount factors for EUR. For the more recent discount factor curve we see the abnormal values greater than 1 due to the negative interest rates

4.3.1   Par-Interest Rate

Let us make a practical example for the usage of the discount rates. Assume two capital goods' export of a present value of 1 financed by a credit with identical repayment terms. One export goes to a country with a discount curve identical to the EUR curve for 2010 and the other to a country with a curve like 2020. How should they differ? The only difference is the interest rate on the credit. Assume there are N semi-annual instalments of $1/N$ each plus interest at a rate of z. Then the present value is

$$\text{PV} = 1 = \frac{1}{N} \sum_{i=1}^{N} df(0.5 \cdot i) + \frac{1}{N} \sum_{i=1}^{N} (N+1-i) \cdot \frac{1}{2} \cdot z \cdot df(0.5 \cdot i). \qquad (4.21)$$

From here we get

$$z = 2 \cdot \frac{N - \sum\limits_{i=1}^{N} df(0.5 \cdot i)}{\sum\limits_{i=1}^{N} (N+1-i) df(0.5 \cdot i)}. \qquad (4.22)$$

We calculate now these interest rates and show them in Fig. 4.7. As could be anticipated the most recent yield curve gives negative interest rates, while the older one shows a comprehensive shape. Again, these interest rates, given their discount functions, make sure that the present value of the credit receivables is at par.

This is an important feature because it motivates the fact that credit insurance, more precisely OECD Arrangement, does not take interest into account for premium calculation. If it did, it was a clear double counting because interest is in the export value as present value. Now, where interests charged in the export contract are

Fig. 4.7 Interest rate calculation for OECD type of credit

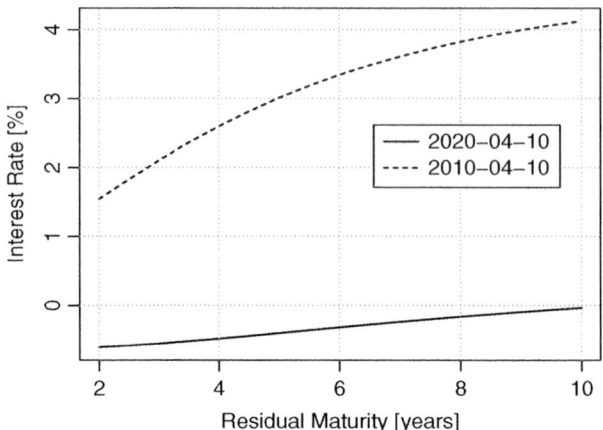

massively higher than needed for the present value – they should be nearly risk-free because of the credit insurance – then they should be considered not fair. ECA would also insure the premium; therefore, excessive interests are even more unfair.

Equation 4.22 can be generalised. Suppose we have the variable capital payments C_i with $\sum_i C_i = C$ or the relative capital payments c_i with $\sum_i c_i = 1$ and the interest rate z. We assume $t_0 = 0$. Then the present value of such a stream is

$$C = \sum_{i=1}^{N} C_i \cdot df_i + z \cdot \sum_{i=1}^{N} \left[C - \sum_{j=1}^{i-1} C_j \right] \cdot (t_i - t_{i-1}) \cdot df_i \qquad (4.23)$$

or relative:

$$1 = \sum_{i=1}^{N} c_i \cdot df_i + z \cdot \sum_{i=1}^{N} \left[1 - \sum_{j=1}^{i-1} c_j \right] \cdot (t_i - t_{i-1}) \cdot df_i. \qquad (4.24)$$

And from here follows the "par-interest-rate" z as

$$z = \frac{1 - \sum\limits_{i=1}^{N} c_i \cdot df_i}{\sum\limits_{i=1}^{N} df_i - \sum\limits_{i=1}^{N} \left[1 - \sum\limits_{j=1}^{i-1} c_j \right] \cdot (t_i - t_{i-1}) df_i}. \qquad (4.25)$$

We can define S_1 and S_2 such that Eq. (4.24) transformed reads as follows:

$$1 = S_1 + z \cdot S_2, \qquad (4.26)$$

and then we could introduce the margin m and the upfront premium π as

$$1 + \pi = S_1 + (z + m) \cdot S_2. \tag{4.27}$$

The calculation of the upfront premium given a margin or the margin calculation given the upfront premium is simply

$$\pi = m \cdot S_2 \tag{4.28}$$

$$m = \frac{\pi}{S_2}. \tag{4.29}$$

The margin and the upfront premium are linked by a factor S_2 that is dependent on the discount factors of the relevant currency. There is no shortcut or rule of thumb to that.

We could have simplified Eq. (4.23) by defining a new term for the remaining principal structure as follows:

$$R_i = C - \sum_{j=1}^{i-1} C_j = \sum_{j=1}^{N} C_j - \sum_{j=1}^{i-1} C_j = \sum_{j=i}^{N} C_j$$
$$r_i = 1 - \sum_{j=1}^{i-1} c_j = \sum_{j=i}^{N} c_j. \tag{4.30}$$

Example 4.1 (Premium-Margin). With Eq. (4.28) we have a formula to transform margin in premium and vice versa. The link is the term:

$$S_2 = \sum_{i=1}^{N} r_i \cdot (t_i - t_{i-1}) \cdot df_i. \tag{4.31}$$

With the yield curve for EUR from 2010 above we calculate S_2 for the maturities $T = 3a, 5a, 10a$ with equal instalments as $S_2(T) = 1.710, 2.618, 4.613$. Thus a margin of 100 bp translates to a premium rate of 2.618% for 5 years. Without discounting the value is 2.75%, or simply $m(n + 1)/4$ with $n = 10$ semesters. $\triangle$

The example above shows that the upfront premium depends both on the discount rates, but not that heavily, and the principal repayment stream. This in turn depends on the term of the repayments.

Here it is assumed that the premium margin is not defaultable, i.e. it will be paid also after default. Later we will come back to the defaultable margin.

Example 4.2 (Annuity). The OECD Arrangement states that the principal sum of an export credit shall normally be repaid in equal instalments or, when appropriate (e.g. when support is provided for lease transactions or for the export of standalone machinery or equipment), equal repayments of principal and interest combined.

The latter pattern is known as an *annuity*. Recurring payments of an amount W for n times for semi-annual periods at an interest rate of r p.a. The accrual factor is $a = (1 + r/2)$. Beginning at t_0 the balance is B, after a semester it is $B \cdot a - W$, after two $(B \cdot a - W) \cdot a - W$ and after three $((B \cdot a - W) \cdot a - W) \cdot a - W$. By induction we see after k semesters the balance is

$$B(t_k) = B \cdot a^k - W \sum_{j=0}^{k-1} a^j. \tag{4.32}$$

The geometric series can be simplified, because $s = 1 + a + a^2 + \ldots + a^{k-1} = 1 + a(1 + a + a^2 + \ldots + a^{k-2}) = 1 + a(s - a^{k-1})$ and from here $s = (1 - a^k)/(1 - a)$. We deduce W with $B(t_N) = 0$ and $k = N$:

$$W = B \cdot a^N \cdot \frac{a - 1}{a^N - 1}, \tag{4.33}$$

or expanded by a and with $R = r/h$ and $h = 2$, the frequency of payment per year:

$$\frac{W}{B} = \frac{R \cdot (1 + R)^N}{(1 + R)^N - 1}. \tag{4.34}$$

With $R = 0.025$ and $N = 10$ it follows $W/B = 0.1070031$. If the relative export value plus premium is 1.05 then W must become $1.05 \cdot W$. △

4.3.2 Discounting Floating Rates

Most floating rate notes or debt in general is based on an *indicator rate* plus margin. The indicator rate may be a common short-term interest rate, e.g. LIBOR, EURIBOR, OIS or a treasury rate, or an inflation index, consumer price index etc. The main feature is that it will be periodically reset, mainly with an interest payment and thus semi-annually. The normal interest for the period t will be z_t given the index l_t and the *quoted margin m*:

$$z_t = l_t + m. \tag{4.35}$$

With floaters we know the next payment amount and the next index value. Beyond the next index and thus farther in the future the payment amounts are not known. The convention is to take the actual index value for all future unknown payments. The yield to maturity is expressed as *discount margin k*. For short-term instruments like 6M-LIBOR the ACT/360 convention is used. Moreover, f_t are the number of days to the next payment divided by 360 and f_j the number of days in the interest period. The margin m is called "quoted margin". Generally, for the dirty price $B(t)$, i.e. the present value, we use

$$B(t) = \frac{1}{1 + (l_1 + k)(f_1 - f_t)} \cdot \sum_{i=1}^{n} \frac{c_i}{\prod_{j=2}^{i} \left(1 + (l_j + k)f_j\right)}. \tag{4.36}$$

If we have a varying principal p_i to consider, then the cashflows c_i become $c_i = p_i \cdot (l_t + m)$ for $i > 1$ and $c_1 = 1 \cdot (l_1 + m)$. Thus

$$B(t) = \frac{1}{1 + (l_1 + k)(f_1 - f_t)} \cdot \sum_{i=1}^{n} \frac{c_i + p_i \cdot (l_t + m) \cdot f_i}{\prod_{j=2}^{i} \left(1 + (l_t + k)f_j\right)}. \tag{4.37}$$

Floating rate notes are quoted in the market by the discount margins. For additional information see Brown (1998, 43) and Somaia (2011, 6). To determine the margin one needs a procedure as described in Chap. 4.5.

Example 4.3 (Quoted Margin). At inception of the floating rate cashflow stream Eq. (4.37) reduces to

$$B(t_0) = \sum_{i=1}^{n} \frac{c_i + p_i \cdot (l_1 + m) \cdot f_i}{\prod_{j=1}^{i} \left(1 + (l_1 + k)f_j\right)}. \tag{4.38}$$

The price is $B(t_0) = 1$, the relative export value or credit value. Let us assume that $k = 0$, that is the risk-free case. Further, the stream consists of $n = 10$ semi-annual payments of $p_j = 1 - (j - 1) \cdot 1/n$. The index l_1 is the 6M-EURIBOR as of April 2010, i.e. 0.945%. What is m? Eq. (4.38) simplifies to

$$B(t_0) - 1 = \sum_{i=1}^{n} \frac{1/N + p_i \cdot (l_1 + m) \cdot 0.5}{\left(1 + l_1 \cdot 0.5\right)^i} - 1 = 0. \tag{4.39}$$

Now we solve for m, the "risk-free par margin". Obviously, the margin is zero! Suppose the premium rate was 5% for a fixed rate stream. Then we have to solve $B(t_0) = 1.05$. Numerically we get $m = 0.01852$, approximately 2%. This is the path from upfront premia to margin of a variable interest rate. $\triangle$

4.3.3 Swap Curve

An interest swap is an exchange of a fixed interest rate over a given term with a floating rate. Its price is the difference of the two discounted cashflow streams. For calculation purposes it is advisable to add to both streams an equal principal payment to the last payment of the stream. By doing so nothing changes in the valuation because the two "phantom" payments cancel each other. Thus we compare two bonds, a fixed and a float.

Just remind that the typical short-term rate LIBOR l has the accrual $1 + l \cdot f_j$ with f_j the days in the period with the convention ACT/360. The float price is given by the adapted Eq. (4.37), risk-free with no margins, as

$$B_1(t) = df(t_0, t_1) \cdot \left[\sum_{i=1}^{n} \frac{1 \cdot l_t \cdot f_i}{\prod\limits_{j=2}^{i} \left(1 + l_t f_j\right)} + \frac{1}{\prod\limits_{j=2}^{n} \left(1 + l_t f_j\right)} \right] \tag{4.40}$$

$$= df(t_0, t_1)(1 + l_t \cdot f_0) = 1. \tag{4.41}$$

This miraculous simplification from Eq. (4.40) to (4.41) is due to the fact that the accrual and the discounting factor to 1. Discounting the cashflow at n to $n-1$ yields

$$1 = \frac{1 + l_t \cdot f_n}{1 + l_t \cdot f_n} = \frac{1 + l_t \cdot f_i}{1 + l_t \cdot f_i}. \tag{4.42}$$

By induction this leads to $i = 1$ as above to the first term as $(1 + l_t)$. The fixed bond's price is the discounting as follows:

$$B_2(t) = \sum_{i=1}^{n} z_n \cdot f_i \cdot df(t_0, t_i) + 1 \cdot df(t_0, t_n). \tag{4.43}$$

Now the swap rate z_n is determined for the maturity $t_n - t_0$ by transformation to yield:

$$z_n = \frac{1 - df(t_0, t_n)}{\sum\limits_{i=1}^{n} f_i \cdot df(t_0, t_i)}. \tag{4.44}$$

One LIBOR rate thus generates a whole curve.

Example 4.4 (Swap-Curve to Yield). We rewrite Eq. (4.44) with a new variable A_n as

$$z_n = \frac{1 - df(t_0, t_n)}{\sum\limits_{i=1}^{n-1} f_i \cdot df(t_0, t_i) + f_n \cdot df(t_0, t_n)}$$

$$= \frac{1 - df(t_0, t_n)}{A_{n-1} + f_n \cdot df(t_0, t_n)}, \tag{4.45}$$

so that we have

$$df(t_0, t_n) = \frac{1 - z_n \cdot A_{n-1}}{1 + z_n \cdot f_n} \qquad (4.46)$$

with $A_0 = 0$ and finally the zero coupon yields y_n:

$$y_n = h \cdot \left(df(t_0, t_n)^{\frac{-1}{h \cdot n}} - 1 \right). \qquad (4.47)$$

This inductive approach is known as bootstrapping. Remind that the first value z_1 equals the index value, e.g. LIBOR.

We start with the data from the swap rates as of May, 29th on the following grid in years:

```
[1]   1   2   3   4   5   6   7   8   9  10  15  20  30.
```

Now we implement the recursion formula as follows:

```
swprate<-c(0.290, 0.250,0.262,0.303, 0.361, 0.428, 0.493,
0.552, 0.607, 0.657, 0.831, 0.918, 0.966)
swprate<-swprate/100
tt<-c(1:10,15,20,30)
z<-c()
libor<-0.50975/100
tout<-seq(from=1,30,by=0.5)
# interpolate linearly on regular grid
z<-approx(tt, y=swprate, xout=tout, method="linear")$y
df<-c(); df[1]<-1/(1+libor*0.5)
A<-0; y<-c();h<-2
y[1]<-h*(df[1]^(-1/h)-1)
for (i in 1:30){
   j<-i+1
   A<-A+183/360*df[i]
   a<-(1-z[i]*A)/(1+z[i]*183/360)
   df[j]<-a
   y[j]<-h*(a^(-1/(j))-1)
}
y
 [1] 0.002547128 0.002946751 0.002743739 0.002540403
 [5] 0.002601791 0.002663123 0.002872481 0.003082001
 [9] 0.003378796 0.003676008 0.004020002 0.004364662
[13] 0.004699701 0.005035495 0.005340858 0.005646970
[17] 0.005932913 0.006219620 0.006480737 0.006742596
[21] 0.006924404 0.007106715 0.007289543 0.007472904
[25] 0.007656813 0.007841289 0.008026351 0.008212017
[29] 0.008398308 0.008585246 0.008676774
```

Figure 4.8 shows the rather small differences. Nonetheless, one has to be careful in applying the different curves for different purposes. A rate is not just a rate.   △

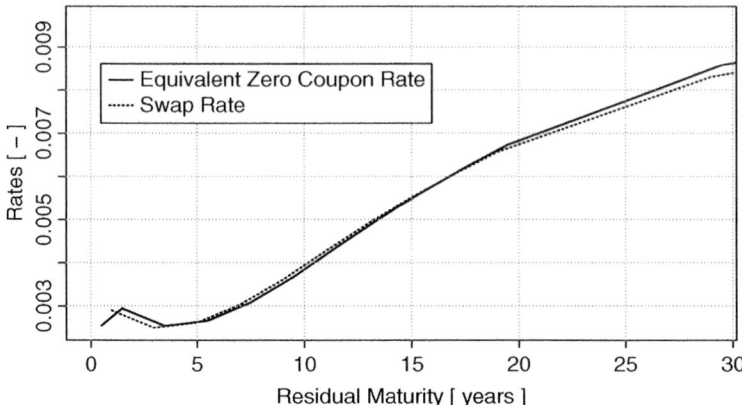

Fig. 4.8 Zero coupon rates from swap rates. There are slight differences due to accrual methods etc

4.3.4   Risk and Interest Rate

There are several interplays between risk and interest rate. One neglected is the different weighting in time. Suppose an export value of 1000, i.e. the present value, for the export in a low-yield and a high-yield country. The last instalment of 50 plus interest is due in 10 years. For simplicity assume a constant rate over the time dimension of either 0% or 15%. Thus the nominal interest rate on the credit is $z = 0$ in the first instance and $z = 0.1447611$ in the second (according to Eq. (4.22)).[1] Now we introduce the *modified duration* as first derivative of the expression of Eq. (4.7) of page 91:

$$D_{\mathrm{mod}} = -\frac{d}{dt} \sum_{i=1}^{N} c_i \cdot (1+y)^{-t_i}. \tag{4.48}$$

And thus:

$$D_{\mathrm{mod}} = \frac{1}{1+y} \sum_{i=1}^{N} t_i \cdot c_i \cdot (1+y)^{-t_i}. \tag{4.49}$$

---

[1]This z semi-annually corresponds to 15% annually by Eq. (4.10).

Now let us take the typical OECD pattern, i.e. semi-annual regular repayments of principal. This yields the following:

$$D_{mod} = \frac{1}{1+y} \frac{1}{N} \sum_{i=1}^{N=20} \left(\frac{i/2}{(1+y)^{i/2}} + z \frac{i/2(N+1-i)}{(1+y)^{i/2}} \right). \tag{4.50}$$

With some fantasy one could recognise a discounted time weighted life of the credit. Supposing $y = 0$ and $z = 0$, i.e. we disregard interest for the calculation, then the formula yields

$$D_{mod,0} = \frac{1}{2N} \sum_{i=1}^{N=20} i \tag{4.51}$$

$$= \frac{1}{2N} \cdot \frac{N(N+1)}{2} \tag{4.52}$$

$$= \frac{N(N+1)}{4N} \tag{4.53}$$

$$= \frac{20 \cdot 21}{80} = 5.25. \tag{4.54}$$

From this we could formulate the following proposition: "The repayment period of the Arrangement is the risk-free modified duration of the principal repayments".

Figure 4.9 shows the complete picture. Now, back to our two exports: the duration of the receivables of the 0%-country is approx. Five years, half the maturity, while the second pattern shows a duration of only 3 years. This means that the second

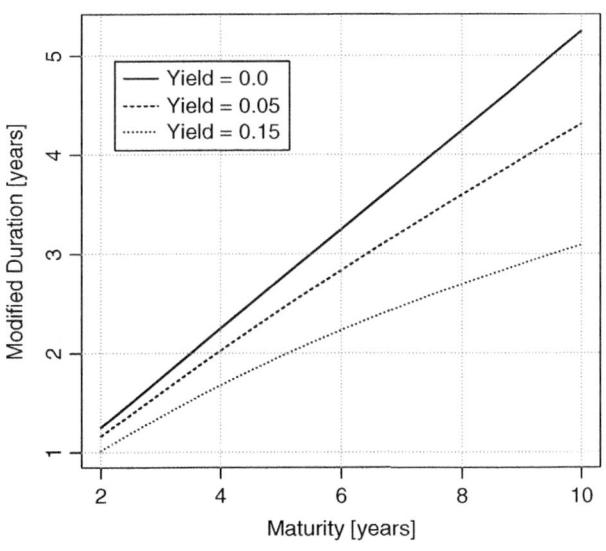

Fig. 4.9 Modified duration of the OECD payment pattern depending on different discount factors

credit is much more front-loaded, i.e. the first payments make up more discounted value than in the low-yield country. This results in a lower credit risk in the high-yield country.

Yet another measure of the repayment pattern is the second derivative of the cashflow stream with respect to yield, the so-called convexity. It is calculated as follows:

$$CX = \frac{1}{(1+y)^2} \sum_{i=1}^{N} t_i \cdot (t_i + 1) \cdot c_i \cdot (1+y)^{-t_i} \qquad (4.55)$$

or with the duration from Eq. (4.49):

$$CX = \frac{1}{(1+y)^2} \sum_{i=1}^{N} t_i^2 \cdot c_i \cdot (1+y)^{-t_i} + \frac{D_{\text{mod}}}{1+y}. \qquad (4.56)$$

The convexity is the measure for the change of duration given a change in yield.

Example 4.5 (Pseudo-Measures). In order to develop a feeling for these two measures, i.e. duration and convexity, we simplify Eqs. (4.49) and (4.55) by setting both the yield to zero as $y = 0$ as well as interest. Then we plot some patterns with their duration, see Fig. 4.10.   △

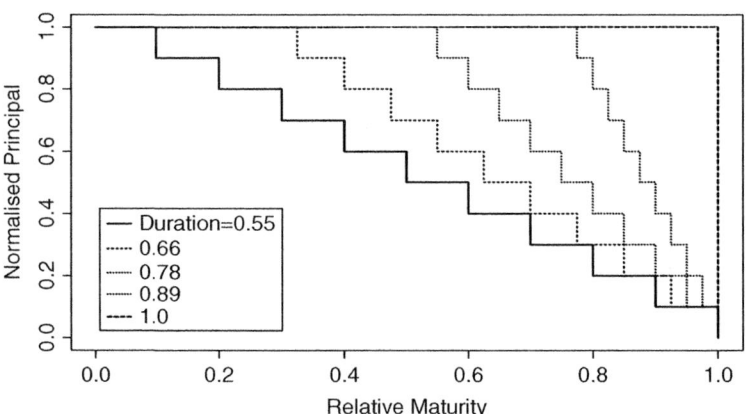

Fig. 4.10 Different repayment patterns with duration. The OECD standard comes with such a duration of 0.55

4.4 Interpolating Yield Curves etc.

We have presented three yield curve models, i.e. Svensson's, Haugen's and the model of Nelson–Siegel (Nelson and Siegel 1987), on page 93. Now some central banks do not like models, e.g. the FED in the USA. The US Treasury posts daily data for chosen maturities from the yields of their outstanding debt instruments. The longest maturity of 30 years is extrapolated as there are no such liquid issuances.

For this situation we have to interpolate the data, or, what results to the same, fit the given data to a model. With interpolation the model is implicit in the method chosen. The interpolation problem arises also with the probability of default curves that are given for certain fixed maturities.

To be clear: the intermediate values do not exist, and therefore interpolated values cannot be right or wrong, at best they are plausible or not. Most people would assume some smoothness of the curve.

Interpolation has the obvious advantage that all given points are matched exactly.

A linear interpolation is very simple but does not give smooth curves. With some pre-knowledge of the shape functions like the logarithm are applied, then linearly interpolated and transformed back. Generally for an x between x_i and x_{i+1} the sought value is

$$f(x) = f(x_i) + \left(f(x_{i+1}) - f(x_i)\right) \frac{x - x_i}{x_{i+1} - x_i}. \tag{4.57}$$

A more sophisticated method are spline functions where often piecewise cubic functions are used. One special algorithm is due to Hiroshi Akima (Wikipedia contributors 2019). It is widely available in numeric libraries (Gebhardt 2016).

An other solution is to use the term structure model with the most parameters, i.e. Svensson's model (Eq. (4.18)), and solve for the parameters. As the model has 6 parameters and the treasury curve has 12 points, some choice has to be made. Or, we apply a least square procedure for fitting.

Example 4.6 (Yield Curve). We build our work on the grid of values as of 2010-04-12 from Table 4.2. We fit the three models to the data and calculate the parameters, as shown in Listing B.5 on page 230. Then we plot the model curves (Fig. 4.11).

The model with the highest number of parameters fits the curve best. It is the model chosen by the ECB. A severe drawback is the initial guess of the parameter to get the solving algorithm working. It needs some experience.

We also show the interpolated values with the aforementioned spline function and the crude linear interpolation. The result is shown in Fig. 4.12. The cubic spline according to Akima's improved version is best, at least in this example.

This example is just one out of a myriad of possible constellations. Nonetheless, we would suggest to use the Akima improved function as a standard. △

Table 4.2 Daily US
Treasury Yield Curve Rates
for two distinct days (Source:
US Department of the
Treasury)

Maturity	2020-04-13	2010-04-12
1m	0.17	0.15
2m	0.29	–
3m	0.26	0.16
6m	0.27	0.24
1a	0.27	0.46
2a	0.25	1.07
3a	0.31	1.65
5a	0.44	2.60
7a	0.63	3.29
10a	0.76	3.87
20a	1.19	4.54
30a	1.39	4.70

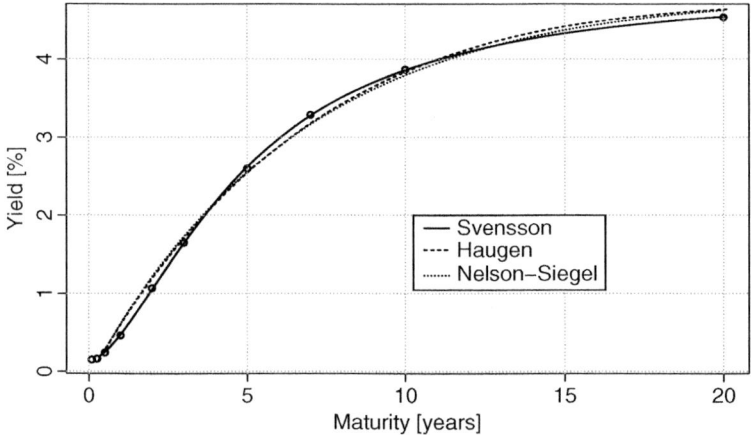

Fig. 4.11 Fitting models to grid data. The ECB used model to fit US Treasury yield is clearly the best, especially in situation where we have several changes in curvature

4.5   Yield Calculation, Implicit Equations

By Eq. (4.12) we see that it is a non-linear equation in y, a so-called polynomial. There are no easy ways to precisely calculate y besides numerical methods. The equation can be rewritten as

$$G(B, y) = B - \sum_{i=1}^{N} \frac{g_i}{(1 + y)^{t_i}} = 0. \qquad (4.58)$$

If the cashflows g_i are given, then B can be derived by Eq. (4.12).

For the solution of equations of the implicit type $G(y) = 0$ there are several numerical methods, from very simple and robust to very fast and less robust.

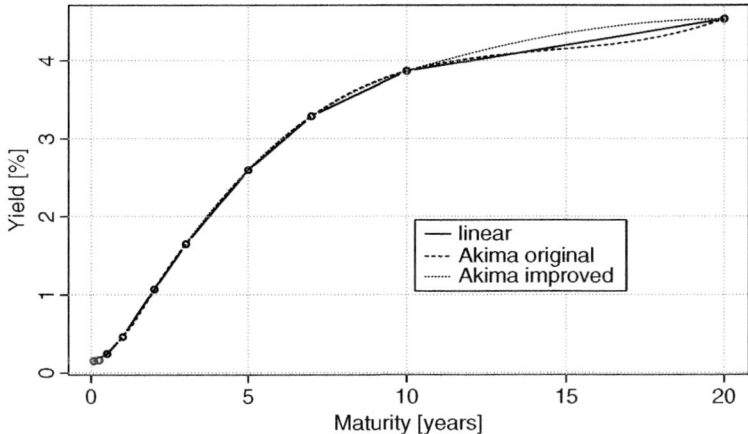

Fig. 4.12 Interpolating yield curves. At the longer end and when there are curvatures the linear interpolation is quite weak

Because computing time is abundant the most basic method will suffice. The algorithm called *bisection* has to evaluate the function $G(y)$ several times until the solution $G(y_n)$ of the n-th iteration is close enough to zero, i.e. $|G(y_n)| \leq \epsilon$.

Algorithm 4.1 (Bisection). To begin with we have to guess an interval that encloses the solution or root. Be the lower bound a and the upper b. Then we evaluate $G(a)$, $G(b)$ and $G_{\mathrm{mid}} = G((a + b)/2)$, the mid-point. Not all three will have the same sign, e.g. be greater than 0, because otherwise there is no zero root in the interval. If $G(a)$ and G_{mid} have the same sign, are thus on the same side of zero, we replace a with $(a + b)/2$. Otherwise, we replace b with $(a + b)/2$ and start a new calculation round until the threshold ϵ is reached or a given maximum number of iterations has been executed. $\triangle$

The main usage in our context comprises the following examples:

- yield to maturity from price,
- margin from defaultable bond and
- quoted margin of a floater (Eq. (4.38)) etc.

Example 4.7 (Finding Roots). The following functions can also be used for solving an implicit equation and finding the root.

```
DefautProbFromFixedBond(d,param),
FixedCouponBondYield(yield,param),
FixedBondDefautProb(mu,param),
GenericBondZSpread(zspread,param).
```

To this end, we have to specify the parameter list, e.g.

```
param=list(c,tvec,dfvec,price=0,h=2,mu))
```

and set the price. If the price is set to 0, then the function calculates the price. Then we have to embed it into the bisection algorithm, i.e.

```
bisect(0,0.2,param=param,FUN=DefautProbFromFixedBond)
```

and chose some appropriate interval, here [0, 0.2], that brackets the sought value. $\triangle$

4.6   Real and Risk-Neutral Probabilities

In the high time of asset pricing theory, end of the seventies of last century, the *fundamental theorem of asset pricing* was discovered (Ross 1978). It states that (Nau 2001, 107): "there are no arbitrage opportunities in a financial market if and only if there exists a probability distribution with respect to which the expected value of every asset's future payoffs, discounted at the risk-free rate, lies between its current bid and ask prices. This is just de Finetti's fundamental theorem of subjective probability, with discounting thrown in".

The market provides risk-neutral probabilities or previsions through the prices. These are implicit and can be extracted.

What does it mean that markets use risk-neutral probabilities while actuaries take real probabilities, i.e. historical frequencies?

If the pricing rests upon taking the expectation of defaultable debt then we use a risk-neutral position. Risk-neutral investors are indifferent about a government bond with an expected value of 100 and a risky bond of the same value. This does not coincide with reality. There is a premium. With risk-neutral probabilities this premium is accounted for. Therefore, using historic probabilities leads to slightly lower prices for risk.

4.7   Price of Risk

The notion of price of risk is used in investment theory. Historically it started with the question about optimal selection of a portfolio of stocks by Harry Markowitz (Markowitz 1952). Then in 1963 William F. Sharp simplified the theory to a *single index model*. Three years later some academics asked the question what happens if all investors used optimal portfolios. The answer was the so-called Capital Asset Pricing Model CAPM. For details see for example Haugen (2001).

The single factor model assumes a relationship between returns and index return as

$$\hat{r}_j = \alpha + \beta_j \cdot \hat{r}_K + \epsilon_j,$$

where α is constant and β_j is the gradient of the linear equation, K is an index, e.g. the market, and ϵ a not explained residual. It turns out that this means

$$E(r_j) = r_f + \beta_j \cdot (E(r_K) - r_f) \tag{4.59}$$

with

$$\beta_j = \frac{Cov(r_j, r_K)}{\sigma^2(r_K)}, \tag{4.60}$$

and r_f the risk-free rate. Is β_j greater than 1, the equity j is more risky than the index K. On the other hand if β_j is less than 1, it is less risky.

We introduce the so-called market price of risk γ as

$$\gamma = \frac{E(r_K) - r_f}{\sigma_K}. \tag{4.61}$$

We note here that the return is defined as the relative change in value of the market capitalisation of a company V_E, that is

$$r_j = \frac{\Delta V_E}{V_E} \approx \Delta \log(V_E). \tag{4.62}$$

Standard beta β is the so-called levered and also equity beta because it inherently reflects the capital structure of the company, i.e. debt to equity ratio. Unlevered beta compares the risk of a company's assets (or equity without debt) to the risk of the market. Unlevered beta, i.e. the beta of the assets, is generally lower than the levered beta or the beta of equity.

The formal connection between the two is as follows (Hamada's equation):

$$\beta_A = \beta \cdot \frac{V_E}{V_E + D}. \tag{4.63}$$

4.8 Distance to Default

There is this famous analogy of a firm's equity being a call option on the underlying asset. Because at the maturity of debt bondholders receive their debts, equity holders take the rest. This is due to Merton (1974) who paved the way for the Black–Scholes formula. The model can easily be visualised as Fig. 4.13. The similarity to the ruin process is evident (see Fig. 3.6).

KMV, a specialised risk management supplier, offered such a model assuming that debt D is homogeneous with time of maturity T, the balance is simply the equation $V_A(t) = V_E(t) + D(t)$ or the value of assets V_A equals the value of equity V_E plus debt D at all times. In addition the market ignores coupons and dividends,

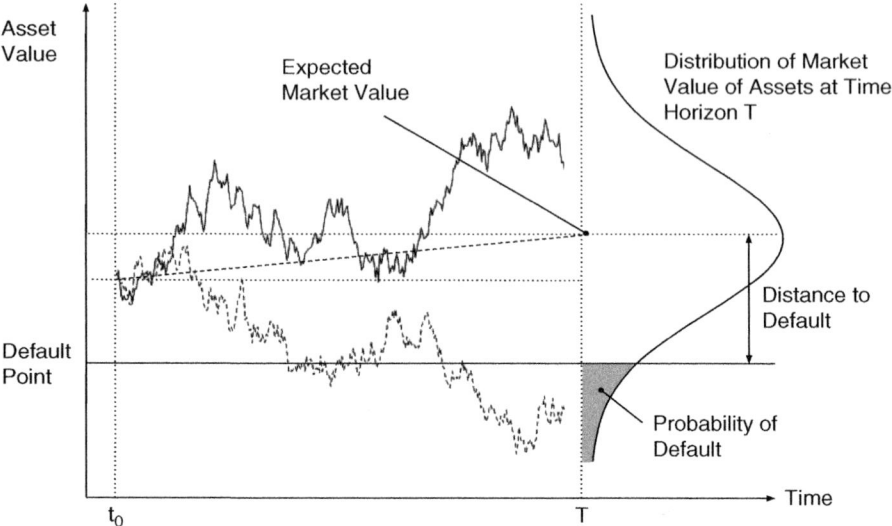

Fig. 4.13 The Merton model with random path of asset value, the distribution of asset values at time horizon and the distance to default. The default point is reached when the asset value falls below the debt. The distribution is assumed to be normal

there are no penalties to short sales etc., and assets are traded and follow a random walk. Thus with the call option analogy:

$$C(S, K, T, \sigma, r) \sim C(V_A, D, T, \sigma_A, r). \tag{4.64}$$

The analogy relates to $S \sim V_A$, the stock price and the asset value and $K \sim D$, the exercise value and the debt. The more tricky problem is to derive σ_A, that is not observable, from σ_E that can be learned from the stock exchange. r is the risk-free interest rate that makes the *risk-neutral* probability of default. The *Black–Scholes* standard price formulae are for calls C and puts P (Hull 2012, 313):

$$C = S_0 \Phi(d_1) - K \cdot e^{-rT} \cdot \Phi(d_2) \tag{4.65}$$

and

$$P = K \cdot e^{-rT} \cdot \Phi(-d_2) - S_0 \Phi(-d_1) \tag{4.66}$$

with

$$d_1 = \frac{\log\left(\frac{S_0}{K}\right) + (r + \frac{1}{2}\sigma^2)T}{\sigma\sqrt{T}} \tag{4.67}$$

$$d_2 = \frac{\log\left(\frac{S_0}{K}\right) + (r - \frac{1}{2}\sigma^2)T}{\sigma\sqrt{T}} = d_1 - \sigma\sqrt{T}. \tag{4.68}$$

The *distance to default* DD, the d_2 of the BS formula, is the distance between the expected value of the asset and the default point. Formally,

$$DD(t) = \frac{\log\left(\frac{V_A}{D}\right) + \left(r - \frac{1}{2}\sigma_A^2\right)(T - t)}{\sigma_A\sqrt{T - t}}. \tag{4.69}$$

From this we can also determine the model's *probability of default d*, i.e. with the cumulative normal distribution function $\Phi()$:

$$d(t) = Pr[V_A \le D] = \Phi(-DD). \tag{4.70}$$

This is also to say that the probability of default is not only a historical concept relating to the letter rating of a firm. There are several ways to derive and thus potentially different values for the probability of default. This method is dynamic as it depends on the stock price, or value of equity, that is fluctuating during a session of the stock exchange, at least for traded stocks. The model is seen as more useful for rating than predictions. We could call it a *market based* credit rating.

For calculating the value we need an additional equation for the volatility σ_A from the option formula as

$$\left| \begin{array}{l} 0 = \Phi\left(DD - \sigma_A\sqrt{T - t}\right) \cdot \sigma_A \cdot V_A - \sigma_E \cdot V_E \\ 0 = V_E - V_A \cdot \Phi(DD) - e^{-r(T-t)} \cdot D \cdot \Phi(DD - \sigma_A\sqrt{T - t}) \end{array} \right|. \tag{4.71}$$

This is a system of non-linear implicit equations to be solved for σ_A and $V_A(T)$. With Eq. (4.69) we get the distance to default.

Example 4.8 (Distance to Default). Let us analyse the data of an American conglomerate with an annual stock volatility of 0.56 and a debt to equity ratio of $D/V_E = 2.36$. Thus $V_A/D = 1 + 1/D/V_E = 1.42$. Assuming $r = 0.015$, $T - t = 1$ and $\sigma_A \approx \sigma_E \cdot V_E/V_A = 0.1667$ we derive $DD = 2.126$ and from here $PD(1) = 0.0167$. From Table A.1 we read approximately and generously BB as 1-year rating. Now the approximation is not good enough and complicates the matter.   △

Example 4.9 (DtD 2). Of course the solution of the system Eq. (4.71) has been implemented in many routines, so in R by the package `ifrogs`. For newer R-releases the library does not work but, as of writing, can be downloaded.[2] We analyse the company RIL that has a debt of 6.07 Trillion INR. The market capitalisation as of 17th June 2020 of 10.97tr INR, a book value of 3.87tr INR and

---

[2]https://rdrr.io/rforge/ifrogs/src/R/dtd.R.

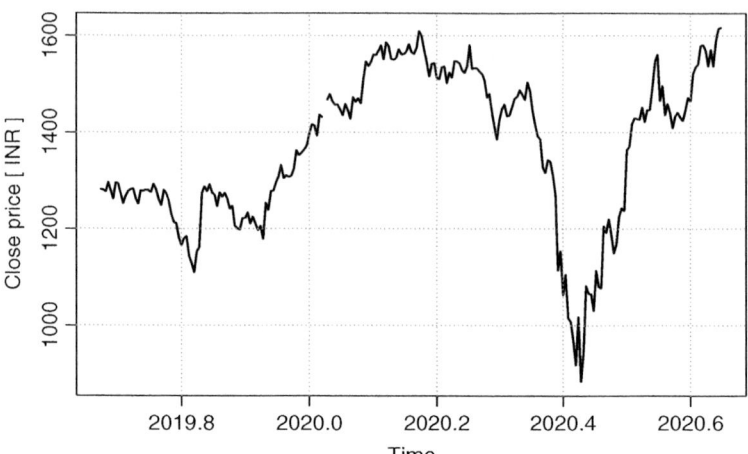

Fig. 4.14 Stock price of the company RIL, quote "RELIANCE.NS", for the last year (Source: yahoo). The Corona effect is very visible

an asset of 10.0tr INR. The volatility can be seen in Fig. 4.14 and calculated over the last 250 days as $\sigma = 0.4475515$. In the code we make use of $\Delta q/q \approx \Delta \log(q)$.

```
library(quantmod)
getSymbols("RELIANCE.NS", src = "yahoo",
from = as.Date("2019-06-17"), to = as.Date("2020-06-17"))

q<-c();j<-0
f<-RELIANCE.NS$RELIANCE.NS.Close
for (i in 1:length(f)){
   if (!is.na(f[i])){q[j+1]<-f[i]; j<-j+1}
}
sqrt(length(q)) * sd(diff(log(q)))
[1] 0.4475515
library(ifrog)
dd<-dtd(mcap=3.95,vol=0.44755,debt=6.07,r=0.076)
dd
     dtd.v    asset.v    sigma.v
2.2410166 9.5750173 0.1840472
pnorm(-dd[1])
     dtd.v
0.0125125
```

The 1-year default rate for this company is 1.25%.   △

Example 4.10 (Z-Score). There exists a simplified version of the calculation of the distance to default. It is based on actual balance sheet information and not expectation for the future and a simplification of the formula. It is known as *Z-score* (Chan-Lau and Sy 2006, 10):

$$DD(t_0) = \frac{1 - \frac{D(t_0)}{V_A(t_0)}}{\sigma_A \sqrt{T}} = \frac{1 - 1/1.42}{0.1667} = 1.8, \tag{4.72}$$

and from here $PD(t_0) = 0.0359$. This corresponds to a rating for 1-year rate for default of B. The official rating of this company is BBB – with a probability of default of 0.25%. The assumption $V_E \cdot \sigma_E \approx V_A \cdot \sigma_A$ is not good enough.

$\triangle$

We have produced the so-called risk-neutral probability of default by using the risk-free rate r. We can also calculate a real-world probability by substituting r with $R = r + s$, where s is the credit spread. Instead of using the formula for the call that represents equity we now take the put option formula that is tied to the call by the so-called put–call parity. In addition we use the real distance to default, i.e.

$$DD^*(t) = \frac{\log\left(\frac{V_A}{D}\right) + \left(r + s - \frac{1}{2}\sigma_A^2\right)(T - t)}{\sigma_A \sqrt{T - t}}, \tag{4.73}$$

where the interest rate is now not risk-free. The put value, or value of the debt at $t = 0$, is

$$D_0 = V_A \cdot \Phi(-DD^* + \sigma_A \sqrt{T - t}) - e^{-r(T-t)} \cdot D \cdot \Phi(DD^*). \tag{4.74}$$

Moreover, the present value of the debt D_0 is the discounted value of the future debt D; thus,

$$D_0 = D \cdot e^{-(r+s)(T-t)}. \tag{4.75}$$

Equating Eqs. (4.74) and (4.75) and with some transformation this yields the spread as

$$s = -\frac{1}{T - t} \log\left(\frac{V_A}{D} e^{r(T-t)} \cdot \Phi(-DD^* + \sigma_A \sqrt{T - t}) + \Phi(DD^*)\right). \tag{4.76}$$

This is an implicit function as DD^* is also a function of s. With a different approach we can distil the spread and relate it to the CAPM model. For this we need the equivalence of a risky discount with a risk-free discount of risky outcomes. It holds, as depicted in Fig. 4.15

$$V = \begin{cases} e^{-y(T-t)} & \text{risky discount} \\ e^{-r(T-t)}[1 - d + d\mu] & \text{risk-free discount of expected value.} \end{cases} \tag{4.77}$$

Fig. 4.15 Two ways to discount a risky cashflow. Either using risk-free rate and default probability (left) or discounting at the yield to maturity (right)

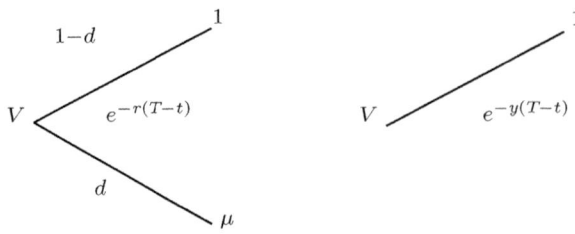

From these two representations we can deduce the spread as difference $y - r$ as

$$y - r = -\frac{1}{T - t} \log(1 - d \cdot (1 - \mu)). \tag{4.78}$$

Now we set for the probability of default d according to Eqs. (4.69) and (4.70):

$$d = \Phi(-DD + \beta\gamma\sqrt{T - t}), \tag{4.79}$$

and thus

$$s_{RN} = -\frac{1}{T - t} \log\left(1 - \Phi(-DD + \beta\gamma\sqrt{T - t})(1 - \mu)\right) \tag{4.80}$$

with

$$\beta\gamma = \frac{r_A - r}{\sigma_A} \tag{4.81}$$

from the CAPM model, i.e. Eqs. (4.61) and (4.60). These formulae are confirmed in Thompson and Jessop (2018, 7). The interesting feature is that Eq. (4.79) does not depend on a rating or a classification. It reaches through to the correlation of a firm or industry representative with the market.

4.9   Default and Survival

Default in credit is akin to death in life insurance. Given your age you have a statistical survival probability for the next year and so forth. The relative tabulations are known as mortality or life tables. Surviving and dying are complementary events. Rating agencies update regularly default events of bonds. For doing so bonds belong to a certain cohort that is followed over time. Such a table from Standard & Poor's is Table A.1 on page 226. It shows per rating class and maturity the cumulated probability of default. Probability is to be understood as empirical frequency.

Let us denominate these probabilities as $D_t(\rho)$, i.e. the default for a rating ρ in t years. The cumulated survival probability is obviously the complement

$$S_t(\rho) = 1 - D_t(\rho). \tag{4.82}$$

The *marginal probability of default*, also called *hazard rate*, $d_t(\rho)$ is derived from surviving up to $t - 1$ and then defaulting in period t. Surviving t has the probability of surviving $t - 1$ multiplied with the probability of not defaulting in t, that is $S_{t-1} \cdot (1 - d_t) = S_t$. From this we can separate

$$
\begin{aligned}
d_t(\rho) &= 1 - \frac{S_t(\rho)}{S_{t-1}(\rho)} = 1 - \frac{1 - D_t(\rho)}{1 - D_{t-1}(\rho)} \\
&= \frac{D_t(\rho) - D_{t-1}(\rho)}{1 - D_{t-1}(\rho)},
\end{aligned}
\tag{4.83}
$$

with $D_0 = 0$ and $S_0 = 1$. From Eq. (4.83) we can infer from induction that the following formula holds

$$S_t(\rho) = \prod_{i=1}^{t} (1 - d_i). \tag{4.84}$$

The implicit assumption in these formulae is that the probabilities of default are independent from each other.

Example 4.11 (Life Table). Life tables begin with 100,000 live births and then record the survivors by age. In the table below we see life tables of 1881 in Germany for men and for US men in 2017. The probability to reach 80 years was $S_{80} = 5.035\%$ respective is 50.6%, a massive increase. The marginal death probability for not reaching 60 years given you were 50 is $d_{50,60} = 1 - (S_{60}/S_{50})$, numerically $1 - 31124/41228 = 25\%$ and for the USA 7.35%.

Age	Germany 1881	USA 2017
0	100,000	100,000
13	61,320	99,162
20	59,287	98,746
30	54,454	97,229
40	48,775	95,188
50	41,228	92,082
60	31,124	85,316
70	17,750	72,691
80	5035	50,573

Table 4.3 Survival rates
from default rates, as
typically tabulated in life
tables

Maturity	A-	B-
0	100, 000	100, 000
1	99, 933	93, 115
2	99, 820	85, 917
3	99, 706	80, 620
4	99, 585	76, 953
5	99, 414	74, 208
6	99, 240	72, 171
7	98, 995	70, 582
8	98, 814	69, 514
9	98, 677	68, 766
10	98, 553	68, 133
11	98, 610	67, 730
12	98, 480	67, 060
13	98, 370	66, 630
14	98, 260	66, 080
15	98, 170	65, 600

We could also transform the survival figures in cumulated rates of death, analogously to $D_t = 1 - S_t/100000$. △

Example 4.12 (Survival Rate). We show the "life table" in Table 4.3, i.e. the survival rates, of two ratings from Table A.1 of page 226.

△

From the concept of expected loss we need besides the probability of loss also the amount that can be recovered in case of a credit event.

4.10 Recovery Rate

The *recovery rate* μ is the percentage of the value of a security or insured interest when it emerges from a credit event. With marketable instruments, e.g. bond, it is the market value of the defaulted security. It is therefore the valuation of distressed sales, which is based on 30-day post-default trading prices.

In insurance, where resolution of claims can take longer, it is the rather the share of the covered interest that can be recovered. This type of recovery rate is dubbed "ultimate". Generally, its sibling is the so-called loss given default, a somewhat odd term, calculated as $1 - \mu$.

The estimation of the recovery rate hinges upon many factors. First, it may depend on the priority of the credit in a bankruptcy proceeding, collateral or earmarked securities or assets, but also on the strength of the juridical system, the

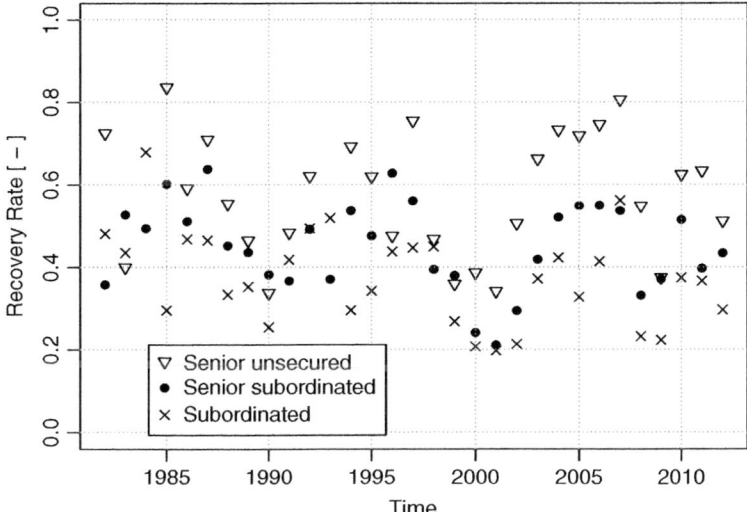

Fig. 4.16 Time series of recovery rates (Source: Moody's). Clearly visible the high fluctuations over time. No real "cycles" are observable. The more senior the higher the recovery

Table 4.4 Empirical recovery rates by Moody's (Moody's 2018, 8). The rates fluctuate wildly in order to average the figures. In prior years there were only rates for senior secured bonds

Priority Position	Volume-weighted 1983–2017
1st Lien Bank Loan	63.74%
2nd Lien Bank Loan	27.73%
Senior Unsecured Bank Loan	40.21%
1st Lien Bond	53.80%
2nd Lien Bond	43.63%
Senior Unsecured Bond	33.48%
Senior Subordinated Bond	26.34%
Subordinated Bond	27.55%
Junior Subordinated Bond	13.97%

rule of law in the pertinent jurisdiction etc. as well as the economic activity and not least the industry.

Recovery rates exhibit significant variation over time and show pro-cyclicality (see Fig. 4.16). In times of economic expansion recovery rates are higher. They tend to be lower in times of declining economic activity. Table 4.4 shows a marked correlation between priority and recovery in the sense of the better the higher. The market convention for CDS takes a recovery rate of 40%.

The credit rating agencies differ very much in their interest for recoveries. Especially Standard & Poor's does not show any figure in their annual update of default rates.

Default probability d and recovery rate μ form a couple and are useful only together. This comes from the paramount importance of expected loss EL and expected value EV, in its simplest form as

$$\text{EL} = d \cdot (1 - \mu) \tag{4.85}$$

and the expected value

$$\text{EV} = d \cdot \mu + (1 - d) \cdot 1. \tag{4.86}$$

It is quite intuitive that expected loss and expected value add up to 1, the risk-free value 1:

$$1 = \text{EL} + \text{EV}$$
$$\text{Risk-free Bond} = \text{Risk insurance} + \text{Risky bond.} \tag{4.87}$$

Example 4.13 (Beta Distribution). Because recovery rates range in the interval $(0,1)$ the most appealing distribution to fit the empirical values is the beta distribution that has a finite support and counts two parameters. We take the data from Moody's for the years 1982–2012 (Moody's 2013) and plot the fitted distribution by seniority as in Fig. 4.17. Now in simulation studies of a portfolio one could draw both a default rate or frequency of losses, from negative binomial for example, and the recovery rate from the beta distribution. The rather large dispersion contributes substantially to the potential portfolio loss.

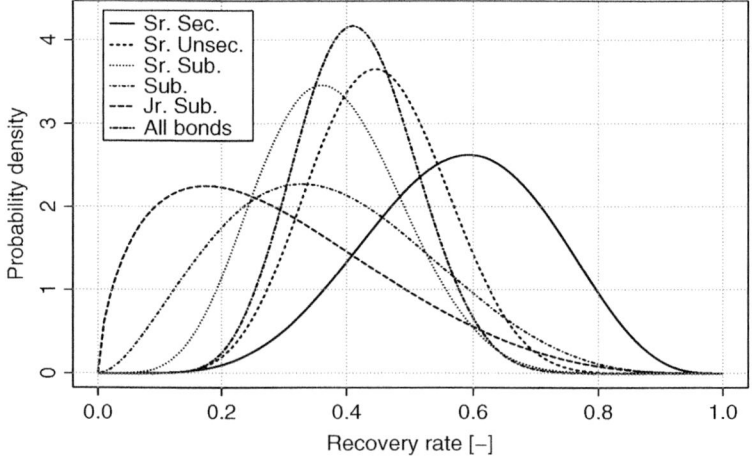

Fig. 4.17 Recovery rates as beta distributions. The skewness transits from left to right with increasing seniority as the recovery does. The overall mean is very much 40%

A R-code is in a nutshell as follows:

```
> library(fitdistrplus)
> x<-read.table("~/R/recoveryrate.txt",header=F)$V3/100
> fit <- fitdist(x, "beta")
> fit
Fitting of the distribution ' beta ' by maximum likelihood
Parameters:
        estimate Std. Error
shape1 11.24064    2.820112
shape2 15.76021    3.979417
> y<-dbeta(0:100/100,shape1=fit$estimate[1],
            shape2=fit$estimate[2])
```

△

4.10.1 Bond Pricing

For each coupon payment date we can calculate the expected value with two states: either survival with probability S_i or default with $S_{i-1} \cdot d_i$ and the outcomes c and $\mu \cdot (1 + c)$. Then we discount with the risk-free rate as

$$b_i = \left(S_i \cdot c + S_{i-1} \cdot \mu \cdot d_i \cdot (c + 1)\right) \cdot df_i. \tag{4.88}$$

For pricing a fixed coupon bond we can generalise as follows (Fons 1994, 28), see the Fig. 4.18:

$$B = \sum_{i=1}^{N} \frac{S_i \cdot c + S_{i-1} \cdot d_i \cdot \mu \cdot (c + 1)}{(1 + r_i)^{t_i}} + \frac{S_N}{(1 + r_N)^{t_N}}. \tag{4.89}$$

Now we can compare the different bond pricing formulae, i.e. Eq. (4.14), 4.13 and 4.89 summarising as follows:

$$B(y, \ldots) = B(r, z, \ldots) = B(r, d, \mu, \ldots), \tag{4.90}$$

meaning: either the yield to maturity or the Z-spread with risk-free rates or the default probabilities with recovery and risk-free rate produce the same result. The Z-spread incorporates both default rates, a vector, and recovery rate, the yield to maturity and both Z-spread and risk-free discount rate. The main difference is that the latter has one parameter more that means that the bond price can be influenced

Fig. 4.18 Scheme for
pricing bonds with default
and recovery rates

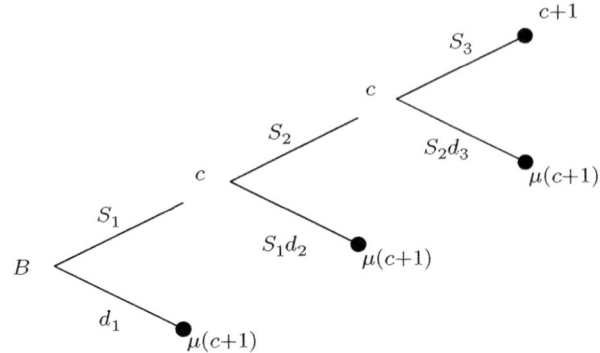

more granularly. This is the possibility to model rating as probability of default, as
issuer rating, and recovery with respect to mitigants, collateral etc. With CDS prices
on the market it is assumed regularly a recovery rate of 0.4. From Eq. (4.90) we
can draw a very important conclusion. Because the risk premium is the difference
between the risk bond and the risk-free bond we can deduce for the premium P:

$$P(y, \ldots) = P(r, z, \ldots) = P(r, d, \mu, \ldots). \qquad (4.91)$$

The yield of a bond or the spread or default rates and recovery with structural
features of the instrument determines the premium.

4.10.2 Default Intensity

Default intensity λ is an other name for the hazard rate that in turn is the marginal
default rate. From the survival rates $S(t)$ the marginal (infinitesimal) hazard rate is
given by (Hull 2012, 523)[3]

$$\lambda(t) = -\frac{1}{S(t)}\frac{dS(t)}{dt} = -\frac{d\log(S(t))}{dt}. \qquad (4.92)$$

---

[3]With the chain rule it follows:

$$\frac{d}{dt}(\log S) = \frac{1}{S} \cdot \frac{dS}{dt}.$$

Solving for $S(t)$ yields

$$S(t) = \exp\left(-\int_0^t \lambda(t)dt\right) \tag{4.93}$$

From here the cumulative default rate $D(t)$ is simply $D(t) = 1 - S(t)$. Now simplifying the average hazard rate $\bar{\lambda}$ can be estimated from the credit spread z as

$$\bar{\lambda} = \frac{z}{1 - \mu}. \tag{4.94}$$

This can be used to get a first crude estimate from bonds for the probability of default. A rule of thumb calculation for different seniorities or priorities starts from the fact that the probability of default is only dependent on the issuer. Therefore one can assume the following approximation for the spreads z_i given their recovery rate μ_i where i is the seniority

$$\frac{z_j}{1 - \mu_j} \approx \frac{z_k}{1 - \mu_k}. \tag{4.95}$$

This is very helpful for traders.

4.11 Markov Chains

A *Markov chain* is a stochastic model describing a sequence of possible events in which the probability of each event depends only on the state attained in the previous event (Wikipedia contributors 2020). In continuous time, it is known as a Markov process. This model is used to describe rating migration that is the probability $m_{ij}(i = B \rightarrow j = B-)$ of a rating subject of class B to migrate to class B − within a period.

In credit insurance we are only considering default or not default, and the migration is not so important as with investment managers. But we have the situation where an insurance is committed well ahead of the potential credit events. The rating as important ingredient to the premium calculation is projected from the commitment date to the cover period. Therefore a transition of rating in this time lap could be significant.

The Markov matrix **M** is a table that contains the probability of transition from a rating to a rating. The diagonal elements are the probabilities for remaining at the given rating. When a migration to the default rating happens then there is no further migration possible. Therefore, the last row contains only zeros besides the rating D for default that has the probability 1.

The mathematics for a discrete Markov chain implies that given a transition matrix one can determine the transitions for an arbitrary number of transitions N by multiplying the matrix $\mathbf{M}$ according to

$$\mathbf{M}_N = \mathbf{M}^N. \tag{4.96}$$

Now the data from the S&P study of Vazza and Kraemer (2018) for time horizon 1, 3, 5 and 7 years show clearly that this property does not hold. This is also known in the literature for quite a long time.

What we could try is to define a transition function $\mathbf{U}(t)$ for all t based on a chosen empirical matrix. Thus we have achieved at least some degree of coherence. Let us think of the 3-year transition matrix. In continuous time and with a scalar value m based on an input u_n we would look for a solution like

$$m(t) = u_n^t = \exp(t \cdot \log(u_n)). \tag{4.97}$$

Now comes the surprise, the same is valid for matrices, i.e.

$$\mathbf{M}(t) = \exp(t \cdot \log(\mathbf{U})). \tag{4.98}$$

This is possible because the exp and log functions can be represented by Taylor's series of terms that contain multiplications of matrices.[4] These are well defined. This calculus does not always work but in our example it behaves well. Schönbucher (2003, 223–254) gives a good overview.

How is the transition matrix used in pricing? We want to assess the value of a bond. In a very simple example let us assume in one time step a given bond is due. From our transition matrix we know the rating i today and the future ratings j with probability $m_{i,j}$. Then the value today is the risk-free discounted weighted average of the bond prices, i.e.

$$B(t_0) = df(t_0, t) \sum_{j=1}^{N} m_{i,j} \cdot B_j(t). \tag{4.99}$$

This is a risk-neutral pricing. In the set of B_j-prices there will be one value μ, the recovery rate as one probability will lead to default.

So, what about premia? The very same procedure: calculate the transition matrix for the lead time, i.e. between commitment and inception of the cover, calculate the premia for all ratings, and take the weighted average with the appropriate row of the transition matrix. As a variation we could disrespect the possibility to have a better rating and thus considering only the downside.

---

[4]It holds $\log(\mathbf{I} - \mathbf{X}) = \mathbf{X} - \mathbf{X}^2 + \mathbf{X}^3 - \mathbf{X}^4 + \ldots$.

If this is deemed too cumbersome then some average factors may be used with respect to the lead time and forward rating.

Example 4.14 (Two-state World). Let us assume there are only two states, viz. survival $m_{1,1} = 1 - 0.0056$ and not $m_{1,2} = 0.0056$. This is the 1-year default probability of a BB rating. Then the transition matrix looks as follows:

$$\mathbf{M} = \begin{pmatrix} m_{1,1} & 1 - m_{1,1} \\ 0 & 1 \end{pmatrix} = \begin{pmatrix} 0.9944 & 0.0056 \\ 0 & 1 \end{pmatrix}.$$

By multiplication we get

$$\mathbf{M}^2 = \begin{pmatrix} 0.9888 & 0.01117 \\ 0 & 1 \end{pmatrix}$$

and

$$\mathbf{M}^3 = \begin{pmatrix} 0.9833 & 0.01671 \\ 0 & 1 \end{pmatrix}$$

etc. It is quite obvious that the values of $m_{1,2}$, the default probabilities, correspond to the cumulated default probabilities $D_t(\rho)$ under the assumption of constant marginal probability of default. The values are for $t = 1 \ldots 10$: 0.01117, 0.02221, 0.04393, 0.08593, 0.1645, 0.3019, 0.5127, 0.7625, 0.9436. This example shows that the two-state world is just a special case of the world with transitions. $\triangle$

Example 4.15 (Transition Function). Let us take the 3-year transition matrix estimated from several rating agencies, see Table 4.5. It contains a column for not rated. In order to have a Markov matrix we have to re-base the values by accounting for

Table 4.5 Transition table for 3 years, mixed from several rating agencies

Rating	AAA	AA	A	BBB	BB	B	C	D	NR
AAA	68.84	17.28	2.61	0.49	0.30	0.05	0.06	0.08	10.30
AA	1.91	67.15	15.34	2.08	0.50	0.15	0.03	0.19	12.69
A	0.10	4.38	68.77	10.00	1.51	0.40	0.08	0.38	14.39
BBB	0.04	0.44	8.20	62.98	7.26	1.60	0.24	1.02	18.24
BB	0.03	0.12	0.84	10.03	50.18	9.59	1.15	3.59	24.48
B	0.01	0.05	0.25	1.18	9.91	45.17	4.44	10.39	28.61
C	0.00	0.00	0.07	0.69	2.32	12.70	27.36	31.63	25.25

the non-rated and to add a row with zeroes and a 1. This yields

$$
\mathbf{U}_3 = \begin{pmatrix}
0.767 & 0.193 & 0.029 & 0.005 & 0.003 & 0.001 & 0.001 & 0.001 \\
0.022 & 0.769 & 0.176 & 0.024 & 0.006 & 0.002 & 0 & 0.002 \\
0.001 & 0.051 & 0.803 & 0.117 & 0.018 & 0.005 & 0.001 & 0.004 \\
0 & 0.005 & 0.100 & 0.770 & 0.089 & 0.020 & 0.003 & 0.012 \\
0 & 0.002 & 0.011 & 0.133 & 0.664 & 0.127 & 0.015 & 0.047 \\
0 & 0.001 & 0.004 & 0.017 & 0.139 & 0.633 & 0.062 & 0.146 \\
0 & 0 & 0.001 & 0.009 & 0.031 & 0.170 & 0.366 & 0.423 \\
0 & 0 & 0 & 0 & 0 & 0 & 0 & 1
\end{pmatrix}
$$

This matrix is the input to Eq. (4.98). With our R libraries we simply execute the following code:

```
library(expm)
U.3<-read.table("~/R/markov.txt")/100
U.3<-as.matrix(U.3)
Q<-1/3*logm(U.3)
Q
               [,1]            [,2]            [,3]            [,4]
[1,] -8.944115e-02   8.376699e-02   3.014050e-03    0.001006721
[2,]  9.468920e-03  -9.118595e-02   7.468799e-02    0.004593810
[3,]  1.905906e-04   2.177192e-02  -7.855288e-02    0.049370984
[4,]  1.728672e-04   8.440106e-04   4.269515e-02   -0.093946291
[5,]  1.109450e-04   5.154238e-04   8.800139e-04    0.062405479
[6,]  3.132418e-05   1.763497e-04   1.168125e-03    0.001040329
[7,] -9.658940e-06  -6.372695e-05  -3.557826e-05    0.003946563
[8,]  0.000000e+00   0.000000e+00   0.000000e+00    0.000000000
               [,5]            [,6]            [,7]            [,8]
[1,]  0.001157160    2.376285e-05   3.302433e-04   0.0001331929
[2,]  0.001517472    3.987689e-04   6.594172e-05   0.0005296332
[3,]  0.004821139    1.041148e-03   2.899720e-04   0.0010677337
[4,]  0.040980502    5.291499e-03   8.600657e-04   0.0030665205
[5,] -0.147395392    6.517883e-02   5.674671e-03   0.0125995251
[6,]  0.072269902   -1.661072e-01   4.260624e-02   0.0487338709
[7,]  0.006997177    1.175666e-01  -3.442612e-01   0.2158749926
[8,]  0.000000000    0.000000e+00   0.000000e+00   0.0000000000
```

Now we can calculate the transition matrix $\mathbf{M}(t)$ for arbitrary time horizons by Eq. (4.98). With R: `M<-expm(t*Q)`. $\triangle$

4.12 Joint Default

We encounter often the situation where one debt is additionally guaranteed by another entity. For the creditor there is only a loss when both parties, i.e. obligor and guarantor default. This situation is known as *joint default*. Very simplistically, often it is assumed that the weaker of the two has already defaulted so that there is only the better of the two as obligor. This may be acceptable when the rating of the two differs strongly. Nonetheless, there is a method to estimate the joint default better.

Assume we know the probability of default of the guarantor A to be p_A and the respective for the debtor B p_B. Furthermore, be p_{AB} the joint default probability that A and B default together and ρ_{AB} the *default correlation*. The indicator variable $\mathbf{I}_{\{A\}}$ is defined as 1, if A defaults and 0 otherwise. From that we take the definition of the correlation, yielding

$$\rho_{AB} = \frac{E[\mathbf{I}_{\{A\}}\mathbf{I}_{\{B\}}] - E[\mathbf{I}_{\{A\}}]E[\mathbf{I}_{\{A\}}]}{\sigma_A \sigma_B} \tag{4.100}$$

$$= \frac{p_{AB} - p_A p_B}{\sqrt{p_A(1 - p_A)p_B(1 - p_B)}}. \tag{4.101}$$

From here we determine the joint default probability with an assumed known correlation as

$$p_{AB} = p_A p_B + \rho_{AB}\sqrt{p_A(1 - p_A)p_B(1 - p_B)}. \tag{4.102}$$

Suppose the ratings of A and B are given, and the correlation between the bank A and the corporate B is low, i.e. 10%, then we can calculate the joint default probability and from reverse looking up the default table we can infer the joint rating.

Example 4.16. U has a rating of BBB and V is rated B+. According to Table A.1 on page 226 this means a 1-year default rate of 0.17 and 2.10%. With a correlation of 0.1 Eq. (4.102) yields $p_{AB} = 0.00062$. Looking up the table, we find that this value leads to a rating of A-. Thus the joint rating is better than each of the two ratings. See Listing B.19 on page 240. △

This method is limited to two parties. For more than two we have to make some assumptions. Generally speaking the joint rating should be at least as good as the better of the single ratings but in most cases even better.

Now we have a method of treating the joint default under the assumption that the correlation can be estimated. The correlation is the lower the less common economic and political background factors influencing the standing of the two companies. A guarantee of the mother company is strongly correlated with its affiliated entity. A foreign bank on the other hand will have a very low correlation.

Equation (4.102) is just a discrete 1-year joint default probability. There exist one or more generalisations under the name of *copula*. The simplest copula is the Gaussian that needs the bivariate normal distribution $\Phi_2(x, y, \rho)$. It is the integral of the following density:

$$\phi_2(x, y, \rho) = \frac{1}{2\pi \sigma_x \sigma_y \sqrt{1 - \rho^2}} \exp\left(-\frac{1}{2(1 - \rho^2)}\left[x^2 + y^2 - 2\rho xy\right]\right).$$

(4.103)

Here x and y are normalised variables and ρ is the correlation. From the well known article of Li (2000) the following copula formula has been widely used (and abused) (Li 2000, 16):

$$D(t_1, t_2) = \Phi_2\left(\Phi^{-1}(D_1(t_1)), \Phi^{-1}(D_2(t_2)), \rho\right).$$

(4.104)

$D_i(t)$ is the cumulated default rate as a continuous function of rating i. In sophisticated circles this formula has been dubbed "the formula that killed Wall Street" or "formula from hell" because of its use in securitisation rating in the sub-prime disaster.

The parameter ρ is not known and must be estimated. For the sake of simplicity we would rather recommend to stick with the 1-year formula.

Example 4.17 (Copula). We continue the example above and use Eq. (4.104). We generate a curve starting with zero correlation up to 1. With R this may look as follows:

```
library(pbv)
x<-0.0017; y<-0.0208; r<-0.1
q<-c()
for (i in 1:100){
q[i]<-pbvnorm(qnorm(x),qnorm(y),(i-1)/100)*10000
}
```

Figure 4.19 shows the result. With a correlation of 1 the value must be the smaller default rates of the two items. A more realistic picture would emerge by using a fatter t-distribution with small degree of freedom instead of the normal.   △

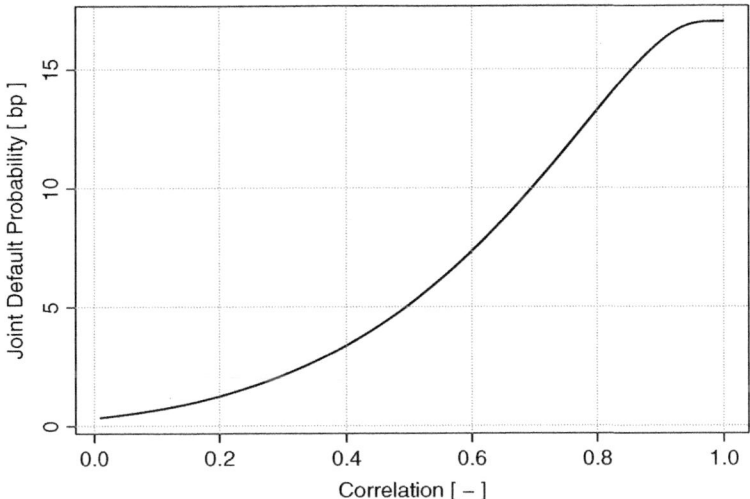

Fig. 4.19 A copula approach to joint default

4.13   Risk Assessment for Default

The credit or default events covered are categorised as either (i) political risk or (ii) commercial risk. The commercial risks pertain to the buyer. The foreign buyer can be one of the three classes:

- a sovereign buyer,
- a public and
- a private buyer.

Sovereign buyers are a foreign state, its government, ministries or institutions that can validly bind the state. Their main feature is that such entities cannot be liquidated by bankruptcy procedures.

Public entities are institutions that belong wholly or with a majority stake to the state. Often they are utilities providing some basic services. They can in many cases become bankrupt.

The vast number of buyers is private entities, corporations or limited companies for which the bankruptcy code was designed. Thus a risk assessment must consider the class of buyer as well as the events to be covered.

The well known OECD Arrangement composes the final assessment of a buyer by discerning the country risk (see Fig. 4.20) and the commercial risk. Rating agencies try *inter alia* universal ratings where both political and commercial risks are merged into one letter rating (see Figs. 4.21 and 4.22).

For pricing purposes the risk assessment produces a rating that will be a parameter of a pricing formula. As we know from Senate hearings in the USA of

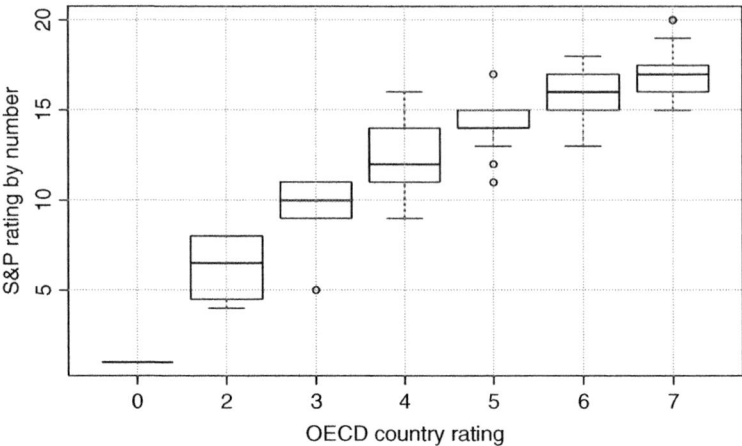

Fig. 4.20 Relation between OECD country risk and S&P rating. The correlation is 0.892, i.e. very high. The lonely rating "0" belongs to Singapore

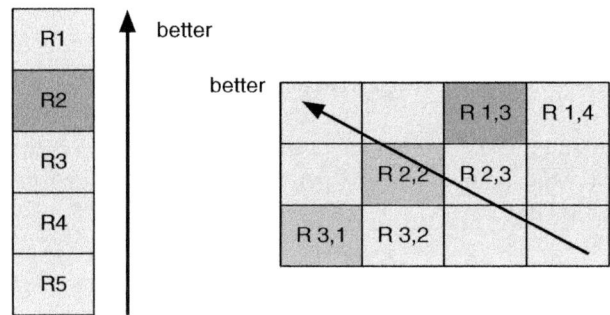

Fig. 4.21 Rating schematically. Whether one uses a one or two dimensional rating does not matter. Because of unambiguous ordering the two dimensional collapses into one dimension

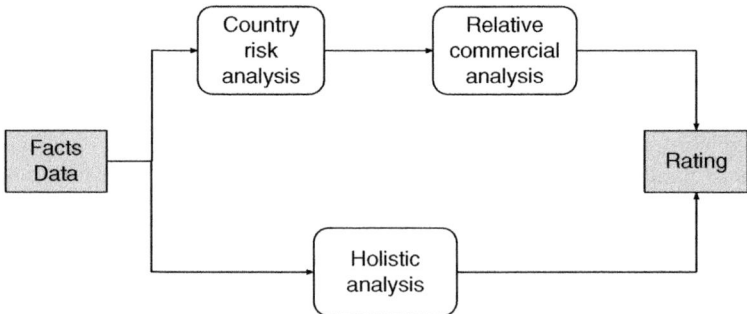

Fig. 4.22 Universal and relative rating. In the end we need one rating, irrespective of how it was determined

rating agencies that took place in the aftermath of the sub-prime securitisation crisis in 2008, a *rating is an opinion*. Opinions can be argued but their derivation should at least follow a clear and comprehensive process. A rating is an *ordinal* risk scale.

Generally speaking, the problem of assigning a rating consists in valuing multidimensional data pertaining to the party to be assessed and condensing these information into one figure. So it is about finding out which data is relevant and how to consolidate it.

4.13.1 Scoring

The most obvious mechanism is creating an index that in turn is most often a weighted sum of normalised scores. Formally:

$$\text{Score} = \sum_{k=1}^{N} w_k \cdot X_k, \tag{4.105}$$

where w_k are the weights and X_k are the scores. The numerical score is then mapped to a rating, i.e. an ordinal number. This is just the simplest method.

Assessing the scores implies a historic view, taking the variables from the past, e.g. the last three financial reporting. Deep down this is a frequentist's approach to statistics. As we are coping with export a two stage approach could seem obvious, i.e. analysing the country and the credit quality relative to the sovereign obligor. That is the approach taken in the OECD Arrangement, motivated further by the fact that once only sovereign risk was assessed and the commercial risk was added.

The risk of error, i.e. assigning not the right rating, is inherently mitigated by the insurance principle that requires a homogeneous and large portfolio. Here the central limit theorem is levelling out errors. But if this principle is not followed, risk may be amplified. For the credit insurance company the diversification is important. For the government the maxim of *equal treatment* can be an additional restriction to observe.

4.13.2 Factors, the 5 Cs

A rating as a trustworthy assessment of an entity's or person's creditworthiness must be based on multiple considerations. In the USA the 5 C mnemonic is used as a guiding star. It comprises the following dimensions or factors (Tirole 2009):

1. character,
2. capacity,
3. capital,
4. collateral and
5. conditions.

Although originally used for rating individuals it is also possible to apply the mnemonic to corporations. For a successful company there are two major preconditions that are:

- liquidity and
- profitability.

Now, character makes reference to the credit history, the track record and past experience. Character is more of an assessment for small business loans where the owner and his "character" can be judged. It is about whether to grant a loan at all. For larger companies there is a team of managers for whom this item is less relevant but a good reputation may help.

Capacity is interpreted as the ratio of debt to means of paying it back that is earnings or free cashflow. Earnings in their many manifestations, i.e. before income and taxes *EBIT* or before interest, taxes, depreciation and amortisation *EBITDA*, measure the profitability.

Capital or capital structure is the main source of a wealth of indicators. But the main element is the debt ratio that shows how much equity is in the game and how committed the company and its shareholders are. The financial reporting gives many clues about the sustainability of the business and about the financial director. It cannot tell the whole story of a borrower.

Collateral is additional security given to the lender. Normally, it does not reduce the price of the loan but makes the agreement feasible. The collateral may differ widely by quality and the possibility to get hold of it and being able to liquidate it.

Conditions are quite a broad term, ranging from key-man risk to industry status and economic activity. Of course the usage of the loan belongs to this category.

4.13.3 Counterparty Rating

The main three rating agencies, i.e. Standard & Poor's, Moody's and Fitch, are a kind of oligopoly. Together they dominate the market for this kind of information. They produce mainly *issuer ratings* and *issue ratings*. An issuer, which is a company that is or wants to be financed by the capital market, especially by bonds, may pay for a rating or, alternatively, an investor pays. Some studies find that issuer-paid ratings are more favourable than investor-paid ratings.

An *issuer rating* measures the probability that a company defaults with regard to *all* its financial obligations.

An *issue rating* is based on a mix of default risk and the priority of a creditor's claim in a bankruptcy proceeding. Secured debt has a higher recovery rate than non-secured debt. Therefore, secured debt has a higher rating.

Issue specific rating and loan covenants are more relevant in situations of financial liquidation.

4.13.4 Transaction Rating

Priorities of debt in a formal liquidation procedure comprise normally the sequence senior secured, senior unsecured, subordinated secured and subordinated unsecured status.

Senior debt refers to debt that is in the first-lien position in a potential liquidation. It is followed by subordinated debt and then by equity holders. Subordinated debt is also known as mezzanine or junior debt.

Transaction rating in our context hampers comparability. Suppose one guarantee is based on a credit of one million, whereas a second insurer is confronted with ten million. Then a transaction rating cannot be equal. Comparing counterparty ratings is easy though.

From the above it should have become evident which kind of rating is most pertinent to our subject matter. If we base the pricing on a two dimensional space of probability of default and recovery then we need issuer or *counterparty ratings* for assessing the probability of default, and the transaction relevant items, e.g. priority, collateral and other security interests, for the recovery rate or "loss given default". The transaction rating is just detrimentally blurring the two distinct items unless the transaction envisaged is of such extent to change the counterparty rating anyway.

Generally speaking, the risk assessment methodology is dependent on the credit pricing methodology. Using a structural model, e.g. Black–Scholes type of calculation, needs a different risk assessment than using an actuarial method.

4.13.5 Banks

Some analysts like to make a distinction between corporates and banks or financial institutions. The obvious difference is that banks have a rather narrow scope, are massively regulated and are often very international through connected payments systems and their network of corresponding foreign banks. Therefore most banks have a rating by a reputable rating agency.

Banks have always been considered as systemically important for their economy but also as fiefdom for the governments' clientele. In the last decade many banks have been rescued by the lender of last resort or with the help of the government. On the other hand banks are the major purchasers of government bonds. During the financial crisis both banks and insurance companies were supported. But, just to confirm the rule Lehman Bros. was sent into bankruptcy. Financial institutions may have an implicit, but slightly uncertain, guarantee by the lender of last resort.

Banks may be analysed with much greater focus on the financial reporting and the management discussion and analysis. Regulator has improved continuously their quantitative and qualitative data requirements that embody useful risk metrics. Therefore, analysing traditional and international banks is rather simple compared with corporates.

As an example we report here the rather effective methodology of Morningstar (2016), a global financial services firm. Simple does not necessarily imply that it is inaccurate. The four main dimensions, not equally weighted, are as follows:

1. *Business Risk Score* (30%) encompasses various measures of business risk, as well as economic moat and uncertainty assessments.
2. *Bank Solvency Score* (30%) is a ranking based on a bank's capital adequacy, asset quality, profitability and liquidity profile.
3. *Stress Test Score* (30%) is an evaluation of a bank's potential to absorb loan losses while maintaining adequate capital levels.
4. *Distance to Default Score* (10%) (see Sect. 4.8) is a quantitative model using market based inputs that ranks banks based on their likelihood of financial distress.

This method is similar to *CAMELS*, the Capital adequacy, Asset quality, Management, Earnings, Liquidity and Sensitivity to market risk rating system used by US bank regulators.

4.13.6 Sovereign

Rating sovereigns means not to get submerged by irrelevant data. As statistics stems from the state collecting data there is an immensity of data and time series.

A summary study by Elkhoury (2008, 6) shows that 80% of the rating is explained by GDP per capital alone, and 90% by the following variables together:

- GDP per capita,
- GDP growth,
- inflation,
- the ratio of non-gold foreign exchange reserves to imports,
- the ratio of the current account balance to GDP, and
- default history and the level of economic development.

Some studies have also found that for developing countries' rating the two following variables are important:

- increases in international interest rates and
- the structure of its exports and its concentration.

The OECD has its own classification with seven notches that are highly correlated with the sovereign rating of credit agencies, although it is said to measure country risk. We found a correlation of 0.89 between OECD country categories and S&P ratings.

Here again, the depth of the analysis should correspond to the granularity of the pricing methodology.

4.14 Risk Assessment for Non-Performance

During pre-shipment or before the goods are accepted the loans, overdrafts or advance payments by the buyer are at risk.

Pre-shipment risks strongly involve the performance capability of the supplier or manufacturer. Before providing a supplier with export working capital, lenders and credit insurers must consider several factors in order to determine this level of risk.

Similar to buyer risk analysis, the lender begins assessing the strength of the supplier's balance sheet. But the financial reporting does not say much about the performance capabilities or management skills. It is either informing about the finance director or, for SMEs, the skills of the relationship bank. One has to assess non-financial metrics.

The challenge is to accurately assess the manufacturer's ability to produce the product, meet all contractual specifications, being a knowledgeable party to a well-drafted commercial contract, ship according to an agreed upon time frame, satisfy all essential country regulations and accurately consider duties and taxes. It is important that the lender pays diligent attention to the quality of the supplier's management. The performance is a prerequisite for the receivables to become due, the basis for liquidating the loan.

The skills of the supplier are a function of its experience with producing the good, the good not being completely new or having novel components, the size of the good being extra ordinary, the experience in international trade etc. The benchmark are similar goods having been successfully manufactured in the recent past. The main relationship bank may be in a better position than the insurer to understand the export in question. Some non-financial metrics could be:

- industry reputation,
- customer satisfactions and loyalty,
- customer query time,
- delivery performance,
- R&D spending and intellectual property,
- propensity to innovate,
- percentage of defects,
- quality management system in place,
- industry, regulatory, standards certifications available,
- capacity utilisation,
- key person risks etc.

The assessing group should develop a standard questionnaire with scores. Very important but time consuming are well prepared site visits.

If the insurer is convinced that there is a possibility to discriminate between the suppliers and their performance capability then the pricing should be adjusted according to such a quality assessment. Credit insurers should have or develop a performance rating.

If the insured loan experiences a loss due to non-performance then the credit insurer has the unfortunate task to go after the supplier.

An alternative is to use the Merton model of distance to default of Sect. 4.8 by finding an adjusted beta to the market volatility.

Summarising: The credit rating analysis has to be as good as the pricing is sophisticated. For a simple pricing the analysis can be simple too. The main question is whether the application is insurable at all.

References

Brown, P. (1998). *Bond markets: Structures and yield calculations*. Cambridge: Gilmour Drummond Pub., in association with International Securities Market Association Ltd.

Chan-Lau, J., & Sy, A. (2006). Distance-to-default in banking: A bridge too far? *IMF Working Papers No. 06/215.*

Elkhoury, M. (2008). *Credit rating agencies and their potential impact on developing countries.* Geneva: UNCTAD. Discussion paper no. 186.

Elton, E. J., Gruber, M. J., Agrawal, D., & Mann, C. (2001). Explaining the rate spread on corporate bonds. *Journal of Finance, 56*(1), 247–277. https://EconPapers.repec.org/RePEc:bla:jfinan:v:56:y:2001:i:1:p:247-277.

Fabozzi, F., & Modigliani, F. (2009). *Capital Markets: Institutions and Instruments* (Pearson International edn., 4th edn.). Upper Saddle River, N.J.: Prentice Hall.

Fons, J. S. (1994). Using default rates to model the term structure of credit risk. *Financial Analysts Journal, 50*(5), 25–32. http://fonsrisksolutions.-com/Documents/Using%20Default%20Rates %20FAJ.pdf..

Gebhardt, A. (2016). Package Akima: Interpolation of irregularly and regularly spaced data. Reference manual, CRAN. https://cran.r-project.org/web/packages/akima/akima.pdf.

Haugen, R. (2001). *Modern investment theory* (5th edn.). Upper Saddle River, N.J.: Prentice Hall.

Hull, J. (2012). *Options, futures, and other derivatives*. Boston: Prentice Hall.

Kuznetsov, A. (2007). *The complete guide to capital markets for quantitative professionals*. New York: McGraw-Hill.

Li, D. X. (2000). On default correlation: A copula function approach. *The Journal of Fixed Income, 9*(4), 43–54.

Markowitz, H. (1952). Portfolio selection*. *The Journal of Finance, 7*(1), 77–91.

Merton, R. C. (1974). On the pricing of corporate debt: The risk structure of interest rates. *Journal of Finance, 29*(2), 449–470.

Moody's (2013). Annual Default Study: Corporate Default and Recovery Rates, 1920–2012. Special Comment. New York: Moody's investor Service.

Moody's (2018). Corporate Default and Recovery Rates, 1920–2017 . Special Comment. New York: Moody's investor Service.

Morningstar (2016). Bank Credit Rating Methodology. In *Ratings and Research*. Chicago: Morningstar Inc. http://news.morningstar.com/pdfs/bank-credit-methodology-march2016.pdf.

Nau, R. F. (2001). De Finetti was right: Probability does not exist. *Theory and Decision, 51*, 89–124.

Nelson, C. R., & Siegel, A. F. (1987). Parsimonious modeling of yield curves. *The Journal of Business, 60*(4), 473–489. http://www.jstor.org/stable/2352957.

Nymand-Andersen, P. (2018). Yield curve modelling and a conceptual framework for estimating yield curves: Evidence from the European Central Bank's yield curves . In *Statistics Paper Series 27*. Frankfurt a. M.: European Central Bank. https://www.ecb.europa.eu/pub/pdf/scpsps/ecb.sps27.en.pdf.

Ross, S. (1978). A simple approach to the valuation of Risky streams. *The Journal of Business, 51*(3), 453–475.

Schönbucher, P. (2003). *Credit derivatives pricing models : models, pricing, and implementation.* Chichester Hoboken, NJ: Wiley.

Somaia, C. (2011). *A Compact Guide to Floating Rate Notes.* Credit Suisse, London: European credit views.

Thompson, A., & Jessop, N. (2018). A Cost of Capital Approach to Estimating Credit Risk Premia. In *Insurance Research.* New York: Moody's Analytics.

Tirole, J. (2009). *The Theory of Corporate Finance.* Princeton: Princeton University.

Vazza, D., & Kraemer, N. (2018). Proceedings of the 2017 annual global corporate default study and rating transitions. Technical report. New York: Standard and Poor's Global Ratings. https://www.spglobal.com/en/research-insights/articles/default-transition-and-recovery-2017-annual-global-corporate-default-study-and-rating-transitions.

Wikipedia Contributors (2019). Akima spline—Wikipedia, The Free Encyclopedia. https://en.wikipedia.org/w/index.php?title=Akima_spline&oldid=926769851. [Online; accessed 3-May-2020].

Wikipedia contributors (2020). Stochastic process—Wikipedia, the free Encyclopedia. https://en.wikipedia.org/w/index.php?title=Stochastic_process&oldid=970552702. [Online; accessed 18-August-2020].

Preliminaries

5

This chapter is a preparation and a context for later analysis. It gives a brief account of the pricing of the OECD Arrangement that rules a certain layer of international trade, i.e. export on middle-long term. Some features are analysed to certain extent in order to show some concepts in pricing that we find problematic.

5.1 OECD Arrangement

The Organisation for Economic Co-operation and Development is an intergovernmental economic organisation with 37 member countries, established to stimulate economic progress and world trade. It is a forum of countries describing themselves as committed to democracy and the market economy, providing a platform to compare policy experiences, seek answers to common problems, identify good practices and coordinate domestic and international policies of its members (Wikipedia contributors 2020).

The OECD Arrangement is an agreement between the participants concerning officially supported export credits.

5.1.1 Scope

From the document we can read (OECD 2020, 10) that it is a Gentlemen's Agreement among the Participants (and no binding law by itself). The members, called participants are Australia, Canada, the European Union, Japan, Korea, New Zealand, Norway, Switzerland, Turkey and the USA. Here the Brexit will extract the United Kingdom from the EU.

Its two main goals are:

- to provide a framework for the orderly use of officially supported export credits, and
- to foster a level playing field for official support in order to encourage competition among exporters based on quality and price of goods and services exported.

This is operationalised inter alia by the definition of the Minimum Premium Rates that should also guarantee the requirement of the WTO, i.e. premia that are adequate to cover all cost in the long run.

Further it is stipulated that these instruments are allowed for official support:

1. Export credit guarantee or insurance (pure cover);
2. Official financing support:

- direct credit/financing and refinancing, or
- interest rate support;

3. any combination of the above.

There are additional limitations to maximum repayment terms and to minimum interest rates. Since February 2017, specific rules apply for credit risk premium to be charged in countries that are not classified and where private market financing is generally available (i.e. market benchmark countries).

5.1.2 Rating System

The Arrangement has evolved from insuring only sovereign risk into covering also commercial risk. For years it has used a quantitative model for country risk. With this expansion discussions revolved around the concept of a universal rating scale for private buyers versus an add-on to or in relation to the country risk. The result is known both from the pricing formula (Eq. 5.1 below) and the Annex IIX of the Arrangement (OECD 2020).

The Table 5.1 is a two-dimensional mapping from country and commercial category to a letter rating. With categories SOV+ it contains an escape to top the sovereign rating. Structurally it is a kind of wedge becoming smaller the higher and thus worse the country category becomes. In country category 7 there is not much choice left. We would suppose that a buyer being worse than B− should not be covered unless there is valuable collateral posted.

For the credit insurer and its customer the rating system is very handy because the country categories are agreed upon by the members and need not to be questioned or argued about. Then the analysis of the commercial category is left. The worse the country the smaller the model risk of erring in the commercial category. In a

Table 5.1 The mapping from OECD ratings to letter rating (OECD 2020, 123)

Country	1	2	3	4	5	6	7
SOV+	–	–	–	–	–	–	–
SOV/CC0	–	–	–	–	–	–	–
CC1	AAA to AA–	A+ to A–	BBB+ to BBB–	BB+ to BB	BB–	B+	B
CC2	A+ to A–	BBB+ to BBB–	BB+ to BB	BB–	B+	B	B– or worse
CC3	BBB+ to BBB–	BB+ to BB	BB–	B+	B	B– or worse	–
CC4	BB+ to BB	BB–	B+	B	B– or worse	–	–
CC5	BB– or worse	B+ or worse	B or worse	B– or worse	–	–	–

later analysis on page 214 we show that the OECD country rating has almost a 90% correlation with the S&P sovereign rating.

The system looks like a typical compromise so that one faction can use the two-dimensional rating while the other faction may use the letter rating in S&P style.

Later on we will see that a given letter rating, say BB–, does not lead to the same premium. There seems to be an inconsistency.

What is understandable but misleading is the fact that OECD member countries are excluded from the rating system and need not rate their peers.

5.1.3 The Minimum Premium Rate

Members of the OECD have agreed on *minimum* rates. This implies that all can feel free to require higher rates if they want to. Charging these premia complies with the requirement of WTO. Thus members in this competitive environment have little motivation not to apply these rates unless governmental pressure is more on fiscal strictness than on export support.

The Minimum Premium Rate of the OECD Arrangement reads as follows in its full beauty (OECD 2020, 126):

$$
\begin{aligned}
\text{MPR} = \Big\{ &\big[(a_i \cdot \text{HOR} + b_i) \cdot \max(\text{PCC}, \text{PCP})/0.95 \big] \cdot (1 - \text{LCF}) \\
&+ \big[c_{i,n} \cdot \text{PCC}/0.95 \cdot \text{HOR} \cdot (1 - \text{CEF}) \big] \Big\} \cdot \text{QPF}_i \cdot \text{PCF}_i \cdot \text{BTSF},
\end{aligned}
$$
(5.1)

with the following definitions:

i	Index for the 1 to 7 country categories
n	Index for the seven buyer categories
a_i	Country risk coefficient
b_i	Constant depending on i
c_i	Buyer risk coefficient depending on i and n
HOR	Horizon of Risk
PCC	Percentage of commercial cover
PCP	Percentage of political cover
LCF	Local currency factor
CEF	Credit enhancement factor
QPF_i	Quality of product factor in country i
PCF_i	Percentage of cover factor in country i
BTSF	Better than sovereign factor

From a structural point of view the MPR-formula above is simply:

$$MPR = (A_i + C_{i,n}) \cdot HOR + B_i, \qquad (5.2)$$

and even more simplified

$$MPR = D_{i,n} \cdot HOR + B_i. \qquad (5.3)$$

This is a linear equation in the time factor HOR. After a very long gestation period this has emerged from the exercise of adding the commercial risk to the sole former sovereign risk. Up to 2011 the old formula was as follows:

$$MPR = A_i \cdot HOR + B_i. \qquad (5.4)$$

All the factors could be called sloppily "fudge factors", because they scale a little up and down the rate. These factors are mainly of small importance, e.g. QPF ranges in $[0.98 \ldots 1.02]$, PCF is only important if the cover exceeds the 95% with an addition of at most of 8.6%. QPF depends on the support product, i.e. insurance, guarantee or loan. Only CEF, the risk mitigation, can reach at maximum 65% of reduction on the commercial risk. The LCF is limited to 30% applicable on the sovereign part of the premium rate.

The *Horizon of Risk* consists of two parts: First, the so-called *disbursement period* DP. This is the phase where the credit builds up, either the bank credit in the form of usage and draw-downs or in the form of deliveries by the supplier. This period lasts often until 6 months before the first repayment by the buyer. The point in time between disbursement and repayment is defined as the *Starting Point of Credit* SPOC.

Second, the repayment period RT. From the average weighted life AWL it follows:

$$RT = 2 \cdot (AWL - 0.25), \tag{5.5}$$

and from here

$$HOR = \frac{1}{2} \cdot DP + 2 \cdot AWL - 0.5. \tag{5.6}$$

This formula is an oddity, but not because of the AWL. It is the DP. The AWL is derived from the pattern that these credit should repay semi-annually in equal instalments. For example, a repayment of 10 instalments means every 6 months 10% of principal has to be paid for 5 years. The repayment period is

$$RT = 2 \cdot \sum_{i=1}^{10} 0.1 \cdot i/2 - 0.5$$
$$= 0.1 \cdot (1 + 2 + 3 + \ldots + 10) - 0.5$$
$$= 0.1 \cdot 5 \cdot 11 - 0.5$$
$$= 5.$$

Assume payment every quarter, then the repayment period RT is given as

$$RT = 2 \cdot \sum_{i=1}^{20} 0.05 \cdot i/4 - 0.5$$
$$= 0.05 \cdot (1 + 2 + 3 + \ldots + 20)/2 - 0.5$$
$$= 0.05 \cdot 10 \cdot 21/2 - 0.5$$
$$= 4.75.$$

For the actual premium Π in monetary units the rate r has to be multiplied by the covered export value V, i.e.

$$\Pi = r \cdot V. \tag{5.7}$$

The premium can also be insured. Then the premium is given by

$$\Pi = \frac{r}{1 - r} \cdot V. \tag{5.8}$$

The premium should be paid upfront. One ought to think of a higher export value $V/(1-r)$ and not a higher premium rate $r/(1-r)$, especially in a minimum premium rate context.

There are additional requirements. For OECD high income countries there is a maximum tenor of 8.5 years, for all others 10 years. Before the start of the credit at least 15% must be paid in advance. The instalment intervals should not be longer than 6 months. For projects there are additional conditions and there are special provisions for specific products, e.g. aircraft, ships, rail, etc. This can be retrieved by OECD (2020).

For transparency reasons a lot of reporting and notification is mandatory for OECD members. The Arrangement contains special provision, or better understandings for some specific sectors:

1. Ship,
2. Aircraft,
3. Nuclear,
4. Renewable Energy/Climate Change/Water,
5. Rail Infrastructure and
6. Coal-Fired Electricity Generation.

Last to mention, the Arrangement is limiting the use of concessional financing for projects that might be supported through commercial financing and to direct tied aid towards developing counties that are less well off.

Besides the Arrangement there are the so-called OECD Sustainable Lending Principles that are harmonised with provision of the World Bank and the IMF. They are not legally binding for the members.

5.1.4 Local Cost

The Arrangement limits the eligibility of local cost. Suppose the total contractual price is 100. Then the export contract value is this total minus the local costs. Only 85% of this value is eligible for cover plus a maximum of 30% of the export contract value as local cost. Therefore, the maximum cover ratio MCR is dependent on the local cost ratio LCR, i.e. the local cost as percentage of total contractual price:

$$\text{MCR} = (1 - \text{LCR}) \cdot 0.85 + \min(\text{LCR}, 0.3 \cdot (1 - \text{LCR})). \tag{5.9}$$

This formula raises to a maximum of 88.5% with over-all local cost component of 23.08% (see Fig. 5.1). This could have been formulated easier.

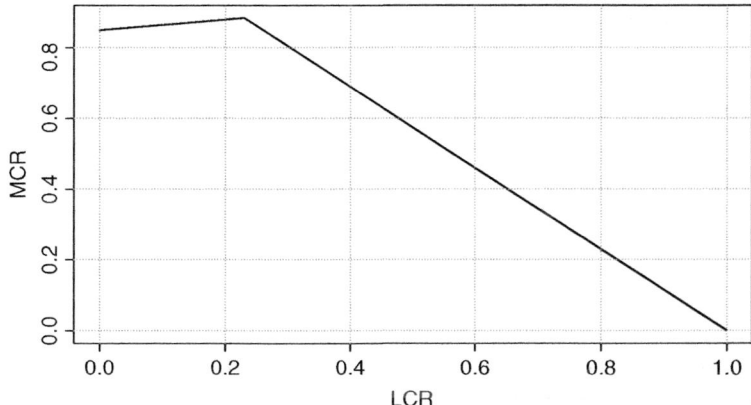

Fig. 5.1 Cover ratio with local cost. With a local cost ratio of less than 25% one can slightly increase the over-all cover ratio beyond 85%

5.1.5 The Interest Rate for Direct Lending

The OECD Arrangement defines the so-called *Commercial Interest Reference Rate* CIRR base rate as the 3, 5 and 7 year government bond yield. The minimum interest rate is set to those rates plus 100 basis point. The markup is not meant to contain the premium or other non-regular banking fees. It can be chosen to either use the 5 year rate for the whole maturity or the three rates for intervals in years [0, 5],]5, 8.5] and]8.5, longer].

These rates are published once per month and updated accordingly. For special sectors there are additional rates for longer tenors.

This minimum interest rate can be compared with the "par-interest rate" of Eq. 4.25 of page 96. In Table 5.2 we see the application of the following formula:

$$CIRR = \text{Base Rate} + 100\,\text{bp}. \tag{5.10}$$

Table 5.2 CIR rates as of 15. April 2020 (Source: OECD). These are CIRR base rates plus 100 bp

Repayment term	USD	EUR	CHF	GBP
Up to and including 5 years	1.50	0.24	0.34	1.16
Over 5 and up to and incl. 8.5 y	1.59	0.32	0.43	1.22
Over 8.5 years	1.78	0.42	0.53	1.31

5.1.6 Some Critical Issues

The Arrangement understandably cannot be a very dynamic and rapidly adapting agreement. It is convened after long discussions within the support agencies, their discussion with their guarding authorities, mainly with the appropriate department of government, and discussions between the participants to the arrangement.

Here the first issue arises: the arrangement is too *slow in adapting* to the market dynamics, new products and new entrants to the field that are not bound or do not adopt the arrangement on a voluntary basis. This has to do with shifts in relative importance of economies that are not captured.

The repayment terms are not flexible enough. There is first the maximum term and secondly the repayment pattern.

Thirdly, the *Horizon of Risk* is an in-comprehensive albeit elaborate construct.

Fourth, the minimum premium is based on the export value, i.e. the present value of receivables, but does not take into account the discount factors and thus the interplay between charged interest rates and the time-value of receivables. The stronger the discounting the higher the relative value of the early, larger payments. This implies a shorter effective time in risk (see Fig. 4.9).

Fifth, the formula is under-complex. Especially the linearity on time, or more precise on the HOR, is way too simple and is at odds with all known price evolutions.

For some exports with a natural local content, be it because of constructions or infrastructure involved in the buyer country, be it for buyer's country aim to support the local industry or acquire practical knowledge in an industry, the maximum allowed local content may be too low.

One could hope, that these restrictions could be supplanted by a premium system that automatically penalises unwanted and rewards wanted behaviour or terms.

Example 5.1 (Consistency). We are comparing two premia with the same letter rating, say B+ in country category 3 and 6. Thus B+ corresponds to both (3,CC4) and (6,CC1). Simplifying Eq. 5.1 by considering only parameters that are country specific yields

$$\text{MPR} = \left[a_i \cdot \text{HOR} + b_i\right] + \left[c_{i,n} \cdot \text{HOR}\right]. \tag{5.11}$$

From Table 5.3 we read $a_3 = 0.35$, $b_3 = 0.35$ and $c_{3,\text{CC4}} = 0.495$ and $a_6 = 0.90$, $b_6 = 1.20$ and $c_{6,\text{CC1}} = 0.1$. By transforming the equation we have $(a_i + c_{i,n}) \cdot \text{HOR} + b_i$. That is for $i = 3$: $(0.35 + 0.495) \cdot \text{HOR} + 0.35$ and for $i = 6$:

Table 5.3 The coefficients
to the Minimum Premium
Rate. From left to right all by
row all figures are strictly
non-decreasing besides row
CC1. This must be an error

i	1	2	3	4	5	6	7
a_1	0.09	0.20	0.35	0.55	0.74	0.90	1.10
b_1	0.35	0.35	0.35	0.35	0.75	1.20	1.80
$c_{i,n}$							
SOV+	0.000	0.000	0.000	0.000	0.000	0.000	0.000
SOV/CC0	0.000	0.000	0.000	0.000	0.000	0.000	0.000
CC1	0.110	0.120	0.110	0.100	0.100	0.100	0.125
CC2	0.200	0.212	0.223	0.234	0.246	0.258	0.271
CC3	0.270	0.320	0.320	0.350	0.380	0.480	n/a
CC4	0.405	0.459	0.495	0.540	0.621	n/a	n/a
CC5	0.630	0.675	0.720	0.810	n/a	n/a	n/a

$(0.90 + 0.1) \cdot \text{HOR} + 1.2$. Now compare

$$\text{MPR}_{3,\text{CC4}} = 0.855 \cdot \text{HOR} + 0.35$$

$$\text{MPR}_{6,\text{CC1}} = 1 \cdot \text{HOR} + 1.2.$$

This is extremely divergent for the same rating. For HOR of 2 years it gives either 2.06 or 3.2%.   △

5.2   Inception of Credit

We have argued that credit is both a situation and a class of instruments. A loan is the instrument that comes to mind first. We have also listed on page 21 different means to document the future payments. Comparing a term loan with a bundle of confirmed letters of credit shows the problem. While for this loan there is a clear stated closing date of the agreement where the money is paid out or the conversion of an overdraft takes place for this bundle of guarantees there may be something called a confirmation date (see Fig. 2.9). We could posit that a credit agreement covering the (fixed) repayments by a lender has a commitment date as start of the credit. Thus the inception or beginning of the credit has a well defined date from the agreements. This is true for buyer's credit or supplier's credit with bank involvement.

For pure supplier credit the credit terms are defined in the commercial contract. There is no need to define a start of credit as with an instrument. Here credit is more akin to credit as a situation. Credit in this sense begins with a performance of the supplier to be paid later or an advance payment by the buyer to be compensated by delivery or a pre-financing by a domestic bank. With supplier credit the definition of inception of credit is not clear.

The OECD Arrangement has tried to synchronise the two product classes by introducing a fictitious *Starting Point of Credit* SPOC. The SPOC separates the so-called disbursement period from the repayment period. For buyer credit, disbursement refers to the period in which drawdowns from a line of credit happen.

For one disbursement there is no period. For supplier credit during this period the manufacturer builds up the credit by producing and then delivering, in part or as a whole.

The Arrangement defines the SPOC by examples and sets a latest condition, i.e. not later than (OECD 2020, 140–142):

- the actual date of acceptance, weighted mean date of acceptance;
- submission of the invoices to the client or acceptance of services by the client;
- at commissioning;
- actual date when the buyer takes physical possession, or the weighted mean date when the buyer takes physical possession;
- date when construction has been completed;
- date when the supplier has completed installation or construction and preliminary tests to ensure it is ready for operation.

Thus for supplier credit the "start of the credit" is an event from the commercial contract. But what is the situation before the start of credit?

The Arrangement has this other notion of *disbursement period* that describes contrary to its name the build-up of the credit situation in the pre-shipment phase. Why this should be of any concern for the repayment to be insured is not easily understandable. The Arrangement gives no clue, it does not even define the disbursement period.[1] After closing the commercial contract and from beginning work on the export to the SPOC is set to be the disbursement period times two. In banking terms it corresponds to the term of a working capital facility divided by 2.

Using this period that increases the premium for insurance cover during a period where there is no insurance cover seems rather odd. The most usual pattern is a single disbursement, i.e. payment by the bank of the whole covered export value on behalf of the buyer. Therefore, the period is mostly a point in time with no duration.

When devising a new framework for pricing this notion of SPOC is not of much use. For the Arrangement it has importance as anchor for the limitation of tenor and as reference for the first repayment, not later than 6 months after SPOC.

Most calculations that we will present in the following will assume the inception of the credit, that is the point of reference for discounting and the like, to be 6 months before the first repayment, if this is of importance. Every "credit" should have a beginning and an end.

The disbursement may be working as a forward period. Because the premium should be paid at the zero point, see footnote, then this time lapse is the gap between fixing the insurance contract with its clauses, e.g. rating of the buyer, interest rates and the commencement of the credit. For this interpretation the influence on the premium seems too heavy handed.

---

[1] In an older version of the Arrangement it is said in a footnote, that the disbursement period begins at the zero point. "The zero point is defined as the date of the first drawing in case of a buyer credit or the first delivery in case of a supply contract."

We will suggest an other way of taking the forward pricing into consideration, viz. as lead time.

5.3   Forward, Lead Time, Disbursement Period, etc.

In Fig. 5.2 we try to depict the general setting of the ECA cover. The subject of the cover, here "Risk Object", is the yellow payment stream of so-called repayments. They are given by date, amount and currency. They represent the credit which started at inception (Fig. 5.2 in blue). This is the domain of the institution in the guise of guarantor or insurer.

Until inception there is a build-up of the credit. There are several paths: (1) the supplier begins to work and uses own capital to ready the deliverable, (2) the supplier may be financed by a financing institution, by a committed credit line from which to draw (*disbursement period*), or (3) there may be an issuance of a bond whose proceed may be partly used and partly re-invested.

The costs of financing the credit, actual for financing institutions (e.g. commitment fees, interests) or opportunity costs from the supplier will be incorporated into the credit to be reimbursed (Situation C and D of Fig. 5.2).

Therefore the financing and costs of the build-up are condensed into the credit (Situation E in Fig. 5.2). The bigger the cost the higher the principal amount and thus the bigger the repayments.

The time dimension is imperative in the determination of the financing cost. In our parlance it is known as "Disbursement period". But it influences the amount of the credit and not primarily and directly the premium. For, why should two identical risk objects differ in premium based on the build-up history? *Therefore we do not consider the "disbursement period" as a genuine variable of the pricing.* Actually it does not show up in the formulae.

On the other hand the time between commitment t_0 and inception t_1 has an influence on the risk that our ability to conjecture a future state of the world or the credit worthiness of an obligor is flawed. The longer the time span the bigger the probability that something relevant happens. Something happening is also a random process which is a possible subject for insurance or risk cover.

Figure 5.3 shows the rating diffusion over time as taken from rating migration tables. Starting with 100% BB, after a year approx. 80% are still there, after 3 years only 35% are still BB. For some export credits the lap between committing the insurance and the inception of the credit or the first repayment can span several years.

Ratings can also become better as shown. For our purposes we are more concerned with the worsening of the credit.

Fig. 5.2 Synopsis of risk
profiles. Incorporation of the
financing cost in the export
credit

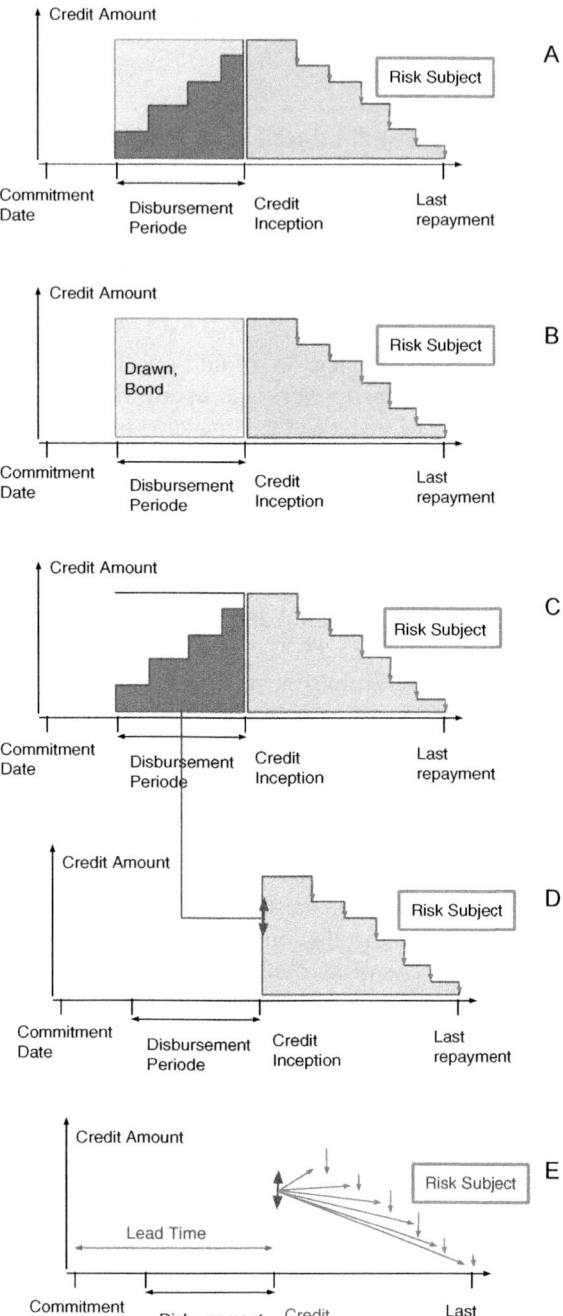

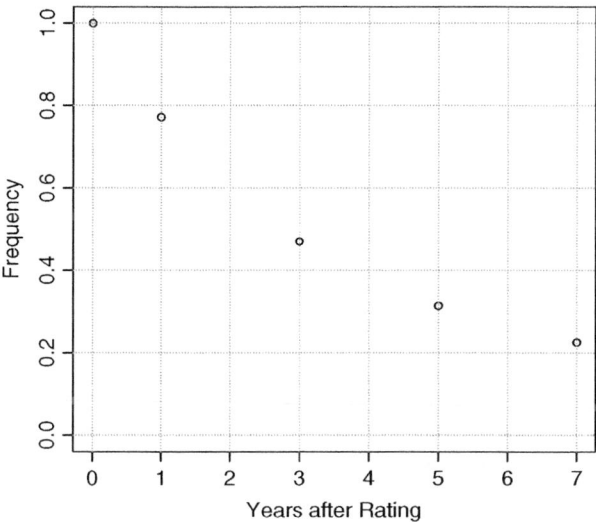

Fig. 5.3 Frequencies of a BB-Rating over time. The curve from S&P default data shows how unstable ratings can be

5.4 Mitigation of Risk

In essence mitigating risk means for the insurance company making an export cover feasible and then reducing the premium by improving the structure of the deal. The higher the risk the higher the premium. We see two fundamental dimensions of risk, the probability of default and the recovery given default. The first depends very much on the scope of the cover while the second is contingent on the exposure evolution over time, the kind of good exported and additional risk sharing. There are factors that affect both dimensions, e.g. the tenors of the repayments. This is especially valid for export on credit terms. For the second type of insurance, i.e. contract guarantees or working capital insurance the basics are a little different.

Here we assume the perspective of the supplier and not of the insurer as it is the scope of credit insurance to make export feasible and not to reduce the burden of the insurance company. On the other hand, the quality of the export contract is not validated by the insurance. Therefore not all risks can be covered.

5.4.1 Reducing the Probability

The most obvious measure is replacing the lower credit with a better one, i.e. requiring an additional guarantee. A better rating has a lower probability of default even more so when we consider the joint default.

Choosing the right tenor can help reducing the risk. But there are two or more counteracting arguments. The longer the higher the probability that the good, if it is a capital good, can earn its cost. On the other hand more can happen in longer periods. A compromise is to look at the useful life of the good as a yardstick and have an amortising pattern for longer tenors.

Agreeing on a payment in the currency of the buyer, if it is easily convertible, shifts the risk of the exchange rate to the supplier who may be in a better position to guard against this risk.

5.4.2 Improving the Recovery

The recovery in absolute terms is dependent on the cover or exposure. Trivially, the lower the exposure the smaller the insured loss. Reducing the cover may just be a feature to make an export insurable.

As the discussion of the work-out has shown the jurisdiction of the claim is important. Therefore the use of certain financial instruments or contractual features may give an opportunity to determine the forum for a later dispute. There may be big differences both in quality and speed. For some problems the jurisdiction is the country of incorporation, e.g. bankruptcy. The design of the loan agreement or commercial contract may be helpful in recovery. Material adverse change clauses or covenants are used to a wide extent in credit agreements (see Table 2.6 and Fig. 5.4). The lender has thus some possibilities to assure payments by the obligor. In (traded) bonds there are less possibilities to devise such clauses. In general there is more control in bilateral credit agreements than in public bonds. Therefore one could argue that the covenants or material adverse change provisions are a kind of risk mitigant.

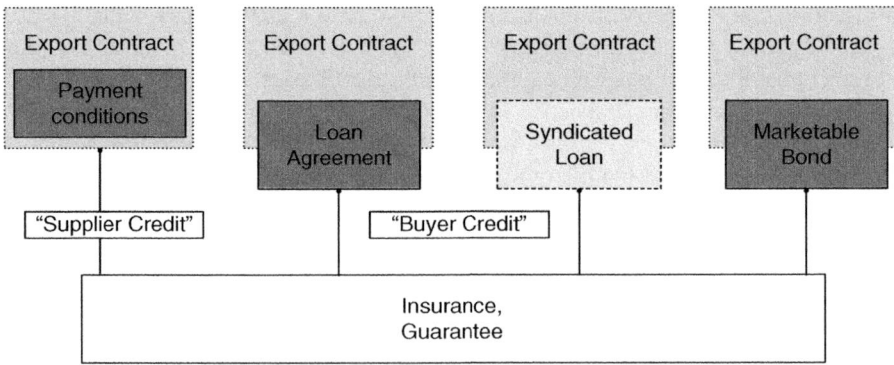

Fig. 5.4 Synopsis of risk different credit agreements

Typical credit enhancements as documented in the OECD Arrangement are

- assignment of contract proceeds or receivables,
- asset based security: mortgage on very mobile and valuable piece of property and property that has entire value in itself,
- fixed asset security ("provide the ECA with more leverage over the use of the asset"),
- escrow account by a party not controlled or sharing common ownership with the buyer.

Remotely controllable assets may be a machinery that works only if attached to the internet and may be switched off by the exporting supplier in case that the obligor does not pay the due. It is a second best solution or lose–lose-situation. But it is a clear incentive to pay as otherwise the machine cannot be used. This is a kind of fixed asset security.

The quality of the transaction and its mitigants are an important variable in the determination of the premium via the recovery rate.

5.5   Accounting for Premia

When the application has been approved the premium is charged most often upfront. The cover is contingent on this payment. The inherent premium loading for administrative cost is recognised in the income statement. The risk premium is a liability on the balance sheet as long as the cover is not effective. This account is called *Unearned Premium Reserve* UPR. It "represents the amount of premium applicable to the unexpired portion of the policy. It is a reserve to assure the return of unearned premiums. It comes about as the natural result of collecting premiums in advance for insurance to extend over a stated period of time in the future" (US Legal 2020).

During the cover period the appropriate amount is booked from the premium reserve into the earned premium account. Thus the earned premium EP accrues correctly.

Now in credit insurance, especially in the OECD Arrangement definition of repayment terms the cover is not constant over the cover period but is decreasing every 6 months. Therefore at the beginning of the period more has to be earned, decreasing steadily.

Defining the *specific premium* as the risk premium for one unit of time and one monetary unit the earned premium of a given day is just the actual exposure times the specific premium π. This is in strict analogy to the plain interest charged on the principal. In simple insurance like motor liability the earned premium is just proportional to the period of cover. Here we have to consider a more complex exposure over time.

Let us assume we have charged a premium and have earned some portion for administrative or operational charges. Then we have the risk premium P. We calculate the area under the exposure or credit principal $p(t)$ from inception t_0 to expiry t_E. The mathematical shorthand looks scary:

$$A = \int_{t_0}^{t_E} p(t) \cdot dt. \tag{5.12}$$

Now the specific premium π is

$$\pi = \frac{P}{A}. \tag{5.13}$$

For an arbitrary period between t_1 and t_2, both $t_i \leq t_E$ and $t_i \geq t_0$, we have

$$\mathrm{EP}(t_1, t_2) = \pi \cdot \int_{t_1}^{t_2} p(t) \cdot dt. \tag{5.14}$$

At time t with $t_0 \leq t \leq t_E$ we have for the UPR

$$\mathrm{UPR}(t) = \pi \cdot \int_{t}^{t_E} p(t) \cdot dt. \tag{5.15}$$

When a claim is filed and accepted the remaining UPR is recognised at once. In the case of rescheduling or changes the credit insurer could just keep the specific premium and only recalculate the new area under the exposure and net it with the UPR.

Example 5.2 (Rescheduling). Given a risk profile of 182 days at 1000, 183 days at 750, 182 days at 500 and 183 days at 250 MU and a premium of 125. The risk premium is 100 (0.8 times 125). The specific premium is derived from the exposure area:

$$A = 1000 \cdot 182 + 750 \cdot 183 + 500 \cdot 182 + 250 \cdot 183 = 456,000.$$

Thus the specific premium is $\pi = 2.193 \cdot 10^{-4}$. Now suppose inception is 1st November 2019. Then, in this year the earned premium is $61 \cdot 1000 \cdot 2.193 \cdot 10^{-4} = 13.38$.

Payment dates are 1st of May and 1st of November. On 15th March 2021 the payments are rescheduled. The next payment of 250 of 1st May 2021 is deferred to November 1st when the residual 500 will be paid. The difference will be the last period

$$\Delta P = \pi \cdot 183 \cdot 250 = 10.03.$$

This amount should be paid by the applicant. If the insurer wants to charge administrative costs for the change, then a loading of 25% would seem reasonable, thus $10.03/0.8 = 12.54$.   △

Example 5.3 (Termination). Suppose for some reason, in accordance with the insurance agreement, the policy terminates early. What should, if ever, be reimbursed? By the very definition of the unearned premium reserve is exactly this amount, possibly after a detraction for handling. △

By keeping the specific premium constant over the life of the cover the insurer need not hassle with a possible change in premium tariff and an implicit promise of grandfathering the premium.

References

OECD (2020). Arrangement on officially supported export credits. Publication, Organisation for Economic Co-operation and Development, Paris. http://www.oecd.org/officialdocuments/publicdisplaydocumentpdf/?doclanguage=en&cote=tad/pg(2020)1.

US Legal (2020). Unearned premium reserve law and legal definition.

Wikipedia contributors (2020). OECD — Wikipedia, The Free Encyclopedia. https://en.wikipedia.org/w/index.php?title=OECD&oldid=955639374. Online. Accessed 10 May 2020.

New Premium Framework

6

We want to build our comprehensive pricing methodology for credit insurance on principles which we present as propositions. By doing so we hope to convince the reader of the soundness of the approach or to channel criticism to the point.

Very generally speaking there are only two broad classes of pricing methods for guarantee like instruments:

1. discounting cashflows and
2. option pricing.

The latter is a generalisation of methods introduced by the Black–Scholes and Merton models. Remember just the distance to default calculus of Sect. 4.8. This approach clearly stands on the first method.

An other sub-group comes from the input data used, i.e.

1. market quotes of identical risk,
2. market quotes of similar risk with adjustments or
3. empirical data from pertinent categories.

We want to develop a framework that can cope with either input data.

In the title of this booklet we have raised the expectation to be concise. This does not, alas, mean that the subject matter can be treated trivially. Especially governments think that their supported exporters or banks should be able to re-perform the calculations. We do not agree that this is a valid argument for over-simplicity.

The premium calculation is not just meant for terms greater than 2 years. It is independent of the residual maturity.

In this chapter we present a new framework for premium in the actuarial world. In the next chapter we will look at a market version of the pricing.

6.1   Foundation

6.1.1   Risk Neutrality

Export credit support is granted by government bodies that act as lenders of last resort. Their over-all financial capacity is much vaster as the capital needed to back this support operation. Therefore it may have the attitude that there is no need of pricing of risk beyond the pure premium or expected loss.

Proposition 1 (Risk Neutrality). *Official credit agencies and insurance on state account are risk-neutral with respect to pricing credit risk cover.*

Concentrations or cumulations should not take place in a homogeneous portfolio. Therefore, there are no discounts or markups for large covers.

This proposition obviously cannot hold for private insurance companies. As the ruin process (Fig. 3.6) shows only a massive endowment or a state guarantee reduces the probability of ruin besides a positive loading. Risk neutrality is only for state business that is not competing with the private insurance market. Because risk capital is not for free for private companies they need a loading for risk to reduce ruin risk. They are bound to the going-concern principle. On the other hand the private market can select customers where the ECA have to accept transactions by their mandate.

Proposition 2 (Proportionality). *The premium is proportionate to the cover, e.g. export value or similar basis.*

6.1.2   No Subsidies

Proposition 3 (Fundamental). *The provision by governments (or special institutions controlled by governments) of export credit guarantee or insurance programmes, of insurance or guarantee programmes shall be effected at premium rates which are not inadequate to cover the long-term operating costs and losses of the programmes.*

The scope of the Pricing provisions is relevant to the remuneration of the credit risk (counterparty risk/transaction risk) for the ECA and represents the pure risk reward component. There are two components to the premium, i.e. losses and costs, and the remuneration of the credit risk should hence be equivalent irrespective of the type of support provided.

This proposition prevents governmental subsidies, that is a tangible financial benefit. It is both unfair between countries but it is also problematic to create inequalities between domestic exporters and non-exporters.

Proposition 4 (Scope). *Premia must cover both (1) risk bearing and (2) operating cost of the institution. We call the first "Risk Premium" and the latter "Operational Cost".*

As long as all participants to an agreement have similar administrative cost there is no problem. On the other hand more efficient and lean producer are not rewarded in terms of cheaper premia.

6.2   Instruments

Insurance, guarantees and lending follow different legal concept, i.e. "utmost good faith" (*uberrima fides*) for insurance and "buyer beware" (*caveat emptor*) for guarantees and lending. Lending and guarantees are more liquid instruments, while insurance is subject to an analysis and due diligence of the representations and other conditions, before claim payment. Therefore a guarantee is generally more valuable than an insurance policy.

Proposition 5 (Structural Differences). *The price for an insurance covering the same risk on the same conditions should be cheaper than a guarantee, $P_{insurance} \leq P_{Guarantee}$.*

The OECD arrangement has a specific factor that ranges in the whereabouts of some small percentage, e.g. $2 \ldots 4 \%$.

6.3   Credit

6.3.1   Credit Events

Proposition 6 (Credit Events). *There should be a list of agreed causes for loss, i.e. Credit Events, discriminating between market and sovereign triggered events. The more events are covered by an instrument the higher should the premium be. The events afflict the obligor and lead to a loss.*

Usually the definition of force majeure in credit support is being interpreted in a very broad sense not to raise disputes with similar clauses in commercial contracts or loan agreements. The scope of an insurance or guarantee defines the probability of default and thus has an impact on the premia.

Credit events should be synchronised between credit insurer, lender and commercial contract. In projects and construction agreements there is much emphasis on force majeure clauses. Credit insurers take a rather comprehensive stance, that is their definition tries to be at least as broad as in the commercial contract.

Fig. 6.1 Common scale   Proprietary Domain   Common Scale
from proprietary systems

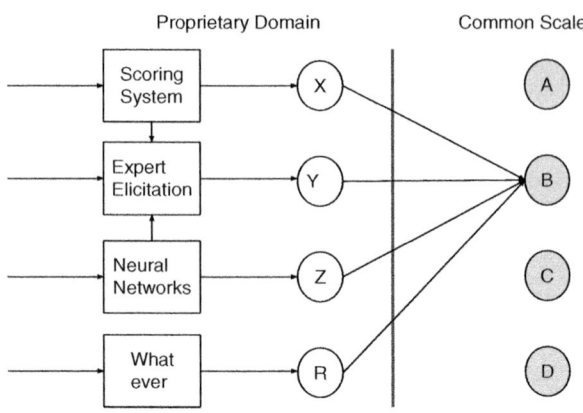

6.3.2   Risk Assessment

The pricing of credit risks of an obligor in the light of market or economic risks
depends on its credit quality.

Proposition 7 (Ordinal Rating Scale). *The credit quality of an obligor, its counterparty rating, is measured by an appropriate ordinal scale[1] called rating. The
premium for a better rated obligor is less than the premium for a worse obligor, all
other circumstances equal.*

The common rating need not imply that all use the same methodology for assessing
the risk. In our view it would be advisable to map the result to a common scale
which in turn would determine the rate of default (see Fig. 6.1) This could also
accommodate a situation where there is a benchmark from a market.

6.3.3   Enhancement

An export credit may be secured or enhanced by additional security packages, e.g.
additional third-party guarantees, or by the exported good itself.

Proposition 8 (Credit Enhancement). *Applicable credit enhancements lower the
premium prior to enhancement. This may affect (1) the ultimate loss via recovery
or (2) the probability that an event occurs. The case of joint probabilities of default
should be considered.*

---

[1]An ordinal scale is amenable to comparison like "better" or "worse", but not to difference or
summation.

6.4   Risk Profile

The underlying credit is a payment stream in the future. Therefore the amount outstanding and covered is time-variant. Typically a credit builds up in a first phase, may have a grace period and then a third phase decreasing by repayments. There are two components, i.e. a principal profile F_i and an interest payment I_i stream, together $C_i = F_i + I_i$. In case of a default the residual principal is due but not the outstanding interests of the future.

Proposition 9. *The whole risk profile should be considered for the premium consisting of principal F_i and Interest I_j while applying the time-value of money. The payment dates need not be synchronous.*

There could be also a margin cashflow if upfront premium is not required. For the repayment part often the start or inception of the stream is not so clear. Therefore we propose an inception point which is given from the data.

Proposition 10 (Credit Inception). *The inception point of the credit is the earliest point in time where the principal of the credit has its highest monetary value.*

Often this point in time is farther in the future such that setting the premium and life of the credit may embed a risk that the information and the risk context change. Therefore this lead time should be considered in the premium (see Fig. 6.2).

   The purpose of this tentative definition is to calculate the credit profile from the data of the credit, thus without the recourse to additional definitions. This may be seen in stark contrast to the Starting Point of Credit SPOC of the OECD Arrangement which in our view is subject to many dependencies and special clauses.

   For the calculation of the present value there must be a point in time as reference for the discounting of the repayments, viz. the inception point.

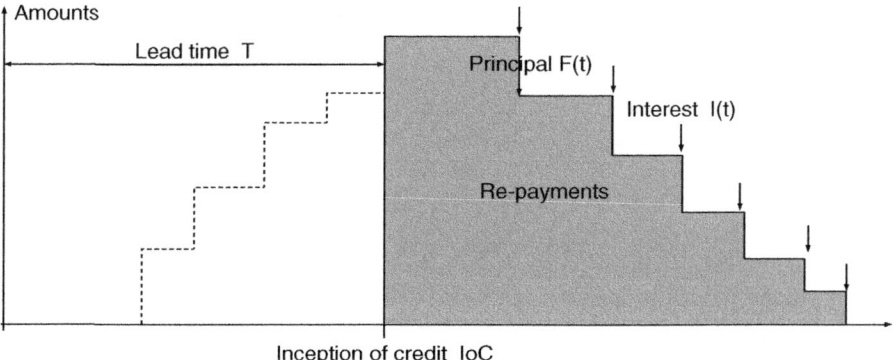

Fig. 6.2 Typical risk profile

Proposition 11 (Lead Time). *The lead time between fixing the premium and inception of the credit should be considered in the premium. The longer the period the higher the surcharge.*

Credit insurers explicitly insure and lenders implicitly self-insure the repayments of the credit.

Having said that, the subject of the cover is the credit, or the repayments and receivables. The lead time would then be the period between committing the cover – and determining the appropriate premium – and the inception of the credit.

With the determination of the premium there is an assumption about the situation which will prevail in the future, i.e. when the repayments are due. The further in the future and thus the longer the lead time, the bigger the uncertainty of the risk situation. What will happen tomorrow is less uncertain than what will happen during the next half year. Now uncertainty is a risk and thus relevant to the premium.

Pricing of financial instrument considers this "forward start", often in derivatives. Assets are modelled as following a diffusion process where the potential asset prices spread from their mean according to a $\sqrt{T}$-law.

We have discussed three possible methodologies, i.e.:

- forward swap rates,
- Markov process and
- a diffusion factor.

Not charging for this lead time at all would imply that a credit beginning tomorrow would require the same premium as an identical credit starting in 1 year's time.

6.5   Premium Principles

There are principles from the actuarial science, which are mainly unspecific to credit insurance and pricings from the credit industry. The latter can be incorporated into the former.

The most basic premium formula in insurance is the "pure premium" given as the expected value of loss $E(L) = EL$. The expectation is the probability weighted outcome and the loss is net of recoveries, i.e. with d default probability:

$$E(L) = d \cdot L + (1 - d) \cdot 0 = d \cdot L, \tag{6.1}$$

where the net loss L equals the gross loss G minus recoveries M, i.e. $L = G - M$.

An alternative name, used in banking, is Loss given Default LGD. Expected Loss may account for the insurance part, there must be a surcharge for the operational cost. This part may be an addition or a multiplicative loading. Thus the premium P is

$$P = E(L) + A = (1 + a) \cdot E(L). \qquad (6.2)$$

Proposition 12 (Pure Risk Plus Loading). *The simplest premium formula is Eq. (6.2), i.e. $P(L) = (1 + a) \cdot d \cdot L$.*

An insurance or lender either indemnifies random events or bears the loss which must at least obey some probabilistic regularities. These are mainly represented by distributions or characteristics thereof. The mean loss (or expected loss) is the pure premium. Therefore, the principle is Premium = Expected loss plus Loading.

Suppose the payments C_t have two components, the principal F_t and the interest I_t, thus

$$C_t = F_t + I_t. \qquad (6.3)$$

In case of a default in t, the interests in $t + 1, \ldots$ are not paid. At the same time the outstanding principal, a residual notional is defined by

$$R_t = \sum_{k=t}^{N} F_k \qquad (6.4)$$

with $R_N = 0$. This definition can be used to calculate the interest I_t from the rate z as (see Eq. (4.23) on page 96)

$$I_t = R_t \cdot z \cdot (t_i - t_{i-1}). \qquad (6.5)$$

For a stream of payments $C_i, i = t, \ldots, N$ there is a simple generalisation. The non-default event is called "survival" $S_t(\rho)$, with ρ the rating, as (Eq. (4.84))

$$S_t(\rho) = (1 - d_1) \cdot (1 - d_2) \ldots (1 - d_t) = \prod_{i=1}^{t} (1 - d_i(\rho)). \qquad (6.6)$$

The cumulative default rate D_t is given by

$$D_t(\rho) = 1 - S_t(\rho). \qquad (6.7)$$

A default in the period t is equivalent to surviving until $t - 1$ and then defaulting, thus $S_{t-1} \cdot d_t$. By risk-free discounting the stream with df_t and the recovery rate μ we get the present value (see Fig. 6.3):

$$B(\rho) = \sum_{t=1}^{N} df_t \cdot S_{t-1} \Big((1 - d_t) \cdot C_t + d_t \cdot \mu \cdot (C_t + R_{t+1}) \Big) \qquad (6.8)$$

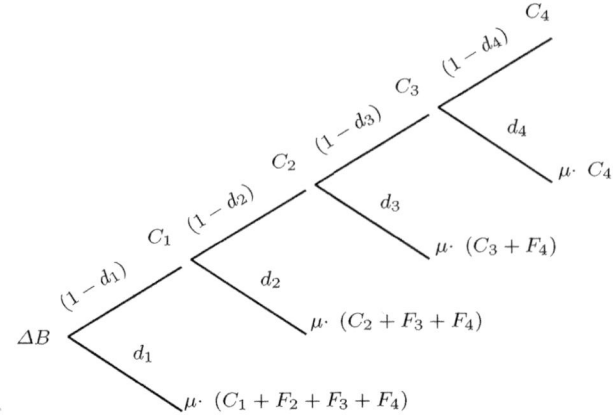

Fig. 6.3 The default graph (schematic), discounting omitted

For a risk-free payment stream the Eq. (6.8) reduced to

$$B(\rho = 0) = \sum_{t=1}^{N} df_t \cdot C_t. \tag{6.9}$$

The difference from risk-free to risky present value can be identified with the pure risk premium P as expected loss of the payment stream, thus

$$\text{Premium} = \text{Risk-free Present Value} - \text{Risky Present Value}, \tag{6.10}$$

or formally

$$P = \Delta B = B(\rho = 0) - B(\rho) \tag{6.11}$$

and therefore

$$\Delta B = \sum_{t=1}^{N} df_t \cdot C_t - \sum_{t=1}^{N} df_t \cdot S_{t-1}\Big((1-d_t) \cdot C_t + d_t \cdot \mu \cdot (C_t + R_{t+1})\Big), \tag{6.12}$$

after some algebraic transformations:

$$\Delta B = \sum_{t=1}^{N} df_t\Big(D_t \cdot C_t - S_{t-1} \cdot d_t \cdot \mu \cdot (C_t + R_{t+1})\Big), \tag{6.13}$$

where we use D_t as the cumulated default rate from Eq. (6.7).

Proposition 13. *Equation 6.10 gives the pure risk premium based on expected value of a stream of payments. It is the difference of the risk-free net present value minus the value of the risky payments.*

The premium based on the expected value can be calculated both (1) as upfront premium and (2) as a per annum rate.

The pure premium as a rate is calculated from Eq. (6.12), where the risk-less payments are discounted with an appropriate rate such that the present value equals the expected value of the payments, i.e.

$$0 = \sum_{t=1}^{N} df_t^* \cdot C_t - \sum_{t=1}^{N} df_t \cdot S_{t-1}\Big((1-d_t)\cdot C_t + d_t \cdot \mu \cdot (C_t + R_{t+1})\Big), \qquad (6.14)$$

where $df_t^* = (1 + y)^{-t} = (1 + r_f + m)^{-t}$. The rate y is the risky rate, which incorporates the risk-free rate r_f and a risk margin or premium margin m. Thus the methodology can handle both representations.

The determination of r^* needs a simple numerical solver for finding the root of the function of Eq. (6.14).

6.6 Term-Congruence

In 1857 the German economist Adolph Wagner formulated the so-called Golden Banking Rule. It says that a bank can stay always sound and solvent if its loans correspond to a financing that is equal in volume, term and payment schedule (Wagner 1857, 167). This rule is still applied in liquidity risk management on the whole balance sheet. Up to the major financing crisis banks tried to profit from the *maturity transformation*, that means borrow on short term and lend for long.

For real assets, i.e. many exported capital goods, this concept of congruence translates into comparing the funding with the useful life of the asset. Thus a regular payment of identical instalments would imply that the utility of the financed asset is linear. This seems a little bit simplistic especially when applied irrespective of the good in question.

Proposition 14 (Congruence). *Pricing should be independent from imposed payment patterns as long as the characteristics of the credit are coherent with the usage of the funded asset.*

6.7 Conclusions

For starting a fruitful discussion concerning the (minimum) premia for export credit
support provided by governments or their agencies we have tried to set some
generally accepted or acceptable propositions. Based on these principles we have
given a sketch of a very simple procedure. We have tried not to re-base already
known methodologies.

Equation (6.10) would then lead to the final representation as

$$\Delta B = \sum_{t=1}^{N} df_t \Big((1 - S_t) \cdot C_t - (S_{t-1} - S_t) \cdot \mu \cdot (C_t + R_{t+1}) \Big) \tag{6.15}$$

$$P = a \cdot b \cdot q(T) \cdot \Delta B, \tag{6.16}$$

with ρ the rating, $C_t = F_t + I_t$ the payments, D_t the cumulated default rates, d_t
the marginal default rate, μ the recovery rate, a a loading for the operational cost and
b a fudge factor for the instrument, i.e. insurance or guarantee. The μ incorporates
the collateral. The premium depends on $P(C_t, a, b, q, \mu, T, df_t, D_t, \rho)$.

It is obvious and well known that the difficulties arise with the details and the
fact that the instruments of the different insurers may vary greatly.

Of course many tedious problems are just shifted into the rating classification.
Now we have to agree on the right value of the input variables, i.e. d_t, μ and the
loadings.

Example 6.1. We apply Eq. (6.13) with data from both Standard & Poor's (Vazza
and Kraemer 2018), update from 2018, and Moody's long time series from
1920 to 2008 (Emery and Cantor 2009) and cumulated default rates from Fitch
(FitchRatings 2020, 9). Because of the different ratings the curves are not directly
comparable. With Fitch we have chosen ratings that show consistent values. We set
the interest rate such that the present value of the risk-free discount equals 1. The
profile is semi-annual instalments of equal amount. The core code is as follows with
the Listing B.12 and B.10:

```
res<-c(); dum<-c()
K<-c(11,12,13,14,15,16)
a<-read.table("~/R/snptab.txt")
for (k in 1:6){
  Sgrid<-c(1,1-a[K[k],2:16]/100)
  for (l in 1:20){
    tvec<-1:1/2
    cvec<-rep(1/l,l)
    tgrid<-c(1/12,2/12,3/12,6/12,1,2,3,5,7,10,20,30)
    vgrid<-c(0.07,0.09,0.11,0.12,0.13,0.14,0.17,0.29,0.48,0.68,
      1.20,1.42)/100
```

```
    Svec<-approx(0:15, y=Sgrid, xout=tvec, method="linear")\$y
    param=list(tvec,cvec,dfvec,2,1)
    gir<-bisect(-0.01,0.1,param=param,FUN=parIntRate2)
    dum[1]<-DeltaPrice(gir,tvec,cvec,dfvec,Svec,0.4,2)[1]
  }
  res<-cbind(res,dum)
}
```

The Figs. 6.4, 6.5 and 6.6 show the premia curves in dependence of the ratings. The worse the rating the more parabolic the curves. We will see later that the marginal default rates decrease with maturity. Therefore the longer the bond survives the better the prospects of surviving thereafter. For better rating the marginal rates do not decrease systematically.

The two premia from different suppliers are not easily comparable. The best match is to be found in the low quality ratings where for long tenors we have 13% with S&P data and 10.5% with Moody's.

We find a non-linear shape of the curves especially in the lower ratings. For the best ratings the curves are increasing with the tenor.   △

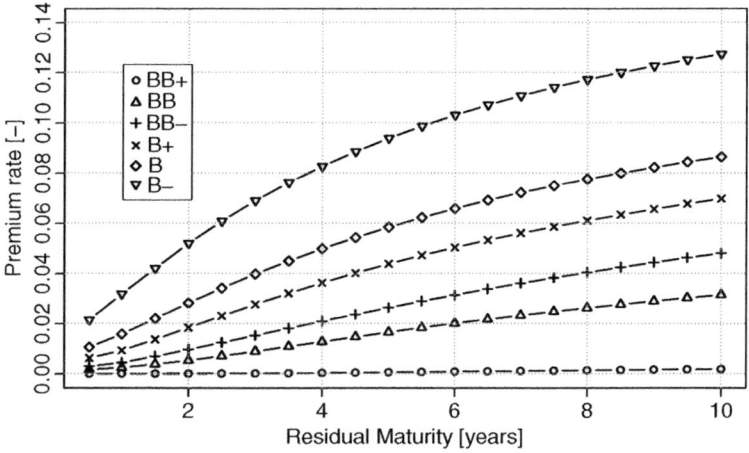

Fig. 6.4 The pure premia from risky discounting with historic default rates from S&P

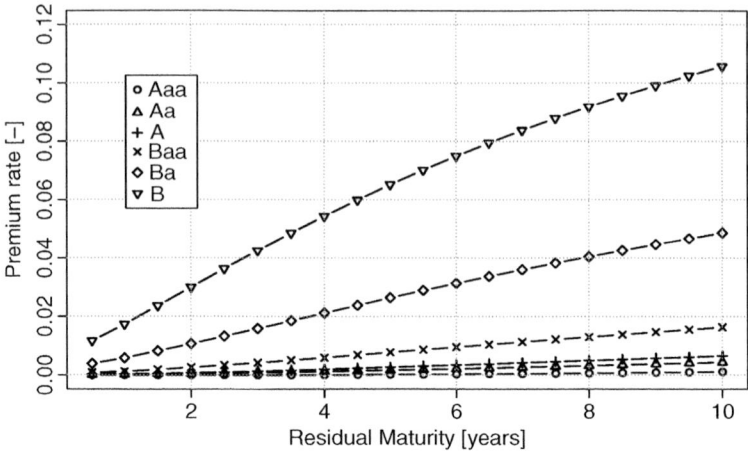

Fig. 6.5 The pure premia from risky discounting with historic default rates from Moody's

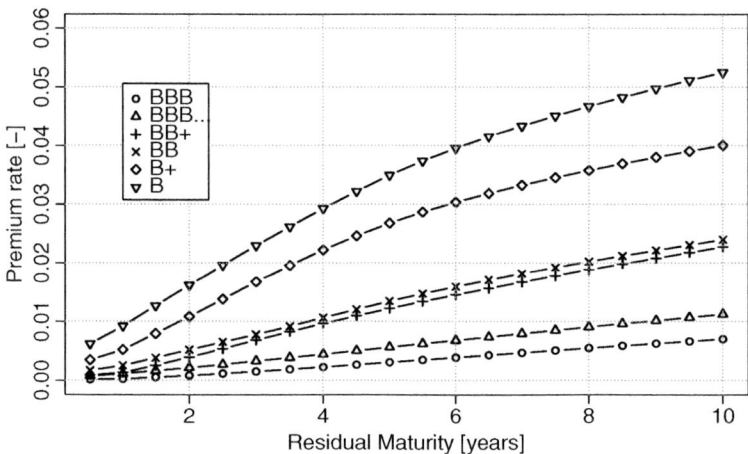

Fig. 6.6 The pure premia from risky discounting with historic default rates from Fitch

References

Emery, K., & Cantor, R. (2009). Corporate Default and Recovery Rates, 1920–2008. Special comment, Moody's Investor Service, Global Credit Research.

FitchRatings (2020). Global Corporate Finance 2019 Transition and Default Study. Study, FitchRatings: Rating Performance Analytics.

Vazza, D., & Kraemer, N. (2018). 2017 Annual Global Corporate Default Study and Rating Transitions. Technical report, Standard & Poor's Global Ratings, New York. https://www. spglobal.com/en/research-insights/articles/default-transition-and-recovery-2017-annual-global-corporate-default-study-and-rating-transitions.

Wagner, A. (1857). *Beiträge zur Lehre von den Banken*. Leipzig: Voss.

Historic Default Rates

7

The new framework of the preceding chapter needs pertinent probability of default. Now both pertinence and probability need to be defined and assessed.

From a subjectivist's point of view probabilities are opinions exactly the same as the claim of the credit rating agencies. The historic approach supposes structural stability, i.e. the meaning of rating does not change, and therefore equates the default probability to frequency. Frequencies can be a starting point for subjectivists who will adjust this pre-knowledge with other information. Here comes the "pertinent" into play. We are looking at an individual buyer or debtor as a member of a certain group, viz. those categorised as something. The question is which group, and as it will often not exist, which group is the most appropriate. Reliable default data from credit insurers do not exist. This gap is bridged by resorting to similar ratings of the best proxy industry.

The second dimension of "pertinent" is time. What is the situation today or over the period of interest in relation to the historic period? The first point is dealt with in the risk assessment; the second may depend on many arguments.

7.1 Data Collection

The rating agencies publish historic default data based on the debt instruments that were rated by them. From the theory developed so far we can bring default in line with life tables by using the survival rates instead of the cumulated default rates.

7.1.1 Cohort and Period

Now we will go a little into life tables of which at least two common distinct types of life expectancy exist, viz. for (1) cohorts and (2) periods.

© The Author(s), under exclusive license to Springer Nature Switzerland AG 2021   167
C. Franzetti, *Pricing Export Credit*, Management for Professionals,
https://doi.org/10.1007/978-3-030-70285-4_7

A cohort is a group of individuals born in a given year and transposed a portfolio of debts existing in a given year.

As (Ortiz-Ospina 2017) writes, "When we can track a group of people born in a particular year, many decades ago, and observe the exact date in which each one of them died then we can calculate this *cohort's life expectancy* by simply calculating the average of the ages of all members when they died". Now, it is obviously not possible to know this metric before all members of the cohort have died. Therefore, actuaries commonly track members of a particular cohort and predict the average age-at-death for them using a combination of observations for past years and projections for future years.

An alternative approach (Morgan 2020), the *period life expectancy*, uses mortality rates from a single year and assumes that those rates apply throughout the remainder of a person's life. This means that any future change to mortality rates would not be taken into account. Therefore, period life expectancies tend to be lower than cohort life expectancies because they do not include any assumptions about future improvements in mortality rates.

"Period life expectancy would match cohort life expectancy only if there were no change in age-specific mortality rates over time. This is an extremely unlikely scenario".

The analogy with debt instruments has some limitations, e.g. there is residual maturity and at inception is not uniform. There will be much more data for short-lived credits than for longer terms.

Standard & Poor's uses the concept of *static pool* that groups into a cohort all issuers of a given rating in a given year. Having an observation period of 40 years means that there are 40 times the number of rating classes static pools. The pools are thought as buy-and-hold portfolios. Therefore, an issuer of a bond issued in t will also enter all pools after t until maturity or default. Suppose the issuer defaults in $t + 3$ then the bond would have been part of pool $t, t + 1, t + 2, t + 3$. The system would record a 4 year default in the first pool, a 3 year default in the second and so on (see Fig. 7.1).

There is another decision to be taken: are we basing the cohort on the original issue rating at inception of the debt or do we consider transitions and consider the

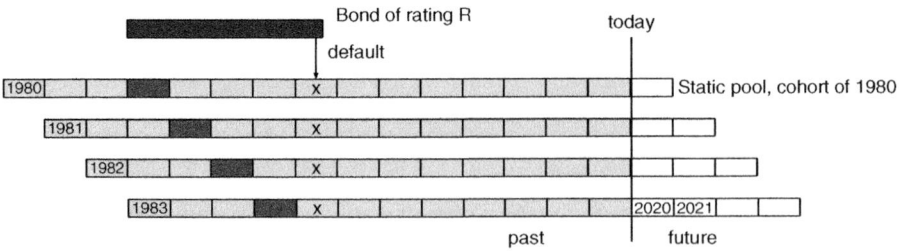

Fig. 7.1 Static pools and default. The bond is an element of several pools and defaults for each pool in a different relative maturity

rating a start date of the cohort? Some academics used the former method, but Moody's and other agencies' corporate default studies are often based on pools of issuers holding a given rating on the cohort date regardless of original rating or time since issuance (Hamilton and Cantor 2006, 5). This implies that the same debt instrument may be included in different cohorts of different ratings.

7.1.2 Averaging

Reality has it that bonds in cohorts withdraw, i.e. leave the pool when their rating is withdrawn. Mostly bonds are bought back or issuing companies enter into mergers. This means that in our model we do not have to cope with two states, i.e. survive or default, but with the three:

1. survive,
2. default or
3. withdraw.

With a withdrawal rate $w(t) = w_t$ we have to incorporate the adjusted survival rates as

$$W(t) = \prod_{i=1}^{t} (1 - d_i) \cdot (1 - w_{i-1}) \cdot w_i \tag{7.1}$$

$$D^*(t) = \prod_{i=1}^{t} (1 - d_{i-1}) \cdot d_t \cdot (1 - w_{i-1}) \tag{7.2}$$

$$S^*(t) = \prod_{i=1}^{t} (1 - d_i) \cdot (1 - w_i). \tag{7.3}$$

Now Hamilton and Cantor (2006, 15) claim that by using the coupons c_t as

$$c_t = \frac{r_t + d_t}{1 - d_t} \tag{7.4}$$

all terms involving w_t disappear such that the withdrawal has no impact on the present value of the bond. r_t is the risk-free rate. Thus, much ado about nothing. The marginal default rate, the hazard rate, is given as

$$d_{y,\rho}(t) = \frac{x_{y,\rho}(t)}{n_{y,\rho}(t)}, \tag{7.5}$$

where y denotes the cohort by start year, ρ the rating, t the period under investigation, $x(t)$ the number of defaults in period t and finally $n(t)$ the number of elements in the cohort at the beginning of period t.

Now comes the averaging as simple unweighted sums of all cohorts y in Y containing the maturity t (Hamilton and Cantor 2006, 7):

$$\bar{d}_\rho(t) = \frac{\sum\limits_{y \in Y} x_{y,\rho}(t)}{\sum\limits_{y \in Y} n_{y,\rho}(t)}. \qquad (7.6)$$

From these values we derive the survival rates $\bar{S}_\rho(t) = \prod\limits_{i=1}^{t} (1 - \bar{d}_\rho(t))$ and $\bar{D}_\rho(t) = 1 - \bar{S}_\rho$.

These rates are based purely on the count. Alternatives have been tested using volume-weighted default rates. By doing so a default of a big borrower is more important than a small one. This approach may be more appropriate for estimating the recovery rate.

The take home message is that there are many different ways to skin that cat. Rating migration and withdrawal blur the picture.

7.2   Applying for Pricing

Standard & Poor's denies altogether the link between empirical historical default rates collected by life table methods and the probability of default, by saying: "Many practitioners use statistics from this default study to estimate the 'probability of default' and 'probability of rating transition'. It is important to note that S&P Global Ratings' credit ratings do not imply a specific probability of default". Now, subjectivists are not scared by this statement. The much bigger question is about the discrepancies with observed prices in the market. These corporate spreads are the difference between the spot rate on corporate bonds in a particular rating class and spot rates for treasury bonds of the same maturity. Such spreads incorporate an assumption about recovery that is not present in the default tables.

Elton et al. (2001) show in their study that the spread has three main components, viz. expected loss, tax component and a risk surcharge ("risk premium"). According to Hull (2012, 528–530) the difference can be attributed between historic and market based spreads to several facts:

- Bond markets are illiquid and have wide bid/ask spreads. Research shows that this argument does not explain the discrepancies.
- Traders are risk-adverse and far from applying risk-neutral utility. Their concern is with systemic risk.
- Highest explanatory power is given to the fact that bonds do not default independently best shown by the default cycles and their high volatility. In the insurance parlance this would be a loading.
- Bond traders are for profit institutions.

The uncritical use of historic default rates is not recommended. It is an absolute minimum requirement not to be undercut.

7.2.1 Adjusting Withdrawals

The adjustment for those elements of a cohort leaving it for causes other than default is with the denominator $n(t)$ in Eq. 7.5 above. For the unadjusted approach, the denominator evolves as

$$n_{y,\rho}(t) = n_{y,\rho}(0) - \sum_{i=1}^{t-1} x_{y,\rho}(i), \qquad (7.7)$$

whereas adjusted we have according to Hamilton and Cantor (2006, 8)

$$n_{y,\rho}(t) = n_{y,\rho}(0) - \sum_{i=1}^{t-1} \left(x_{y,\rho}(i) + w_{y,\rho}(i) \right) - 0.5 \cdot w_{y,\rho}(t). \qquad (7.8)$$

From the studies we know that, besides for the best rating, withdrawals are increasing with the rating index that is the "B" cohort has larger withdrawals than the "BB" cohort. This shows up in the different curves of Fig. 7.2.

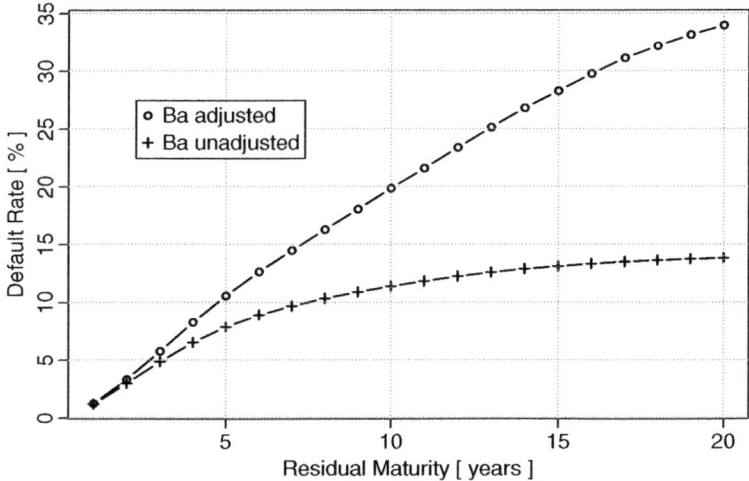

Fig. 7.2 Effect of adjusting for withdrawal. For illustration purposes the graph shows adjusted and unadjusted for withdrawals default rates of Moody's Ba cohorts from 1970 to 2005 (Hamilton and Cantor 2006, 14)

7.2.2 Scaling

The historic default rates are almost always smaller than those implied by the market. The latter are called the risk-neutral probabilities of default. An obvious but somewhat crude method to bring the empirical default rates more in line with market practice is to scale the empirical default rates $d_{t,\text{emp}}$, to be found in Table A.1, to the average or actual level of market price of default.

We will elaborate on this later in Example 8.5 on page 184 (see Fig. 8.7 on page 186). It shall suffice to say that we envisage a factor of approximately 2. The historic rates should be doubled.

7.2.3 No Arbitrage

We are discussing both private credit insurance companies and state agencies, i.e. ECAs, here. The latter need not produce profits but must ensure to cover all costs, both from risk and from operations, by premia. A second mainstay is the level playing field argument. Exporting countries' support should not undercut the market. This leads to low premia that must be upheld by minimum premia.

Exposures from credit insurers are not marketed. The transfer to the capital market by some nascent securitisations has no substantial weight. Therefore the credit insurance exposures are not exposed to any kind of arbitrage. It is not possible to manage a portfolio of credit exposures with a handful of CDS on the market.

Therefore, applying empirical default rates for pricing is feasible without causing disruptions. But it supposes that the sponsors of the credit insurance have deep pockets with a very long time horizon and penalise customers in good times and help more than due in bad times of the cycle.

We should look for an alternative as we do in the next chapter.

References

Elton, E. J., Gruber, M. J., Agrawal, D., & Mann, C. (2001). Explaining the rate spread on corporate bonds. *Journal of Finance, 56*(1):247–277. https://EconPapers.repec.org/RePEc:bla: jfinan:v:56:y:2001:i:1:p:247-277.

Hamilton, D. T., & Cantor, R. (2006). Measuring Corporate Default Rates. Special comment, Moody's Investor Service, Global Credit Research.

Hull, J. (2012). *Options, futures, and other derivatives*. Boston: Prentice Hall.

Morgan, E. (2020). Period and cohort life expectancy explained: December 2019, Office for National Statistics, UK Government. https://www.ons.gov.uk/ peoplepopulationandcommunity/birthsdeathsandmarriages/lifeexpectancies/methodologies/ periodandcohortlifeexpectancyexplained.

Ortiz-Ospina, E. (2017). "Life Expectancy" – What does this actually mean? https:// ourworldindata.org/life-expectancy-how-is-it-calculated-and-how-should-it-be-interpreted. Online. Accessed 18 August 2020.

Market Version of the Framework

8

Insurance pricing rests either on empirical data that assumes to a certain extent that the underlying structure has some stability over time and thus is a valid predictor for the future. Or, data for pricing may be extracted from traded instruments that derive their price from the market, which in turn is the will and subjective estimate of the party to the instrument or agreement. In this chapter we apply the framework to input data from the market.

8.1 Motivation

The famous Austrian economist Friedrich von Hayek would say in an abridged version: "Market is where there is public data". Data about credit is in the Credit Default Swap market. It is arguable whether a bilateral private credit contract reflects the market, albeit one party is active on the financial market. Some analysts make the heroic assumption that a bank is by its very nature the "market". But this approach fails the above characterisation as market producing public data because parties often restrain from giving transparency on their pricing.

We think it a good starting point to look at CDS that are priced continuously. The obvious drawback is threefold:

- Pricing varies strongly within rating categories,
- there is only a very limited number of issues and
- the prices can be very volatile.

Especially the third point is contrasting the philosophy that the government and its agencies should give planning certainty. Therefore, often actual high frequency prices are mixed with stable historic prices, again matched by the same rating.

The problem of scarce data is often tackled by using proxies. Here also a universal rating gives a first indication. Generally, mixing and taking averages dampens the volatility.

Pricing, because of its reliance on ratings that are opinions, is not only an objective endeavour. So the outcome is not true, but hopefully adequate and produced by a due process.

8.2   OECD Market Pricing

The rather convoluted description of market pricing can be found in Schleich and Shin (2017). The Arrangement defines five so-called authorised *market benchmarks*, enumerated below:

1. Uncovered tranche of export credits,
2. Name-specific (or related entity) credit default swaps (CDS) or corporate bonds,
3. Loan benchmarks,
4. Benchmark market curves and
5. The TCMB-BAP model as floor.

Because the TCMB-BAP is a floor, it has to be calculated anyway. Actually it would make no sense to calculate the other benchmark or try to retrieve them because most ECAs are prone to charge the minimum. But, with the provision that the CDS or pertinent bond spreads according to number 2 of the list above are allowed to be lower than TCMB-BAP, the floor can be undercut.

The calculation begins with a so-called *Bond Premium* π_B and an *Actuarial Premium* π_A. Calculation means just the interpolation of values. The first table is the spread between corporate bond market yields in the United States (using essentially BVAL Sector Curve for USD US Non-Financials) updated annually and dollar swap rates.

The upfront premium is derived from the discounting of the so assessed rate with the CIRR base rates that could be negative.

$$\text{TCMB} - \text{BAP} = \max\left(0.0015, \pi_B, 0.65 \cdot \pi_B + 0.35 \cdot \pi_A\right) \tag{8.1}$$

with

$$\pi_A = 0.6 \cdot \frac{dr_{S\&P} + dr_{Moody} + dr_{Fitch}}{3} \frac{1}{T}. \tag{8.2}$$

Both $\pi_B(\rho, T)$ and $\text{DR}(\rho, T) = (dr_{S\&P} + dr_{Moody} + dr_{Fitch})/3$ with rating ρ are interpolated at T from the respective tables.

The tables are updated once a year. There is a backstop to contain volatility. The variation from year to year is kept low.

Now the applicable rate is determined from the spreads, if available, and the minimum that is the historic default rates called MAP for "Minimum Actuarial Premium". Formally:

$$s_{\text{MB}} = \max\left(\text{MAP}, \min(s_{\text{TCMB–BAP}}, s_{\text{SLoan}}, s_{\text{CDS}}, s_{\text{Bond}})\right). \qquad (8.3)$$

Here we have a slight inconsistency as default rates and swap rates are made comparable by the recovery according to Eq. (4.95). The upfront premium is calculated by discounting with the appropriate CIR-rate.

Example 8.1 (TCMB-BAP). As of writing, we retrieve some data from an existing Indian conglomerate. Its CDS spreads are volatile, but by eye-balling over some 6 months they average around the following spreads:[1] for 1 y 30 bp, 3 y 70 bp, 5 y 120 bp, 7 y 150 bp and 10 y 170 bp. The MIFOR is around 6.25%. The company has a BBB+ rating. △

8.3 CDS Pricing

In a CDS, the buyer of the swap makes fee payments to the swap's seller until the maturity date of a contract. In return, the seller agrees in case that the debt issuer experiences a credit event, to pay the buyer the security's value as well as all interest payments that would have been paid between that time and the security's maturity date.

Thus we have two legs, i.e. the *fee leg* (or premium leg) and the *contingent leg*. The first consists of the fees plus the accrual on default, thus (Beinstein and Scott 2006, 16):

$$s_n \sum_{i=1}^{n} f_i \cdot S_i \cdot df_i + s_n \sum_{i=1}^{n} \frac{1}{2} f_i (S_{i-1} - S_i) df_i$$

$$= (1 - \mu) \sum_{i=1}^{n} (S_{i-1} - S_i) df_i. \qquad (8.4)$$

---

[1] Source: https://www.assetmacro.com.

The notation is as follows:

s_n	Credit default swap rate for maturity n
f_i	Length of time period i in years
S_i	Survival probability up to time i
df_i	Risk-free discount factor for time i
μ	Recovery rate

We can solve Eq. (8.4) for the swap rate s_n:

$$s_n = \frac{(1-\mu)\sum\limits_{i=1}^{n}(S_{i-1}-S_i)df_i}{\frac{1}{2}\sum\limits_{i=1}^{n}f_i\left(S_{i-1}+S_i\right)df_i}. \tag{8.5}$$

Now, in 2010 the specifications changed in order to stricter standardise the CDS contract. The "coupon" payments were restricted to a set of values, e.q 1 or 5%. In order to compensate the difference to the effective rate, an upfront payment was introduced. In combination with standard contract sizes, this helps to equalise the size of cash flows across contracts.

There exists a simplified version of Eq. (8.5) that is derived by Eq. (8.4) by omitting the second, and smaller, term:

$$s_n = \frac{(1-\mu)\sum\limits_{i=1}^{n}(S_{i-1}-S_i)df_i}{\sum\limits_{i=1}^{n}f_i \cdot S_i \cdot df_i}. \tag{8.6}$$

8.3.1 Bootstrapping the Survival Rate

We have to extract the survival probabilities S_i from the term structure of spreads s_i, as these are quoted. We make the followings definitions as terms of Eq. (8.4):

$$U_n = \sum_{i=1}^{n} f_i \cdot S_i \cdot df_i$$

$$V_n = \sum_{i=1}^{n} \frac{1}{2}f_n \cdot (S_{i-1}-S_i)df_i$$

$$W_n = (1-\mu)\sum_{i=1}^{n}(S_{i-1}-S_i)df_i.$$

Then we tediously rearrange Eq. (8.5) to the following form:

$$s_n \cdot \left(f_n \cdot S_n \cdot df_n + U_{n-1}\right) + s_n \cdot \left(0.5 \cdot f_n \cdot (S_{n-1} - S_n) \cdot df_n + V_{n-1}\right)$$
$$= (1 - \mu)\left((S_{n-1} - S_n) \cdot df_n + W_{n-1}\right),$$

and from here we transform to:

$$S_n = \frac{(1 - \mu)S_{n-1} + W_{n-1}/df_n - s_n\left(0.5 f_n \cdot S_{n-1} + V_{n-1}/df_n + U_{n-1}/df_n\right)}{1 - \mu + s_n \cdot 0.5 \cdot f_n}. \tag{8.7}$$

and

$$S_n = \frac{S_{n-1}\left(1 - \mu - s_n 0.5 f_n\right) + \left(W_{n-1} - s_n(V_{n-1} + U_{n-1})\right)/df_n}{1 - \mu + s_n \cdot 0.5 \cdot f_n}. \tag{8.8}$$

With the anchors $S_0 = 1$ and $U_0 = V_0 = W_0 = 0$, follows

$$S_1 = \frac{1 - \mu - s_1 \cdot 0.5 \cdot f_1}{1 - \mu + s_1 \cdot 0.5 \cdot f_1}. \tag{8.9}$$

Bootstrapping means to calculate $S_2, S_3, \ldots S_n$ with the recursion Eq. (8.8) beginning at S_2.

Example 8.2 (Survival Rates from CDS). In Table 8.1 we have two lists of prices from Bloomberg for sovereign CDS. With spreads and yield curve we have almost all ingredients to calculate the survival rates. The recovery rate μ is assumed as 0.4

Table 8.1 CDS market data and risk-free discount rates for 13th September 2019

	Egypt		Slovakia	
Maturity	Spread	Zeroyield	Spread	Zeroyield
6M	56.86289	0.16365	13.20974	−0.00766
1Y	56.86289	0.15854	13.20974	−0.00810
2Y	106.2062	0.15494	21.41691	−0.00864
3Y	187.2445	0.15082	30.51752	−0.00878
4Y	265.8125	0.14901	41.92411	−0.00860
5Y	344.2387	0.14720	53.31968	−0.00822
7Y	411.8193	0.14597	73.18660	−0.00769
10Y	430.9893	0.14500	87.84624	−0.00522

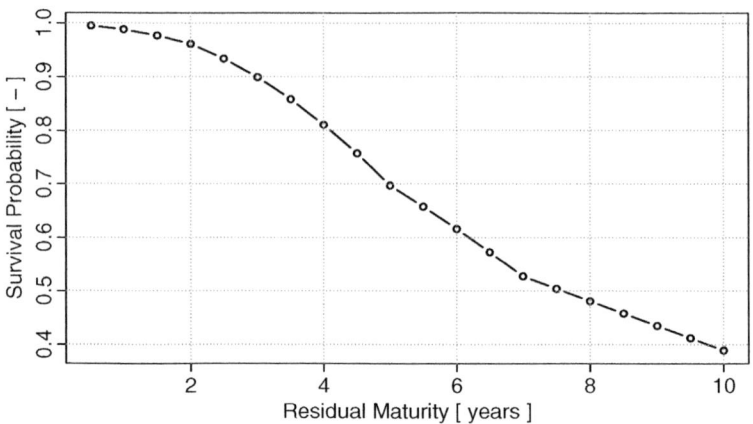

Fig. 8.1 The survival probabilities as calculated from CDS prices. Input data is from Table 8.1

as a standard. Thus, we have to apply Eq. (8.8). We use the code of Listing B.13 of page 235. The result is shown in Listing B.17 and in Fig. 8.1.   △

8.3.2   Risky Annuity and Forward Swap Rate

In the parlance of CDS trading the fee leg of one basis point is called the *risk annuity* A_t:

$$A_t = \frac{1}{2} \sum_{i=1}^{t} f_i \big(S_{i-1} + S_i \big) df_i. \tag{8.10}$$

A forward CDS is a protection that starts at a future date t_1 but is contracted today t_0 and matures at t_2 with $t_2 > t_1 > t_0$. This is called also a *forward start* CDS. The present value of a CDS from t_1 to t_2 is identical to a buy of a protection from t_0 to t_2 minus a CDS from t_0 to t_1. With the risky annuities and the designation of the forward CDS spread as s_{t_i,t_k}, the given spot curve as $s_{t_0,t}$ we can write

$$s_{t_0,t_2} \cdot A_{t_2} - s_{t_0,t_1} \cdot A_{t_1} = s_{t_1,t_2} \cdot (A_{t_2} - A_{t_1}) \tag{8.11}$$

and therefore

$$s_{t_1,t_2} = \frac{s_{t_0,t_2} \cdot A_{t_2} - s_{t_0,t_1} \cdot A_{t_1}}{A_{t_2} - A_{t_1}}. \tag{8.12}$$

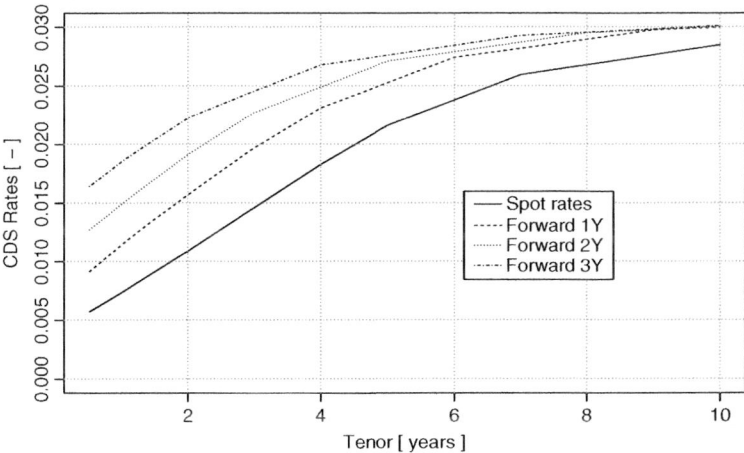

Fig. 8.2 Forward CDS rates. This upward sloping swap price curve leads to higher forward rates. This means that hedging or insuring a future credit risk is more expensive than covering the risk now. A flat curve, i.e. constant swap rates, means that forward and swap rates are identical

Example 8.3. We want to compare a CDS starting in 1, 2 or 3 years with the spot rate of CDS, starting immediately. With the lead time we have argued that the longer the lead time, the higher the price of the credit insurance cover. So we have to calculate three CDS, i.e. for 2, 5 and 7 years. With Eq. (8.12) we do the calculations given the spot rate and its survival function according to Eq. (8.10). The result is shown in Fig. 8.2.

It seems from the curve that there is a price for forward insuring, that is fixing today the rating of an obligor whose credit starts in the future. Considering the forward swap rates can incorporate this feature. With an upward sloping CDS swap curve the insurance covers are more expensive than an immediate risk cover. This is an implicit embodiment of the concept of lead time.

The analogy with spot and forward interest rates is quite natural. $\triangle$

8.3.3 Available Data

CDS data is available in many forms but only as commercial service. The main provider is IHS Markit. Their service comprises not only CDS spreads but also CDS spread curves on a 10 point grid for eight regions, eleven industries and main letter rating combined.

Region	Industry
North America	Basic materials
Europe	Consumer goods
Eastern Europe	Consumer services
Latin America	Energy
Middle East	Financials
Japan	Government
Asia ex-Japan	Healthcare
Oceania	Industrials
	Technology
	Telecommunications services
	Utilities

Figure 8.3 shows an illustration of the data available for the combination Latin America and some industries. The industry classification needs some further investigation as "Government" is worse than utilities and at 5 years maturity higher than the sovereign CDS spread. Such data can be very helpful in a market based pricing based on industry benchmarks.

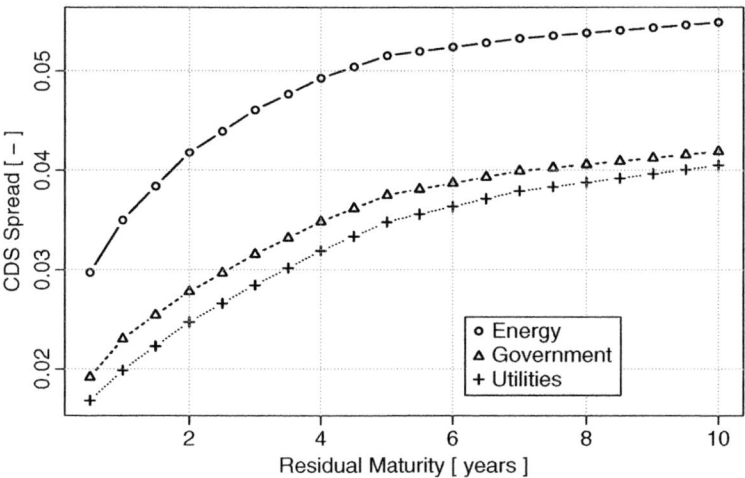

Fig. 8.3 CDS spreads by industry for Latin America and a rating of BB as proxy for Brazil (Source: IHS Markit). Here utilities are better rated than the government. The 5Y CDS spread of Brazil is as of today 235.80 bp or 0.0235

8.4   Calculation

With the bootstrapping algorithm of Eq. (8.8) we can derive the default rates from
the swap rates as it is coded in Listing B.13 on page 235. This is very much the CDS
standard model of ISDA. There are also R community solutions as follows.

ISDA provides several implementations, also in Excel. We take an implementation in R, here from the package `CreditRisk`. A very brief overview can be found
at https://rpubs.com/nmanca1992/352714.

First we read the table as shown in Table 8.1 on page 177. We need both the
CDS prices as to extracted from Bloomberg (or similar provider) plus the risk-free
discount rate (Cimarelli and Manca 2018).

```
library(CreditRisk) \\
cdsdat<-read.table("~/www/cf/affe/CDS.txt",header=TRUE)
```

Then we calculate from this the so-called intensities ($min_int) and from there
CDS characteristics:

```
cal_res.Egypt = calibrate.cds(r = cdsdat$Egypt_zeroyield ,
   t = seq(0.5, 10, by = 0.5), T =tdat,
   cdsrate=cdsdat$Egypt_Spread/10000)

cal_res.Egypt
$min_int
[1] 0.009088705 0.008776412 0.033122264 0.071297670 0.112754311
0.139849528 0.121694907
[8] 0.101318118

$error
[1] 1.461036e-07
```

Now we call the function `cds2` and get:

```
tmp.Egypt = cds2(t = seq(0.5, 10, by = 0.5), T = tdat, tr = tdat,
   r = cdsdat$Egypt_zeroyield, tint = tdat,
   int = cal_res.Egypt$min_int,
   R = 0.005, simplified = F, RR = 0.4)

tmp.Egypt
   T    Survival    PremiumLeg ProtectionLeg         Rate          Price
 0.5  0.9954660  0.002287775   0.002612182  0.005709001  0.0003244069
 1.0  0.9911072  0.004397507   0.004931905  0.005607615  0.0005343982
 2.0  0.9646708  0.008079226   0.017385293  0.010759257  0.0093060673
 3.0  0.9069008  0.011076296   0.040956117  0.018488182  0.0298798207
 4.0  0.8186388  0.013421362   0.072250823  0.026916354  0.0588294614
 5.0  0.7166354  0.015202186   0.103704585  0.034108446  0.0885023993
 7.0  0.5542198  0.017583812   0.144668009  0.041136704  0.1270841975
10.0  0.3986708  0.019484345   0.172478081  0.044260683  0.1529937365
```

From the survival rates you get easily to the cumulated default rates by means of:

$$D_t(\rho) = 1 - S_t(\rho), \qquad (8.13)$$

where D_t is the cumulated default rate and S_t the survival rate. In order to get a sense of how these market data relates to the historic rate data we plot the curves together, see Fig. 8.4.

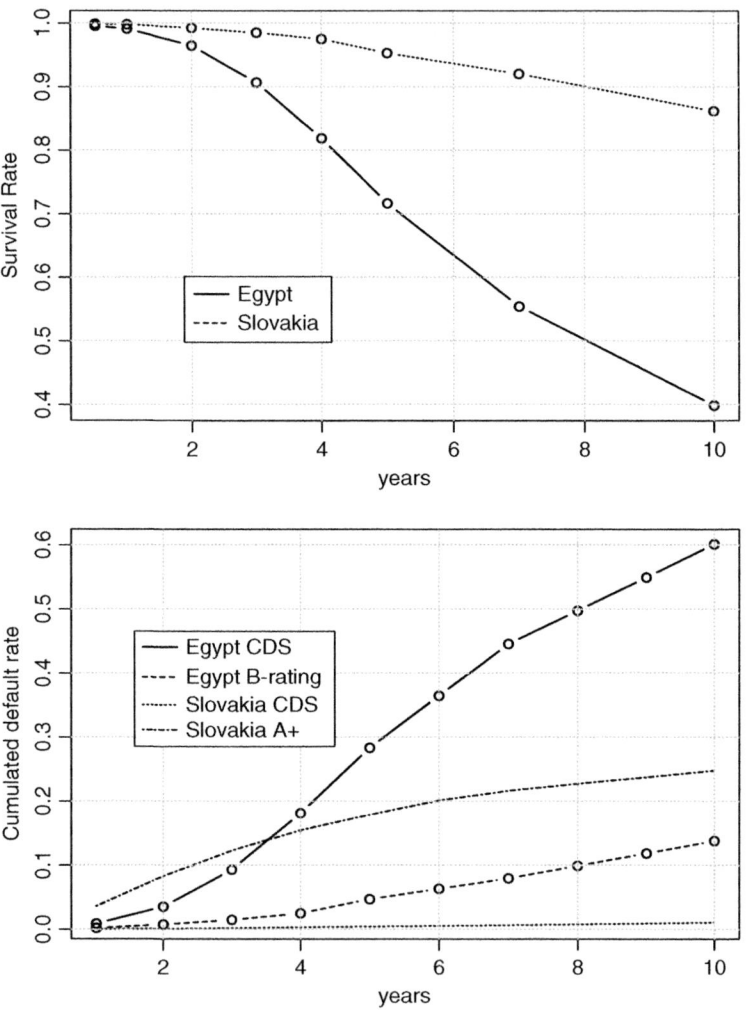

Fig. 8.4 Comparison of market survival and default rate curve of Egypt. As of analysis there are substantial differences. For Slovakia the market rate is better for Egypt it is worse than the historic default rate. CDS prices are just snapshots in time

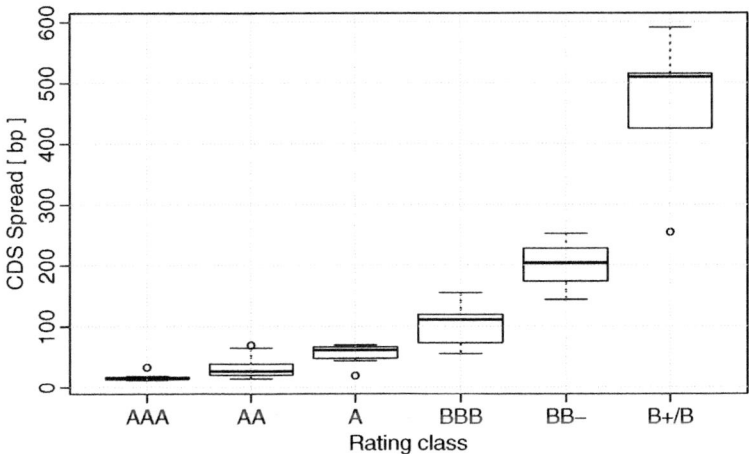

Fig. 8.5 Sovereign 5 year CDS spreads as of June, 9th 2020 (Source: http://www.worldgovernmentbonds.com/sovereign-cds/), grouped by rating classes. The thick horizontals are the medians, the box delimits the first and third quartile of the data. The spreads increase exponential with the rating

Example 8.4 (Fitting Curve to CDS Spreads). Both experience and the Fig. 8.5 suggest an exponential curve. We guess the following curve:

$$\hat{s} = b_0 + b_1 \cdot \exp(b_2 \cdot X) + b_3 \cdot X + \epsilon. \tag{8.14}$$

S is the CDS spread and X is the rating number, i.e. 1 for AAA, 2 for AAA$-$, 3 for AA$+$ and so forth. With initial guesses for the four parameters we perform a non-linear least square fitting as follows:

```
g<-nls(y ~ b0+b1*exp(x*b2)+b3*x,
       start=list(b0=0,b1=1.5,b2=bx,b3=0))
coef(g)
     b0       b1       b2       b3
14.4512   0.8241   0.4068   4.8290
```

The result is shown in Fig. 8.6. As we know this is just a snapshot in time. The following list (Table 8.2) is just an excerpt of the data used. △

The fitted 5 year spread by rating number x in basis points is

$$s(x) = 14.4512 + 0.8241 \cdot \exp(0.4068 \cdot x) + 4.8290 \cdot x. \tag{8.15}$$

From here we can infer the default rate $d(x) = S(x)/(1 - \mu)$ and compare it with the average historic default rate by Table A.1 where we have to transform $D(x)$ to $\delta(x) = (1 - D(x))^{1/5} - 1$. The difference is the actual risk surcharge by the market, called "risk premium" in the bond trader parlance. See Fig. 8.7. The relative

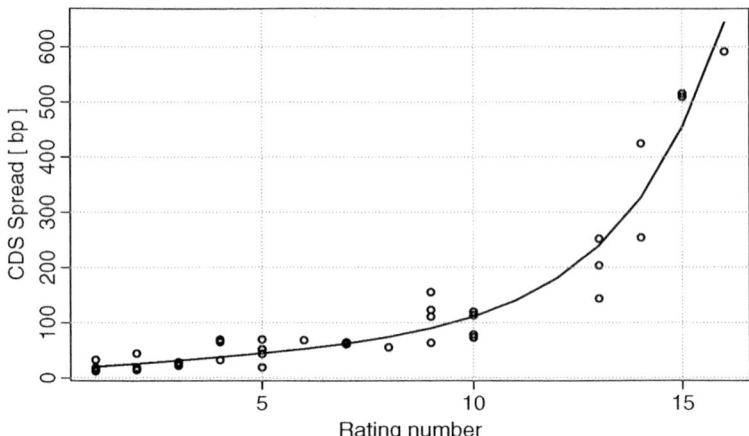

Fig. 8.6 Fitting a curve to the CDS by rating. The chosen curve seems quite appropriate

difference between the two curves of Fig. 8.7 is the bigger the better the rating. For investment grade sovereign it can be more than ten times larger.

Example 8.5 (Scaling). We could infer that just a multiplication will not suffice to scale the historic to the actual default rates. A more sophisticated model is to map the actual default rates $d_a(t)$ from the historic probabilities $d_h(t)$ for a given tenor t. Because the curves have an exponential dependency on the rating index ρ, we suggest the following model for a given t:

$$\hat{d}_a(\rho) = b_0 \cdot \big(d_h(\rho)\big)^{b_1} + b_2 + \epsilon. \tag{8.16}$$

The data above shows the 5-year CDS spreads for sovereigns. We transform the spreads into default rates by the use of the formula: $y = (1 + CDS/0.6)^5 - 1$. The cumulated default rates are taken from Table A.1. The non-linear least square function

```
g<-nls(y ~ b0*q^b1+b2,start=list(b0=1,b1=1,b2=0))
```

produces the parameters:

```
> coef(g)
        b0          b1          b2
2.81703651  1.13823402  0.02961933
```

A linear scaling would produce the following:

```
> g<-nls(y ~ b0*q,start=list(b0=1))
> coef(g)
        b0
2.421537
```

Now this exercise should be performed for all tenors. Here we are just satisfied with a crude estimate for the 5-year tenor.   △

Table 8.2 For illustration
some sovereign rating and
CDS spreads as of mid-2020

Rank	Country	Rating	Spread	Rating number
1	Canada	AAA	33.0	1
2	Denmark	AAA	12.7	1
...				
6	Singapore	AAA	18.6	1
7	Sweden	AAA	13.6	1
8	Austria	AA+	14.7	2
9	Belgium	AA	24.0	3
10	France	AA	27.3	3
...				
12	United Kingdom	AA	28.6	3
...				
19	Qatar	AA−	65.0	4
20	Chile	A+	69.8	5
21	China	A+	43.9	5
...				
24	Spain	A	68.6	6
25	Malaysia	A−	64.7	7
26	Poland	A−	61.4	7
27	Philippines	BBB+	55.7	8
28	Indonesia	BBB	111.1	9
29	Italy	BBB	155.3	9
...				
34	India	BBB−	113.6	10
35	Russia	BBB−	78.6	10
36	Brazil	BB−	204.0	13
37	Greece	BB−	144.1	13
...				
40	Turkey	B+	424.9	14
41	Egypt	B	516.1	15
42	Ukraine	B	510.0	15
43	Pakistan	B−	591.8	16

Example 8.6 (Historic vs. CDS Survival Rates). We apply the same pricing formulae both for the historic and the market survival rates. For this purpose we resume our example from the Egyptian sovereign CDS spreads from page 181. The rating is given as B. The two premia curve are depicted in Fig. 8.8.

The differences are quite evident. This follows from the difference in survival rates. This example shows that the market may differ substantially from historic averages also with respect to preferences of tenors. The comparison reveals that the CDS data is more benign in the short run but more severe in the long than the historic data. The historic may not be adequate for all circumstances.   △

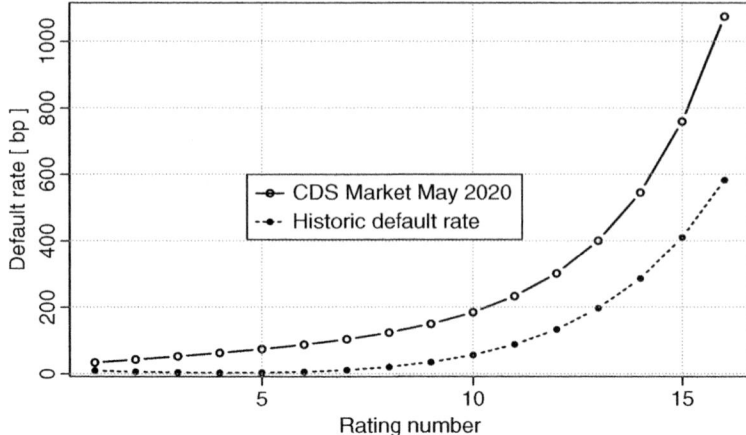

Fig. 8.7 Difference between historic and market default rates. Traders are not risk-neutral but charge a "margin" above the historic, empirical default rate. Shown is the 5-year marginal default rate from sovereign CDS and S&P default rates. Both data sets are fitted to the same model

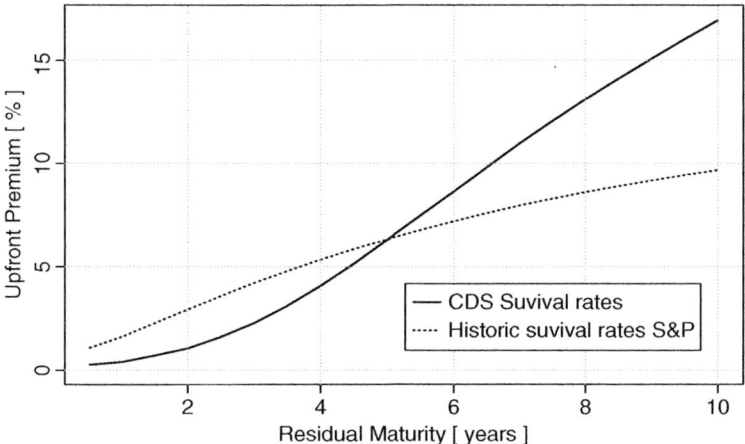

Fig. 8.8 Historic vs market premia. We calculate the premia with a recovery rate of 0.4 for Egypt's CDS and its historic survival rates with the same S&P rating

8.5   Bond Prices

For bonds there exist two important prices, i.e. the *clean price* and the *dirty price*. A bondholder's account would recognise with the passage of every day of a small interest earned, called accrued interest. Selling the bond from his perspective means selling the residual proceeds. This is the clean price. On the other hand the cashflow belonging to the accrued interest, the coupon, has not been paid yet. A buyer would consider the net present value of the cashflows as the price, called dirty price. On

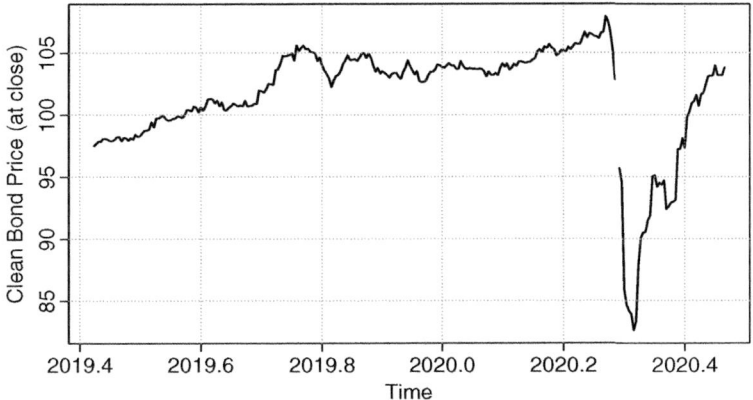

Fig. 8.9 Clean bond prices at close of an Indian conglomerate. The price as of 2020-05-21 is 103.84. See the crash of March, 13th due to the Corona virus pandemic

most markets where quotes exist for a bond it is the clean price shown. For our purposes—so far we have always considered present values of cashflows—we need the dirty price. From the above follows:

$$\text{Dirty Price} = \text{Clean Price} + \text{Accrued Interest}$$
$$= \text{Net Present Value.} \tag{8.17}$$

For determining the accrued interest we need to know the day count convention used. In Singapore ACT/365 be used. ACT stands for actual and 365 is the length of a year, here without leap years. As of today, May 21th 2020 the next coupon payment will be on May, 30st 2020, this is in 8 days. With a coupon of 3.67%[2] the accrued interest is

$$i_{acc} = 100 \cdot \frac{0.03667 \cdot (183 - 8)}{365} = 1.76.$$

The quoted price (clean) is 103.83 and the dirty price is therefore 105.59. In Fig. 8.9 we see the price series for the last year. The corona virus shock on the market is easily to be recognised. This may serve as an argument for not relying on a spot price.

---

[2]The true coupon rate is presumably 3 2/3%.

8.5.1   Bond Price Spread

How do we assess the price for credit risk from here? First, we can calculate the
yield to maturity of the bond and put it into perspective with the risk-free rate. This
is an average credit spread from the bond.

To this end we execute the following code:

```
pram=list("2020-05-21",TT="2027-11-29",h=2,c=0.03667,
     price=1.0559)
bisect(-0.01,0.2,param=pram,FUN=FixedCouponBondYield)
[1] 0.03075507
```

The yield to maturity is $y = 3.075507\%$. The term to maturity of this bond is 7.53
years. From Table 4.2 we take the risk-free rate r_f for this tenor to be 0.65%. Thus
the average credit spread s for this bond is approximately $3.076\% - 0.65\% = 2.43\%$.
The company issuing the bond has a S&P rating of BBB+.

[Term sheet of a specific bond.]

The second bond of Table 8.3 has a yield to maturity of 0.03065 and a residual
maturity of 4.69 years. The spread is $3.065 - 0.42 = 265$ bp.

The credit spread is a curve over the residual maturity captured only partially by
an average. With these two bonds we have similar values but an unusual decrease
with residual maturity. This unexplained price behaviour may be understood as
an argument against using bonds: they are illiquid, rarely traded and therefore the
quotes only indicative.

Table 8.3   Term sheet of a specific bond. The bond has no optionalities and is senior unsecured

ISIN	USY72570AN72	USY72596BU56
Name	RELIANCE INDS 17/27 REGS	RELIANCE INDS 15/25 REGS
Country	India	India
Issuer	Reliance Industries Ltd.	Reliance Industries Ltd.
Issue volume	800,000,000	1,000,000,000
Currency	USD	USD
Issue price	100	99
Issue date	11/30/2017	1/28/2015
Coupon	3.67%	4.13%
Denomination	1000	1000
Payment type	Regular interest	Regular interest
Maturity date	11/30/2027	1/28/2025
Coupon payment date	5/30/2020	7/28/2020
No. of payments per year	2,0	2,0
Coupon start date	5/30/2018	7/28/2015
Final coupon date	11/29/2027	1/27/2025
Quote	103.83	104.91

From the OECD calculator[3] we take the following spreads for the year 2019 representing Bloomberg BVAL Sector curves, US Non-financial:

Rating	6M	2Y	5Y	10Y	20Y
BBB+	23	55	89	134	194
BBB	27	66	103	152	216
BBB−	44	97	150	211	279

Comparing the average of 243 bp from the actual price of the bond with the interpolated spread at 7.5 years from the table we see a substantial difference: 243 vs. 112. Is this acceptable? Looking up the table in reverse we would infer a rating of BB−. This implies that the investor requires an additional risk premium beyond premium for default.

8.5.2 Survival Rates from Bond Prices

For our mechanics to calculate the premium for arbitrary cashflows, or at least not bullet bonds patterns of standard bonds, we need to extract the survival rates from the bond price through the credit spread. The credit spread is a curve and not just a fixed amount. Therefore, one ought to analyse a whole set of bonds with different maturities. But this is not a realistic scenario at least not for a single name. The second best solution is to take an average rate from the bonds yield to maturity minus risk-free rate and estimate from here the survival rates.

Now we have used the identity of a risky discount, i.e. discounting with a risk rate, with a risk-free discounting while considering the survival probabilities. This is to say that the value of a risky cashflow pattern plus risk premium equals a risk-free bond.

For a regular bond with terminal value $1 + c$ and coupon payments c we can determine the present value of the preceding coupon payment date (Fig. 8.10) either with the yield curve $y(t)$ and its forward discount function

$$df_y(t-1,t) = \frac{\left(1 + y(t-1)/h\right)^{(t-1)h}}{\left(1 + y(t)/h\right)^{th}},$$

thus

$$V_{t-1} = (V_t + c) \cdot df_y(t-1,t), \tag{8.18}$$

---

[3]http://www.oecd.org/trade/topics/export-credits/documents/TCMB-2020-(validity-from-01-feb-2020).xlsm.

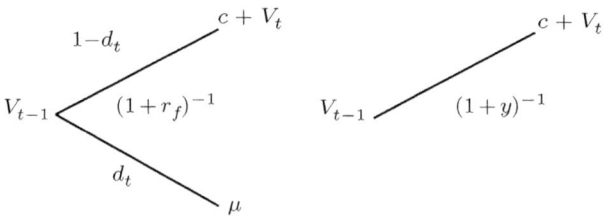

Fig. 8.10 Two ways to discount a risky cashflow. Either using risk-free rate and default probability (left) or discounting at the yield to maturity (right)

or with the risk-free discount with rate $r(t)$ but considering complementary marginal survival probabilities, i.e. default probabilities $d(t)$ in period t and $df_r(t-1,t)$ with the risk-free rate r as above:

$$V_{t-1} = \Big((V_t + c)(1 - d_t) + d_t\mu\Big)df_r(t-1,t). \qquad (8.19)$$

Equating the two representations and solving for d_t gives

$$d_t = \frac{(V_t + c) \cdot \big(df_y(t-1,t) - df_r(t-1,t)\big)}{\mu - (V_t + c) \cdot df_r(t-1,t)}. \qquad (8.20)$$

The value V_T at maturity equates to 1. In the simple case where the two curves are flat, and therefore the spread is constant, we arrive at:

$$d_t = \frac{(1 + c) \cdot \big(df_y - df_r\big)}{\mu - (1 + c) \cdot df_r}. \qquad (8.21)$$

Example 8.7 (Default Probability from Yield). Our bond from above has a coupon payment of $0.03667/2$ semi-annually, a yield of $y = 0.03075507$ and a risk-free rate of $r = 0.0065$. Let us assume a recovery rate of $\mu = 0.4$. Therefore the flat periodic probability of default for a semester is: 0.004146548 or $41.5\,\text{bp}$ and annualised: 0.00831029 or $83.1\,\text{bp}$. △

How good is the constant default probability assumption? For answering that question we look at the patterns of the empirical default curves as represented by studies from S&P and Moody's. Figures 8.11 and 8.12 show an ambiguous picture. We have chosen the very long time series of Moody's in the expectation that patterns would be clearer.

What is consistent is the characteristic shape for poor ratings. It shows an initial increase followed by a steady decrease. The interpretation would be that after having survived the crucial first years the credit becomes much better. For better ratings the curves are less clear. But here the rates are much lower anyway so that relative comparisons over time may exaggerate the real figures. In the better rating ranges a

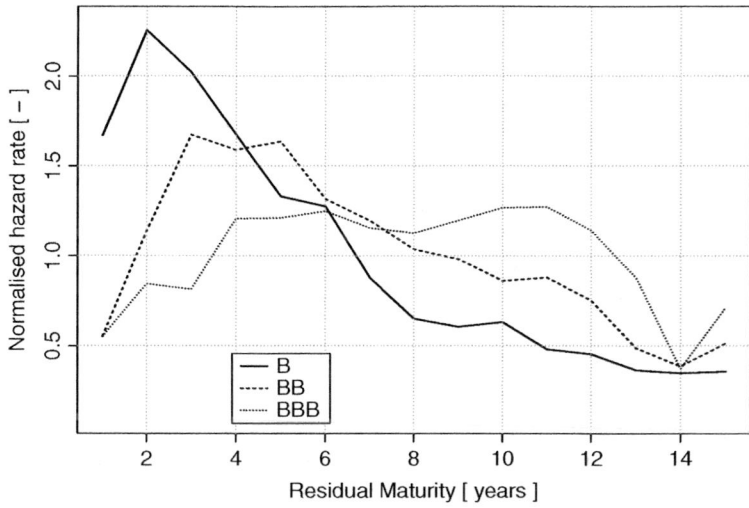

Fig. 8.11 Marginal default rate of Standard & Poor's normalised by mean (Vazza and Kraemer 2018)

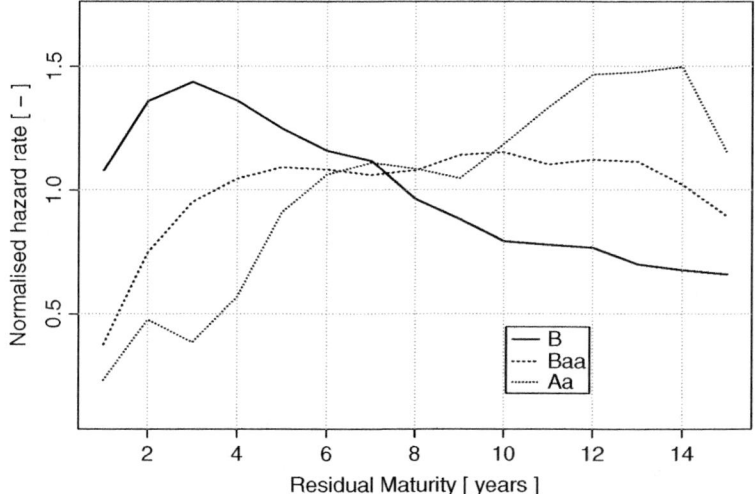

Fig. 8.12 Moody's marginal default rate of Moody's normalised by mean. These rates are collected from 1920 to 2008 (Emery and Cantor 2009)

constant marginal default rate is not completely to be dismissed. The two exhibits are also a warning to overestimate the usefulness of historic rates.

8.6   Conclusions

First we can argue that the calculation of the input date for our pricing model from CDS market prices is straightforward. We show how to do that with a short excerpt or snippet of a program. From there the price for typical ECA style payment profiles has been determined.

The two examples of Egypt and Slovakia show that there may be a massive departure from the historic default pattern. This concerns both the form of the cumulative default rate which is dependent on the yield curve. An inverse curve as in Egypt has a beneficial effect on the short end.

One could easily argue that the rating is not readily updated but lag behind in time. But as the case for Egypt shows its B rating from S&P could not be much worse.

Market prices are volatile by nature and this collides with the stability criterion of official insurance or guarantee prices. Therefore, we here advocate to mix both market and historic prices in order to lower the volatility and augment the certainty.

References

Beinstein, E., & Scott, A. (2006). *Credit derivatives handbook*. Handbook. New York: JP Morgan
Cimarelli, A., & Manca, N. (2018). Package CreditRisk: Evaluation of Credit Risk with Structural and Reduced Form Models. Reference manual, CRAN. https://cran.r-project.org/web/packages/CreditRisk/CreditRisk.pdf.
Emery, K., & Cantor, R. (2009). Corporate Default and Recovery Rates, 1920–2008. Special comment, Moody's Investor Service, Global Credit Research.
Schleich, J., & Shin, S. U. (2017). Information note for guidance on premium rules for officially supported export credits in market benchmark countries. Technical note, OECD Export Credit Division, Paris. http://www.oecd.org/officialdocuments/publicdisplaydocumentpdf/?cote=TAD/PG(2017)7/FINAL&docLanguage=En.
Vazza, D., & Kraemer, N. (2018). 2017 Annual Global Corporate Default Study and Rating Transitions. Technical report, Standard & Poor's Global Ratings, New York. https://www.spglobal.com/en/research-insights/articles/default-transition-and-recovery-2017-annual-global-corporate-default-study-and-rating-transitions.

Minimum Interest Calculation

9

As we have already mentioned there are governmental credit institutions or export credit agencies that offer the so-called pure cover while others do also direct lending. The third variant is that a state owned bank does the funding and the ECA contributes the cover.

In this chapter we try a decomposition of credit price in some constituent parts and make a proposition on how to price the minimum interest rate for pricing.

9.1 Decomposition of Credit

Broadly speaking a credit as future promised payments has three main features:

- funding,
- credit risk and
- servicing.

We proceed along these lines skipping credit as we dwelt extensively on it in previous chapters.

9.1.1 Servicing

As we have especially seen with documentary credits or letter of credits bank lending involves a lot of paper work either as legal agreements for the loan or the security or letters and notifications to trigger a payment. In trade there is a heavy documentation accompanying the physical good, e.g. packing list, or representing it, e.g. bill of lading, etc. Every payment in time must be controlled and managed, irregularities resolved and, in case of delinquent payments, appropriate action taken.

© The Author(s), under exclusive license to Springer Nature Switzerland AG 2021   193
C. Franzetti, *Pricing Export Credit*, Management for Professionals,
https://doi.org/10.1007/978-3-030-70285-4_9

This can stretch as far as in-court restructuring or liquidation. We would call this work servicing.

Today, most banks create new loans and then transfer the servicing duties to a different financial institution or a company that specialises in servicing such loans. With this model it becomes evident that servicing can and must have a clear costing or pricing. For mortgages the fee ranges between 25 and 50 bp per annum.

The existence of such an industry purports the case that credit can not only be thought as decomposed but can effectively be organised as a division of labour.

9.1.2   Funding Cost

Funding can be organised in different ways depending on the status of the financing institution, i.e. is it a bank or not, and the currency of the credit. Banks are allowed by the central banks and as part of the banking system of their domestic currency to *create money*. In order to control the amount of money creation the banks must keep minimum reserves proportionate to the credit outstanding with the central bank.

If a bank would like to extend a loan in another currency than its domestic currency, then the institution must acquire the sum in order not to create foreign money. This is called re-financing. Commercial banks lend and borrow money in the interbank market where up to recently prices were known as LIBOR.

State owned banks supporting export or ECAs working as direct lenders need also money for extending credit. The main source for some agencies is borrowings from the Ministry of Finance of the pertinent country. Some Exim-Banks issue notes and bonds with a state guarantee for this purpose on the capital market. In both cases the funding cost depends on the rating of the state and the term of lending. It can be assumed that the cost of funding is identical to the yields of outstanding notes and bonds of the government. For traditional export countries the government has almost the highest rating in the domestic market. This longstanding assumption has been shaken by the financial turmoil of the last decade.

But, especially for incorporated ECAs or Exim-Banks their creditworthiness may be higher than the sovereign's. This depends on the capital endowment of the institutions and the guarantee structure between state and corporation. Having both a high risk bearing own capital plus a state guarantee makes the institution better than the guarantor.

Another mechanism to derive the cost of funding is through the *Credit Default Swap* market for sovereigns. So bond yields and credit swap rates incorporate a similar rate of return for the credit risk of the sovereign.

Summarising, the funding cost of a lending bank consists of the general opportunity cost to postponing consumption, liquidity preferences for certain maturities and the creditworthiness or rating of the borrower.

Adding to the cost of servicing and the funding of the lender is the credit risk of the foreign buyer or its bank epitomised by the credit insurance premium.

9.1.3 Risk-Free Interest Rate

Risk-free is a fiction. It is best realised by either the debt of the government or the interbank-lending rates. The latter banks have suffered a loss in reputation as the financial crisis and especially the bankruptcy of Lehman Bros ravaged. There is a spread between treasury rates and interbank interest rates.

With concern of funding export credit and a level playing field also between direct lenders and pure cover ECA that must rely on the domestic banking industry it seems obvious that this can be only established by using interbank interest rates and not treasury rates.

The credit and credit derivatives market quotes many spreads against interbank rates ("swap rates") as this is the custom. On the other hand for risk-free discounting the treasury yields are more appropriate when there is not another curve used by the market.

9.2 Rule Proposal

We use Eq. (4.25) as the basis and modify the price that is not 1 anymore as in the risk-free case. Economically this reflects the fact that the price for a cash transaction, i.e. 1, cannot hold for a credit. This is simply due to the additional cost from organising a credit, documenting it, seeking funds and servicing the payments. Now there are upfront cost and running costs. Because of these two types readily identifiable with present value and margin, we need a basis from which to determine the margin and vice versa the present value. We choose here the present value that shall incorporate the financing cost that in turn define the interest rate. The minimum interest rate should depend on the three following variables:

- the set-up cost,
- the service costs and
- the financing cost.

As a proposition we select a 75 pb for setting up the credit plus 25 pb per instalment for servicing. The financing is incorporated in the discount basis which is the swap rate. Thus we have

$$PV = 1 + 0.0075 + 0.0025 \cdot t_N \cdot h, \tag{9.1}$$

with t_N the tenor of the credit in years and h the frequency, e.g. 2 for the semi-annual service of the instalment. The PV value embodies both the admin and set-up fees of the credit and the servicing cost. These two values may be adjusted to the current situation of a bank.

We modify the Eq. (4.25) of page 96 to yield the following form:

$$
z = \frac{PV - \sum_{i=1}^{N} c_i \cdot df_i'}{\sum_{i=1}^{N} df_i' - \sum_{i=1}^{N} \left[\sum_{j=i}^{N} c_j \right] \cdot (t_i - t_{i-1}) df_i'}, \tag{9.2}
$$

where df_i' are discount factors derived from the swap curve which in turn stems from the interbank offer rate of banks in a given country for a given currency. The swap rate is normally higher than the treasury rate and therefore leads by discounting to a higher interest rate.

Stating the obvious shows that the interest rate is not depending on the rating of the credit because the risk of default is absorbed in the premium and the insurance transfers the credit risk to the insurer.

Example 9.1 (Minimum Interest Rate). Let us calculate the minimum interest rate for USD. Here the swap rate is based on a fix leg paying twice a year. Therefore, we transform the given rates R to r as $r = (1 + R/2)^2 - 1$. For small rates there is not much difference. Assume further semi-annual regular instalments with maturity in 5 year. The following code produces a minimum interest rate of 102.2 bp.

```
swap<-c
    (0,0.22,0.189,0.195,0.223,0.273,0.331,0.39,0.445,0.495,0.54)/
    100
tx<-0:10
tvec<-1:10
cvec<-rep(1,10)
dfvec<-vecDfLint(tvec,param=list(tx,swap,opt=T,h=2))
p=1+0.0075+0.002*tx[11]
minIntRate(cvec,tvec,dfvec,P=p)
[1] 0.01021811
```

For a 10-year tenor the rate is 1.596%.   △

Example 9.2 (Comparison in Time). We compare the minimum rate according to Eq. (9.2) for two dates, i.e. August 3rd 2020 and August 1st, 2014. The goal is to demonstrate how the minimum rate depends on the swap rate. As of writing we have still abnormally low rates. The result is depicted in Fig. 9.1.   △

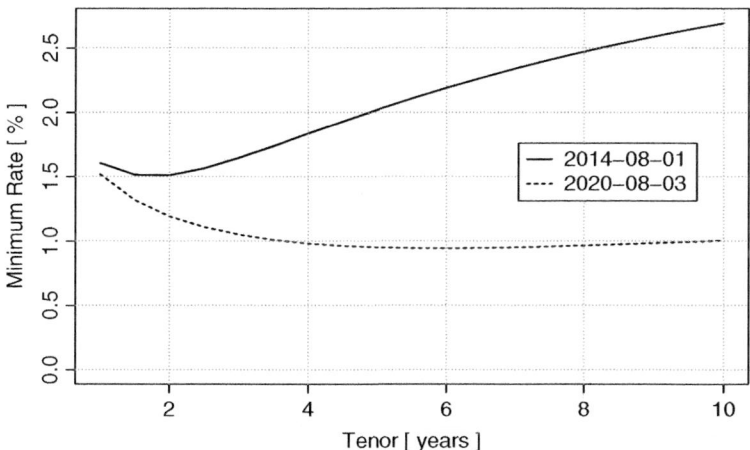

Fig. 9.1 Comparison of the minimum interest rate. In 2014 the swap rates were substantially higher than in 2020. The curves show how the formula embodies the swap rates

Figure 9.1 defies intuition again due to the negative interest rates that are used for discounting. Equation 9.1 as cost function has a fixed part of 75 bp and a recurring part. For longer tenors the fixed part is stretched over more time. Therefore, the average cost can decrease, especially at the short end.

Comparison with OECD Arrangement

10

We compare different features of the OECD Arrangement with our framework. It becomes evident that some features of the minimum pricing are somewhat obscure and may stem from a political process of compromise.

10.1 General Remarks

The comparison is hampered by the fact that the OECD rating system is not consistent. The mapping from a two-dimensional assessment to a general, universal letter rating as it is widely use in the industry, especially by credit rating agencies, is not consistent. Therefore for a given rating, e.g. BB+ of Standard & Poor's style, has several corresponding combinations of country and customer rating. A look at Table 5.1 on page 139 shows this one to many relation.

The second impediment is the difference with respect to the tenor. While OECD has this nebulous concept of horizon of risk, starting point of credit and disbursement period, our proposal is much clearer: inception of the term loan and lead time. A possible makeshift would be to assume the lead time and the disbursement period equal and consequently to identify the inception with the SPOC that separates the disbursement period and the risk period.

What does the comparison reveal? The OECD pricing is constructed foremost on the consensus of the participants and much less on any known theory. Therefore, the bigger the differences, the bigger presumably the resistance to a new pricing although the intuition should be: the greater the need for a change.

The new framework has a more genuine treatment of repayment profiles. While the OECD operates with equivalences, e.g. averaged lives, to fit deviations from the standard to it, the framework is just a general method. It has no preferred pattern that determines the pricing.

© The Author(s), under exclusive license to Springer Nature Switzerland AG 2021   199
C. Franzetti, *Pricing Export Credit*, Management for Professionals,
https://doi.org/10.1007/978-3-030-70285-4_10

A comparison with the private market is difficult as the prices are not transparent, the products may differ and the tenors are shorter. The comparison is therefore more with the pure trading of credit risk with CDS. The framework is consistent with the pricing of CDS, even more so as the CDS prices can build the basis for the premia.

Pricing of the third risk group besides political and commercial, i.e. the contract risks, is not considered here.

10.2   Minimum Pricing

10.2.1 Missing Discounting

The OECD Arrangement defines a standard pattern, i.e. regular semi-annual repayments, and coerces non-standard patterns to the standard by means of equivalences. Thus identical HOR, everything else constant, leads to identical premia and to identical risk perception. In Fig. 10.1 we have three different patterns all with HOR $= 2.5$. Now in country with high interest rates and potentially high devaluation one would clearly prefer those patterns that are front loaded as those payments are more valuable than those effected later. Secondly, the default probability increases with time. Therefore more payments later mean higher risk. We conclude that the standard OECD formula is less risk sensitive as it needs to be. The framework presented here uses discounting, both for the time value of money and the default curve, as the standard. Therefore, it is much more risk sensitive and adequate.

The new framework is heavily reliant on discounting and considers the time-value of money throughout. It needs not resorting to some sort of equivalence, e.g. average weigthed life etc.

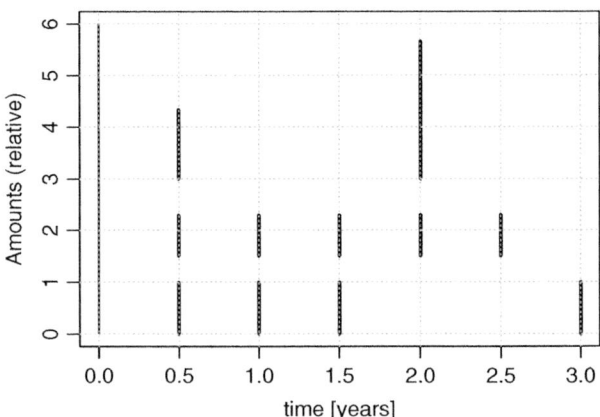

Fig. 10.1 Three payment pattern with same HOR and same principal

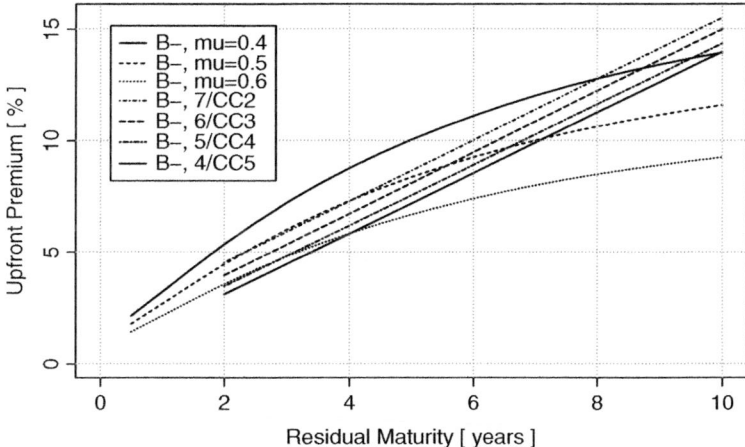

Fig. 10.2 Comparison between this proposal and the OECD-MPR for a B-Rating. This has several possibilities with the OECD, i.e. country risk 4 with CC4, country risk 5 with CC3, etc.

10.2.2 Time Penalty

The OECD formula is linear in HOR, an equivalent for the tenor of the credit. Linearity means a constant marginal increase of the premium with time. As HOR is a risk parameter this means that the risk between 2 and 1 year is the same as between 6 and 5 years. This is empirically, i.e. by historical default rates, disproved. Figures 10.2 and 10.3 show the linearity versus the increasing marginal premium. The latter corresponds better with reality. In the better rating fields the OECD-MPR are systematically higher than the rates of the new framework using the historic default rates. The linearity on the other hand is similar.

10.2.3 Missing Coherence

The OECD Arrangement uses a dual rating system consisting of a combination of country and commercial risk assessment and a credit agency style one-dimensional letter rating. Now credit insurance premium is not consistent because the mapping is not.

Secondly, the table of coefficients has some irregularities that are hard to understand. This adds to the problem above.

The framework uses just one letter rating that follows the fiction of a universal assessment scale. Therefore, such a flaw cannot arise.

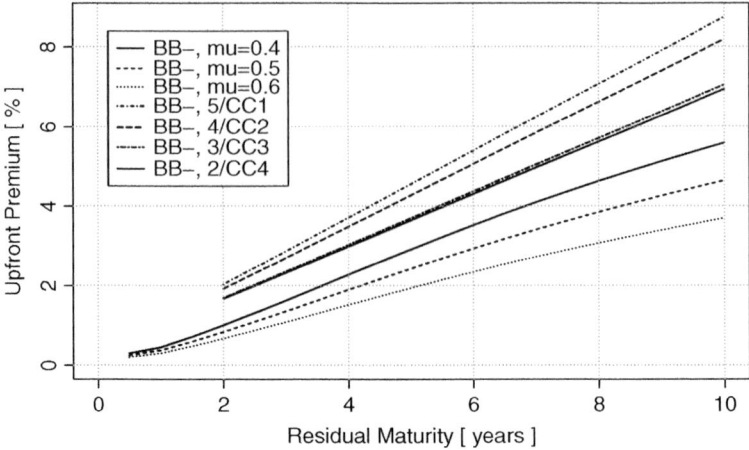

Fig. 10.3 Comparison between this proposal and the OECD-MPR for a BB-Rating. Here the new framework with historic rates is systematically lower than the OECD-MPR

10.3   Market Pricing

The comparison of market pricing is flawed as the OECD has its own definition or understanding of market. Characteristic for securities market is the volatility that mirrors the actual economic activity. In times of stress the volatility can be massive. Now the pricing especially by state agencies should be reliable, foreseeable and stable. This is at odds with markets. OECD tries to mitigate volatility by averaging "through the cycle" with a cycle period of 10 years. A second critique is the assumption that bank quotes for risk are the market although we have a bilateral, nontransparent contract situation.

The framework just uses market default data from benchmarks and determines from analysis an appropriate recovery rate. Obviously the volatility is high. In order to have greater stability over time it is useful to take averages over given periods. But in order that it is still "market" this period cannot be longer than 1 year.

From a methodological point of view the OECD procedure harbours a problem. It mixes spreads (see Eq. 4.95) with default rates and treats spreads from different instruments all the same although the scope is not identical. The seniority is not considered or differences in recovery. The framework on the other hand uses the same methodology as for historic inputs, i.e. risky discounting.

A numerical comparison is difficult as follows from the said above. Generally, we have the impression that these OECD rates are rather low. They do not incorporate any provision for administrative or operational cost as required in our propositions.

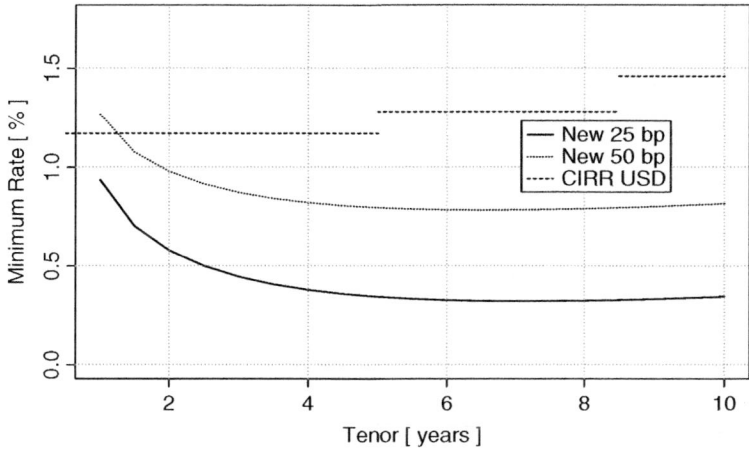

Fig. 10.4 Comparing the minimum interest rate with CIRR as of 2020-08-15. The CIR-rates are strictly non-decreasing while the calculation of the cost is decreasing due to the negative USD swap rates. In one case we have taken 25 bp per instalment as price, a second curve implies 50 bp. The shape rests unchanged

10.4   Minimum Interest

We compare the minimum interest rates as defined by the OECD and sketched in Sect. 5.1.5 with our proposal of Sect. 9.2. The OECD may change their methodology slightly but as a general rule sticks to treasury bond rates plus mark-up. The Arrangement is quite fond to choose equivalent tenors, e.g. weighted average life, for determining market rates or publicly available data instead to discount or consider the whole curve or surface of time dependent rates. This seems to us a spurious simplification.

Our simple costing model assumes a fixed upfront charge for creating the credit and a service charge over the life of the credit.

A quantitative comparison is given in Fig. 10.4 below. We do not consider the quite elaborate mechanisms of commitment fees and forward rates as defined in the Arrangement.

10.5   Restriction

This framework does not make any prescriptions concerning special patterns or maximum tenors in dependence of the import country or local costs. Such restrictions to be found in the OECD Arrangement are, at least in our view, a blend of political and economic considerations. Measures that help less favoured countries to do prosperous trade are welcome.

What we believe in is the congruence of repayments and useful time of capital goods because it takes liquidity strain from the buyer. But this would imply that the repayment pattern be modelled according to the usage of the goods sold on credit terms.

As especially credit agencies are in the sphere of governments and these have a broad scope encompassing global themes like environmental protection it may be efficient to try to act also through export support. But here it is a mined field because historically countries have made different experiences, e.g. atomic reactors, genetically modifies crop, etc.

Other Pricing

11

This chapter is intended to convey some preliminary ideas on the topic of pricing other structures than classical credit of loan type. Concerning common knowledge and literature to these themes is rather scarce. This is due on the one hand to a highly competitive situation and on the other hand to a lack of empirical data. A third reason is the fact that private credit insurance sticks to the traditional business model of relationship. This implies that insurer and insured follow each other through good and rough times and insureds do not jump ship at every occasion. Therefore the pricing will show typical cycles where bad times are followed by increasing premia.

Nonetheless, the following is speculative but hopefully inspiring for own explorations.

11.1 Whole Turnover

Credit insurance may be bought for different structures of risk that form a continuum, i.e.

- single buyer,
- multi buyer and
- all buyers.

In the last case we speak of *whole turnover*. In many cases, it makes sense to cover single transactions with their own trade credit insurance policy when a particularly large sale is involved, or when selling to companies that are new to the industry, or located in unstable nations. The type of cover thus depends on the structure of the turnover. In the following we will treat multi-buyer as special case of whole turnover albeit with a reduced pool of risks.

Fig. 11.1 Schematic pool of
risks. Covered are only
receivables in excess of a
retention limit and capped by
a limit, general or specific by
buyer

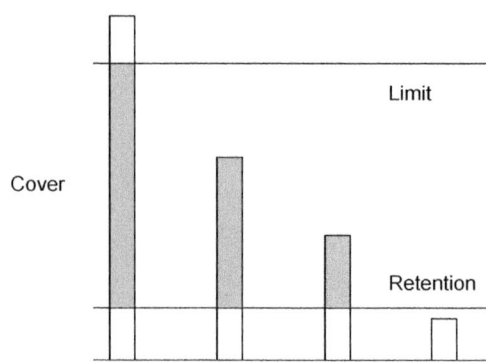

11.1.1 Structure of Business

With whole turnover insurance, a credit insurer promises to cover all eligible
business transacted by an applicant within an agreed period of usually 1 year. Risk
management is exercised primarily through a credit limit set for each covered buyer
(see Fig. 11.1).

The cover ratio is usually 80% to 95%. Premium is payable as a percentage
of insured turnover, which must be declared monthly, quarterly or annually by the
policyholder. Whole turnover policies can be based upon domestic and export trade.

If the suppliers tend to work with a large volume of companies and small
transaction amounts, attritional losses are statistic. The supplier may not need whole
turnover trade credit insurance. This is self-insurance taking advantage of the law of
large numbers.

For those who engage in wholesale trade or international trade with just a handful
of large clients whole turnover policies, as opposed to selective policies, may be vital
because they would face serious financial difficulties if any of their large clients fails
to pay, or fails to pay in a timely manner.

Multi-buyer and whole turnover policies can be structured as "ground-up" or
"excess" policies depending primarily on the strength of the insured's credit risk
management capabilities.

Excess covers are usually cheaper, as the deductible protects insurers from
the initial high-probability credit losses (see Fig. 11.1). Depending on its risk
retention capabilities, the insured can significantly lower coverage costs via a higher
deductible.

11.1.2 Pricing

The easiest way of pricing is a Monte Carlo based simulation and applying the
insurance pricing standard, i.e.

$$\text{Premium} = \text{Expected Loss} + \text{Loading}.$$

Most often there is a draw from a frequency distribution giving the number of losses n and then n draws from the severity distribution, i.e. the distribution of risk amounts in the pool. The parameters are chosen with respect to previous loss experience, projected turnover and trade expectations, and the quality of customers. The expected loss is

$$M = \sum_{i=1}^{n} p_i K_i (1 - \mu) \tag{11.1}$$

with the probability of default p_i, the exposures K_i net of recovery. The variance is

$$V = \sum_{i=1}^{n} p_i (K_i - \bar{K})^2 = \sigma^2. \tag{11.2}$$

A standard pricing could then be

$$\Pi = M + \alpha \cdot \sigma. \tag{11.3}$$

A simple approximation of the total loss of a pool or portfolio of risks has been proposed in the context of securitisation by Moody's. It is called BET, short for *binomial expansion technique*. It was published by Cifuentes and O'Connor (1996). The method uses the well known binomial distribution, i.e.

$$P(k) = \frac{n!}{k!(n-k)!} p^k \cdot (1 - p)^{n-k}, \tag{11.4}$$

that gives the probability of k events out of n with the probability of an event of p. Now the formula is altered by taking the average probability of default $\bar{p}$ and adjusting n by D. Thus

$$P(k) = \frac{D!}{k!(D-k)!} \bar{p}^k \cdot (1 - \bar{p})^{D-k}. \tag{11.5}$$

The integer D is called *Diversity Score* and determined as

$$D = \left\lfloor \sum_{j=1}^{N} \min(K_j / \bar{K}, 1) \right\rfloor, \tag{11.6}$$

whereby K_j is a single and $\bar{K}$ the average exposure. The two special brackets truncate the value to the lower integer. The expected value of the distribution is $m = \bar{p} \cdot D$. From this condition that the expected value has to remain the same after the transformation ($m = M$), we derive the average default rate $\bar{p}$ as

$$\bar{p} = \frac{M}{D}. \tag{11.7}$$

There exists also an extension trying to take correlation between the elements of the pool into consideration. This is achieved by the *Alternative Diversity Score D_A*:

$$D_A = \frac{n}{1 + (n-1)\rho}, \tag{11.8}$$

where ρ is the average correlation.

Example 11.1 (Small Portfolio). We generate 20 random numbers x_i in the range [0.2,1.2] and then take them minimum function as $x_i = \min(x_i, 1)$. The sample is shown in Fig. 11.2. The mean is 0.62892 and the standard deviation 0.24829. Let us suppose the probability of default is for all elements equal to 5%. Then the expected value is 0.03145. The diversity score $D = 16$ and $\bar{p} = 0.03930762$.   △

In accordance with Eq. (11.3) we set the premium as

$$\Pi = D \cdot \bar{p} + \alpha \cdot \sqrt{D \cdot \bar{p} \cdot (1 - \bar{p})}. \tag{11.9}$$

Example 11.2 (Simulation). In order to generate the cumulated probability of default we can use a Monte Carlo approach. The classical method is to model a frequency and the severity. In our case of the small portfolio we can just use the twenty risks. Often the negative binomial discrete distribution is used for the

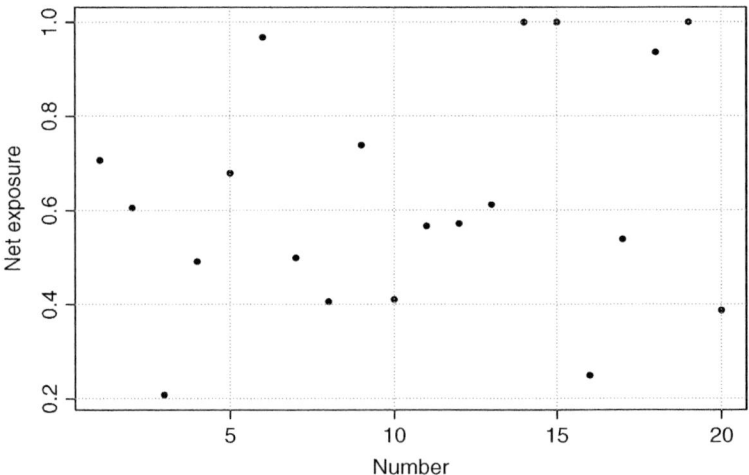

Fig. 11.2 Random sample of exposures in the range between 0.2 and 1. where the losses are truncated

number of credit events. We draw a random number of losses n and then take n losses from the risks and sum them. Because we handle rare events we can omit the lack of replacement. This makes the algorithm a little bit easier. From the loss distribution we can take a dispersion characteristic, e.g. a quantile as *value-at-risk*, for constructing the risk loading of the pricing similar to the approach above. The code is as follows:

```
library(purrr)
q<-c();w<-c()
M<-150000
for (k in 1:M){
  n<-rnbinom(1, mu = 1, size = 1)
  q<-rdunif(n,20,1)
  if (n==0){w[k]<-0} else {
    su<-0
    for (l in 1:n){
      su<-su+x[q[l]]
    }
  w[k]<-su}
}
```

The result is plotted in Fig. 11.3. Now the cumulated values are (the total cover is 15.3)

Probability	Mid value	Share of cover
0.76	0.5	0.0327
0.89	1.5	0.0980
0.95	2.5	0.1634
0.98	3.5	0.2287
0.99	4.5	0.2941

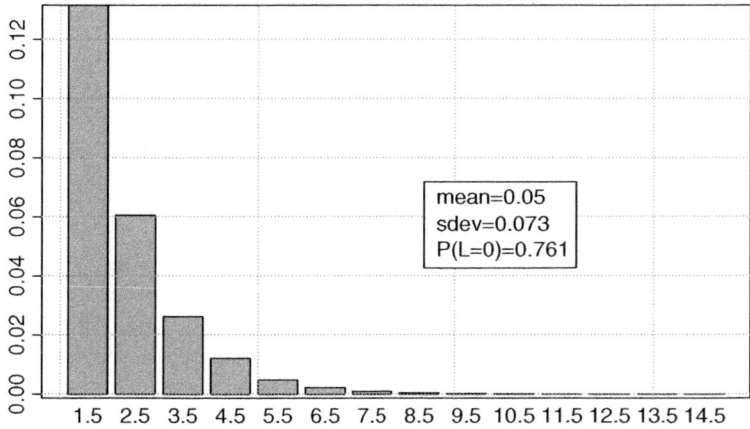

Fig. 11.3 Frequencies of a Monte Carlo simulation of losses. We have assumed a loss frequency of 5%, i.e. one out of twenty. Most often, in 76% of cases there will be no loss at all

Now we could identify the 0.99-quantile minus expected loss (5%) as value-at-risk VaR of 0.2441 ("unexpected loss") and set the premium as

$$\pi = 0.05 + \alpha \cdot 0.2441. \tag{11.10}$$

How to calibrate the input variables and how to choose $0 \le \alpha$ is another question. $\triangle$

11.2   Private Single Credit

For the framework we have assumed very deep pockets of state business that translates into risk-neutral pricing. We have depicted the ruin process which implies that there should be a loading for risk, especially when capital is not almost unlimited. For private insurances capital is a scarce resource that needs managing because it comes at a price. On the other hand, a private insurance can choose and select the transaction it enters while most state business cannot.

A private credit insurer has to load the pure premium, i.e. the expected loss. The most standard formula is just expected loss plus a factor times a risk measure, say θ, analogously to Eq. (11.2) above:

$$\Pi_i = \mathrm{E}(L_i) + \alpha \cdot \theta_i. \tag{11.11}$$

The relation to capital or risk capital, often used as technical provision for the portfolio is by the contribution of each risk to the whole risk capital RC. The risk capital has been calculated as a quantile of the cumulated loss distribution as we did in Example 11.2 above. This figure is called value-at-risk. There are many such risk measures that have nicer properties, e.g. expected shortfall ES.[1] The shortfall is the expected value of the cumulated loss above a certain level. There is a massive body of research done in the last 30 years.

Not going into much detail we assume there is a risk measure for the portfolio RC and it can be partitioned into risk contributions θ_i for each risk L_i according to

$$\mathrm{RC}(\theta) = \sum_{i=1}^{N} \theta_i. \tag{11.12}$$

Then the factor α can be identified with a target return on risk capital similar to the ROE. What seems very easy is not, especially if you want to take care of correlations between the risks. Then one risk contribution depends on the rest of the portfolio or with the assumption of another risk L_{N+1} the θ_i would change. An obvious remedy

---

[1] For value-at-risk the so-called sub-additivity is not always given, formally: $\mathrm{RC}(u+v) \nleq \mathrm{RC}(u) + \mathrm{RC}(v)$. Two portfolios or covers u and v may have together a higher risk than the sum of the stand-alone risks, or differently: merging two portfolios would require additional capital.

is to have a rather homogeneous portfolio that can be achieved through risk limits and reinsurance. Further reading is for example Passalacqua (2006) or Gundlach and Lehrbass (2004).

11.3 Performance Guarantees

As we have seen earlier performance guarantees are "bank guarantees" that are irrevocable and payable on demand. The payment is not an indemnification of loss but a fixed guarantee amount. From a cashflow perspective it is just one payment contingent on the calling by the beneficiary within a given time period. The structure is simple, but the cause of the credit event is not. The ultimate loss is hampered by the "pay first argue later" set-up. The bank will pay unless it is fully evident that the claim is fraudulent. Therefore preventing a call can only be achieved by resolving problems between supplier and buyer directly.

11.3.1 Scope of Cover

A safeguard against unfair or unjustified calling is the uncovered risk share by the bank. Credit insurers want to maintain a certain pressure on the supplier by the bank to resolve issues and not to have the buyer call on the guarantee.

The credit event is the breach of contract by the supplier as interpreted by the buyer as beneficiary. It is quite comprehensive that an insolvency of the supplier can be a root cause of such a breach. The guarantor is covered in as far as he has a cash collateral from the supplier or a credit cover by a credit insurer. Prevention is key.

The potential for subsequent proceedings following a call should be considered from the outset.

Again, the scope of guarantees is to support performance and not to enforce payment.

11.3.2 Pricing

The pricing of bank guarantee has not attracted much attention in the literature. Banks price off the table. Assume a situation as in Fig. 2.22 on page 50. If we then consider Fig. 11.4 we see some ingredients of a potential pricing. These are the probabilities of:

- a covered event materialising,
- an unjustified calling and
- a breach of contract.

It makes not much difference whether only unfair calling is covered because recourse may be frustrated.

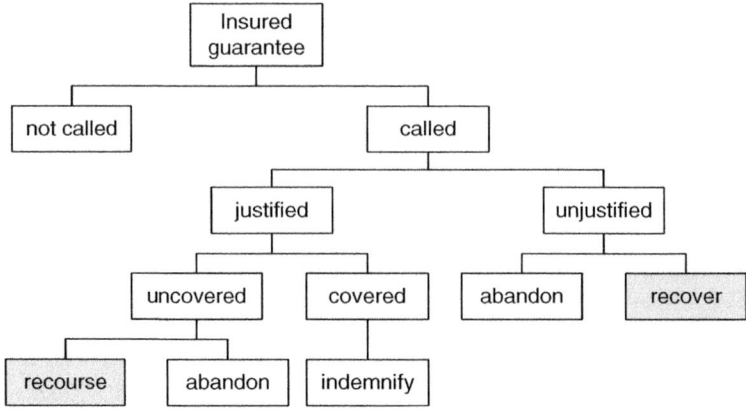

Fig. 11.4 Guarantee payout paths. With justified calling the supplier is the risk, with unfair calling it is the buyer

The credit insurer pays the bank under the counter guarantee in any case of a calling. In case of a justified calling its causes are not insured, i.e. with a breach of contract by the supplier, the insurer ultimately can try to take recourse to the supplier, if this seems worthwhile or abandon the claim. If the calling is unfair one can try to recover from the buyer after having received a positive ruling by the court or arbitration award. But recovering comes at costs and risks may be too high pursuing. The covered events are the failure to perform due to political risk and force majeure or government action.

For the guarantor the cost of the instrument is relatively low as he or she does not have to investigate the validity of the claim. But for the insurer behind this is not true.

Finding reliable data on pricing or on frequencies is very hard also due to the fact that disputes are settled through negotiation or arbitration. Court decision range around 0.1%.

For the insurer covering both the guarantor and the supplier the risks are additive and independent. Therefore also the premium is additive.

This means finding three prices for:

1. political, transfer and government action,
2. unfair calling,
3. non-performance.

The first risk is just a part of country or sovereign risk of the destination country. Here the difficulty is to separate the creditworthiness of the sovereign from the rating.

The second, unfair calling is according to all sources available very rare. Therefore we could just chip in some 10 bp as one source suggests and do no further analysis.

None-performance or a dispute is avoided by both or all parties in order to have the transaction done. Therefore one main ingredient to the performance is the insolvency or bankruptcy of the supplier during the export.

The following is a little bit of experimental. Most banks price guarantees off a table. Some add up fees and come to a sum that may be dependent on the cover period, e.g. quarterly fees, or are independent from the cover length. As a range indication bank guarantees start from 50 bp and end at 200 bp. As these products are used since eons the price should have converged to something above the expected loss plus margin for operations.

11.3.2.1 "Political" Risk

We summarise under the heading "political" political and transfer risk as well as government action. We need some at least categorical, better some quantitative data describing these causes of credit event that leads to a loss and to a potential indemnification. The above is rather a narrow definition that excludes events like pending election, etc.

The OECD knows the term *country risk* which excludes the risk of the creditworthiness of the sovereign. That implies that country risk is narrower than sovereign risk for which besides ratings there exist also market opinions in the form of CDS spreads. Taking sovereign risk as a proxy for political risk may be too far fetched but sovereign risk encompasses political risk.

There are not so few providers of political risk indices for countries because this is of quite vast interest. These indices are scores of underlying measures. For example, BMI Research has a Short-Term Political Risk Index that comprises four equally weighted variables:

- Policy-making process: government's ability to propose, pass and implement its policy.
- Social stability: short-term risks posed by any weaknesses in the economy or society via unemployment, inflation and public unrest.
- Security, external environment: threats to the government's ability to act as sovereign arising from direct challenges to its rule; terrorism and armed secessionism, regional tensions; and constraints on its actions by multilateral agencies or major powers.
- Policy continuity: assess likely policy continuity and explicit reference to the electoral cycle, and the risks of an unconstitutional transfer of power, e.g. coup or popular uprising.

In order to develop a first feeling about the variability of the notion of "political" risk we compare different proxies. Actually, this analysis does not reveal the "best" measure to use. We determine the correlations between the following data:

- S&P letter rating,
- OECD country risk,

- BMI Short-term PRI and
- World Bank Worldwide Governance Indicators.

We choose the last index as the anchor for plotting and calculate the correlations $\mathbf{R}(X_j, X_i)$. We have to bear in mind that the OECD data has no assessment for OECD member countries.

We construct our own indicator from World Bank data as

$$X_{\mathrm{WB}} = 0.125 \cdot \mathrm{CC.EST} + 0.75 \cdot \mathrm{PV.EST} + 0.125 \cdot \mathrm{RL.EST} \qquad (11.13)$$

with

CC.EST	Control of Corruption: Estimate
PV.EST	Political Stability and Absence of Violence/Terrorism: Estimate
RL.EST	Rule of Law: Estimate.

PV-EST measures perceptions of the likelihood of political instability and/or politically motivated violence, including terrorism.

We perform the calculation of correlation between these four indicators and have

S&P	OECD	0.8917
BMI	WB	0.8264
BMI	OECD	−0.7993
WB	OECD	−0.4858
BMI	S&P	−0.7536
WB	S&P	−0.6930

We assume that S&P as opinion on the sovereign risk should have the highest distance to the indicator for "political" risk under the assumption that the other indicator is measuring "political" risk. Thus we infer due to the very high correlation that the OECD measure for country risk is not much different from sovereign risk. On the other hand the World Bank index differs most from the S&P index but little compared to the BMI index for Short-Term Political Risk. If we take PV.EST only then the correlation with the S&P is −0.5997. It is obvious that only the absolute value is of importance and the sign stems from the ranking, i.e. the higher the better or the higher the worse.

From this correlation study we assume that 60% to 70% of the default probability of a sovereign is the "political" risk of the country. Therefore we set

$$d_{\mathrm{pol}}(t) = 0.65 \cdot d_{\mathrm{sov}}(t). \qquad (11.14)$$

11.3.2.2 Unfair Calling

Pricing of this credit event is difficult because of few data. Actually a court or an arbiter has to assess the fact and make an award. The only indication known to the author refers to a frequency of 10 bp cited by Marxen (2018, 110) in a footnote as Graf v. Westphalen (1981). It can be assumed that demand guarantees are called with a frequency of 3 to 5%.

There are ECAs offering protection to this isolated risk. So they should know. For example the Swedish insurer EKN covers: "protection against your buyer requesting payment from the issuing bank even though you have discharged your contractual obligations." Concerning the premium the ECA says: "EKN charges a premium, which reflects the transaction risk. The premium is expressed as a percentage of the guaranteed amount. (...) The size of the premium depends on the import country, the beneficiary and the exporter's ability to effect the transaction." Now, this description is not identical with our understanding of the risk.

As long as we lack better information we assume a premium contribution of 10 to 20 pb p.a. This makes the unjustified calling a rare event, e.g. "rain in the desert". Unjustified calling as a fraudulent practice is not confined to guarantees but inherent in all contracts.

We set therefore the premium contribution of unjustified calling to

$$\pi_{\mathrm{unf}}(t) = 0.0015 \cdot t. \tag{11.15}$$

11.3.2.3 Non-performance

Here we can relate to the analysis of Sect. 4.14 on page 133. We argued that it is useful to construct a rating model for performance. Now we have to translate the rating into a useful parameter of a default model. The main components of the rating are financial stability and management and operational skills. This may have a systematic and an idiosyncratic, i.e. company specific, part.

We determine the default probability using the Merton model that is a Black–Scholes framework in conjunction with the CAPM. This means using Eq. (4.79)

$$d = \Phi(-DD + \beta\gamma\sqrt{T-t})$$

and Eq. (4.69)

$$DD(t) = \frac{\log\left(\frac{V_A}{D}\right) + \left(r - \frac{1}{2}\sigma_A^2\right)(T-t)}{\sigma_A\sqrt{T-t}}$$

for evaluating the system Eq. (4.71).

Bringing everything together we have for the default rate for non-performance a generic formula:

$$d_{\text{Perf}} = F\left(\beta, \gamma, \sigma_E = \beta \cdot \sigma_K, \frac{V_E}{D}, T, r_f\right). \tag{11.16}$$

It will be calculated by the function dtd of Example 4.9 on page 111, viz.:

```
dtd(mcap,vol,debt,r)
```

We calculate the parameters from the market, here the German DAX index over a year with the help of some R code:

```
library(BatchGetSymbols)
a<-BatchGetSymbols(
  tickers="^GDAXI",
  first.date = as.Date("2019-08-13"),
  last.date = as.Date("2020-08-13"),
  freq.data = "daily")

b<-a$df.tickers$price.close
 sqrt(length(b)) * sd(diff(log(b)))
[1] 0.3157511
 length(b) * mean(diff(log(b)))
[1] 0.1010003
```

Rearranging Eq. (4.63) we can deduce from Table 11.1 the ratio

$$\frac{V_E}{D} = \frac{\beta}{\beta_A} - 1. \tag{11.17}$$

The risk-free rate for 1 year and EUR is -0.62%. The volatility is $\beta \cdot \sigma_K$. The price of risk is $\gamma = (0.1010003 + 0.0062)/0.3157511 = 0.3395$. Thus, as an example, with $\beta = 1.$, $V_E/D = 0.1$ it follows:

```
> dtd(mcap=0.1,vol=0.3157511,debt=1,r=-0.0062)
    dtd.v    asset.v   sigma.v
3.1654709 1.1062157 0.0285566
```

and finally

```
> pnorm(-3.1654709+0.3395)
[1] 0.002356877
```

So, we have a probability of default over 1 year of approximately 24 bp.

In Sect. 4.14 we have gone into details about assessing the quality of non-performance. In the formulae above there is no such variable. Now we would advocate to use a fudge factor for accommodating the findings of the assessment. In our view it would suffice to have three qualities, viz. "normal", "better than normal" and "worse than normal". For the better and worse we have to define a multiplicand for the variable d_{Perf} as $\chi_i \cdot d_{\text{Perf}}$.

Table 11.1 Beta values of a choice of industries, for illustration purposes (Source: http://pages.stern.nyu.edu/~adamodar/New_Home_Page/datafile/Betas.html compiled by Aswath Damodaran)

Industry	Beta	Unleveraged Beta
Auto & truck	1.10	0.53
Telecom (wireless)	1.14	0.60
Farming/agriculture	0.89	0.63
Homebuilding	0.83	0.66
Telecom. equipment	0.89	0.84
Retail (automotive)	1.33	0.87
Business and consumer services	1.07	0.89
Household products	1.03	0.94
Auto parts	1.21	0.95
Chemical (specialty)	1.14	0.96
Healthcare products	1.04	0.98
Chemical (basic)	1.37	0.99
Building materials	1.23	1.02
Environmental and waste services	1.27	1.05
Electronics (general)	1.15	1.07
Aerospace/defence	1.23	1.08
Metals and mining	1.31	1.09
Machinery	1.25	1.10
Construction supplies	1.36	1.10
Semiconductor	1.29	1.24
Office equipment and services	1.65	1.24
Paper/forest products	1.54	1.25
Steel	1.62	1.29
Drugs (pharmaceutical)	1.36	1.29
Electrical equipment	1.44	1.31
Engineering/construction	1.60	1.33
Shipbuilding and marine	2.17	1.57
Computers/peripherals	1.75	1.64

11.3.2.4 Summarising

For the premium of the performance guarantee we need to sum the three parts from above and determine recovery rates for the different risks covered. This yields

$$\pi_{PG} = \chi_i \cdot d_{Perf} \cdot (1 - \mu_1) + d_{pol} \cdot (1 - \mu_2) + \pi_{unf} \cdot (1 - \mu_3). \tag{11.18}$$

Now these recoveries may be rather low, lower than the often used 40%. This is to be considered the pure risk premium. In order to cover also operational costs there is the need for a loading, either additive or multiplicative or both. Some 50 bp are always a good start.

Example 11.3 (Performance Guarantee). We compare two premia from two very different industries, i.e. Telecom Equipment and Engineering exporting to the same country on comparable terms. We suppose German supplier shipping to Brazil, the guarantee with a tenor of 1 year.

Brazil has a sovereign CDS spread of approx. 200 bp for 5 years. Thus we set in accordance with Eq. (11.14) $d_{\text{pol}} = 67$ bp from $(1.02^{0.2} - 1)/(1 - 0.4)$. The unfair calling is 15 bp.

From Table 11.1 we read off the two betas as 1.14 and 1.6, respectively. The leverage V_E/D results as 0.9 and 0.2 and the drift $\beta(r_f - r_K)$ as 0.122 and 0.172. Thus

```
beta1<-1.14
beta2<-1.6
a<-dtd(mcap=0.9,vol=beta1*0.3157511,debt=1,r=-0.0062)
b<-dtd(mcap=0.2,vol=beta2*0.3157511,debt=1,r=-0.0062)
pnorm(-a[1])
      dtd.v
0.002735303
pnorm(-b[1])
      dtd.v
0.02594987
```

Assume a recovery rate of 20% then it results: Telecom: $p = 0.8 \cdot (67 + 15 + 27) = 87$ bp and Engineering: $p = 0.8 \cdot (67 + 15 + 259) = 273$ bp.   △

11.3.3 Working Capital, Manufacturing Insurance

Working capital guarantees cover very much the same as non-performance guarantees or better, the insolvency of the manufacturer. The political risk during manufacturing is covered by a manufacturing guarantee. Here the value of the collateral based on the re-usability of the assets is key.

These two ingredients are part of the performance guarantee also. Therefore, the premia for non-performance could be applied to working capital guarantees while the political risk premium is to be used as a basis for manufacturing insurance. We have argued for the market volatility, the beta and the leverage of the industry as a starting point seconded by idiosyncratic features like quality of the management, etc. (see Sect. 4.14) for an assessment and pricing. By using the market volatility the pricing becomes dynamic.

References

Cifuentes, A., & O'Connor, G. (1996). The binomial expansion method applied to CBO/CLO analysis. Technical report, Moody's Investor Service, Global Credit Research.

Graf v. Westphalen, F. (1981). Neue Tendenzen bei Bankgarantien im Außenhandel? *Wertpapier-Mitteilungen, 35*(12):294–305.

Gundlach, M., & Lehrbass, F. (2004). *CreditRisk+ in the Banking Industry*. Berlin: Springer.

Marxen, K. (2018). *Demand guarantees in the construction industry: a comparative legal study of their use and abuse from a south African, English and German perspective*. Baden-Baden: Nomos.

Passalacqua, L. (2006). A pricing model for credit insurance. *Giornale dell'Istituto Italiano degli Attuari*, LXIX.

Conclusions 12

From the discussion so far it seems quite improbable that the pricing of OECD Arrangement can further be used in an OECD that is under siege by different sources. Moreover, it is inadequate to attract the new exporters that have not been part of the OECD. There are several points of attack.

First, the pricing is lacking a strong theoretical and transparent foundation. Up to now this has been hidden by its relative simplicity. Nonetheless, it creates a level playing fields for those abiding to the rules, but this is too general a feature for weighing in positively. Nobody can explain how many parameters have been determined. There is no transparency from the yearlong experience from the covers. What are typical recovery rates, empirical frequency of default? The statistics are not available.

The concept of horizon of risk with its split into a disbursement and a repayment period, separated by the so-called SPOC, is hard if not impossible to reduce to a comprehensive model. One could suppose that it is an attempt to unify supply patterns with lending, to make two different credit situations equivalent. It is well known that this concept is very hard to sell to applicants. The SPOC is just a parameter to affect the premium. Most ECAs offer some pre-shipment products that are potentially overlaying the disbursement period, better credit build-up period, that begins at the so-called zero point.

Trying to approach the financial market pricing by creating two ways of rating, either in two dimensions by country and customer or with a universal rating, is not consistent. The country rating is an expert elicitation buttressed by an own country risk model. These ratings differ often massively from market opinion. There is a bias because OECD countries are exempt from being rated. Politically this makes sense especially when experts could be induced to try to steer geopolitical interests, e.g. sanctions.

The joint default is not treated but by assuming the weaker of the two potential obligors is already defaulted such that only the better of the two needs to be considered. This is not a very sophisticated method which could easily be improved.

C. Franzetti, *Pricing Export Credit*, Management for Professionals,
https://doi.org/10.1007/978-3-030-70285-4_12

The Arrangement contains many rules concerning eligibility and financial restriction. Requiring an advance payment seems very reasonable but the instalment patterns may be too restrictive to accommodate the new realities of international trade and to be adequate for all types of exported goods or services. The concept of matching the repayment with the useful life of the supply is inherent but not differentiated by products.

Not everybody will concord with this critique either fully or at all. But, nobody can deny the fact that the trade world has changed and needs better and acceptable pricing.

The framework presented here gravitates around some few but fundamental concepts. We try to develop pricing around principles. Thus reader may accept or reject them. But it is a transparent way to create a common understanding and basis. These principles stem from longstanding practice, most going back even centuries, some come from the prolific seventeenth century when insurance was founded.

Figure 12.1 shows the scheme underlying the new framework. Left are the inputs connected to the variables to be used. Then well established methods lead to the premium which can be transformed to a margin. As depicted, some variables may

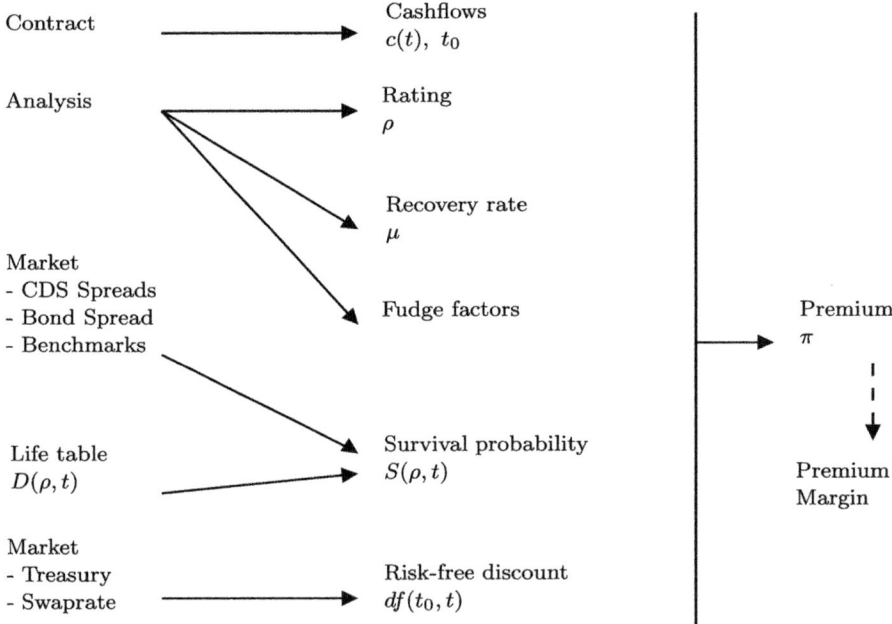

Fig. 12.1 New framework schematically

have several sources, and some inputs are needed in several variables. It needs four basic inputs:

1. contract data,
2. analysis results,
3. default and recovery data, either from market of historical,
4. interest rate data.

Then it uses finance fundamentals like time-value of money, discounting, spread calculus or simply the fundamental theorem of asset pricing of Chap. 4.6 on page 108. It says that under the correct probabilities the price of financial instruments is their expected value.

Thus the framework has a strong foundation in theory and empirical data. This is a very big step forward especially compared to pricing systems that come from expert elicitation and have a potential bias of political compromise.

The analysis has also shown that input variables fluctuate very much with economic circumstances. We are using default and recovery data from the bond market as a proxy for export credit. It would be highly desirable to collect more pertinent data, not only for default but also for recovery where the discrepancies with the market may be greatest.

The world has become more complex and sophisticated. Therefore, simplicity and stability for pricing very fluent risks are not appropriate anymore. This collides with state action that values these notions very highly. But it is not possible to read the premium off a table. This means also that the credit insurer must become more sophisticated with pricing. These are only superficially considered disadvantages of the framework presented here. But we know from almost a whole business life that mathematics is often regarded falsely with too much respect or as a theoretical nuisance to the manager. There is this spurious dichotomy of expert and manager. It seems that managers cannot be experts and vice versa.

The framework leaves enough space to be filled by others. We hope that this booklet may be stimulated to spend some time and energy to contribute additional or controversial ideas. We do not claim to get everything right.

Private credit insurer is in a better pricing position as they may select their customers and must price competitively but are otherwise free to agree conditions. They have the going concern maxim from the shareholders. Insurer may "pay" this freedom with some state oversight and regulation. But because credit insurance is still a niche product regulation is not the most sophisticated.

Coming back to the epigraph, we hope very much to be the "somebody else" who climbed the ladder later to finish the job for you.

Ω

Data

A

C. Franzetti, *Pricing Export Credit*, Management for Professionals,
https://doi.org/10.1007/978-3-030-70285-4

Table A.1 Cumulative Default Rates in Percent estimated from several rating agencies and normalised. Values have been adapted to have them not decreasing downwards and to the right. This is for illustration and calculation only. The rating names are in S&P-style

Rating/Tenor	1	2	3	4	5	6	7	8	9	10	11	12	13	14	15
AAA	0.01	0.03	0.13	0.24	0.35	0.46	0.52	0.60	0.65	0.71	0.73	0.76	0.79	0.85	0.91
AA+	0.02	0.05	0.13	0.13	0.35	0.46	0.52	0.60	0.65	0.71	0.73	0.76	0.79	0.67	0.74
AA	0.02	0.05	0.13	0.22	0.36	0.49	0.62	0.73	0.82	0.93	0.96	1.02	1.12	1.18	1.25
AA−	0.03	0.09	0.18	0.26	0.34	0.49	0.62	0.73	0.82	0.93	0.96	1.02	1.12	0.82	0.87
A+	0.05	0.10	0.21	0.35	0.46	0.56	0.68	0.80	0.94	1.10	1.13	1.26	1.42	1.60	1.76
A	0.06	0.15	0.24	0.36	0.50	0.68	0.87	1.04	1.24	1.48	1.53	1.66	1.78	1.86	2.02
A−	0.07	0.18	0.29	0.42	0.59	0.76	1.01	1.19	1.32	1.45	1.39	1.52	1.63	1.74	1.83
BBB+	0.11	0.32	0.56	0.79	1.06	1.35	1.56	1.82	2.07	2.33	2.36	2.53	2.73	2.99	3.26
BBB	0.17	0.43	0.68	1.07	1.46	1.84	2.20	2.56	2.94	3.33	3.37	3.66	3.90	4.02	4.24
BBB−	0.27	0.81	1.46	2.19	2.94	3.62	4.24	4.81	5.28	5.72	5.52	5.86	6.16	6.61	6.97
BB+	0.35	1.17	1.99	2.92	3.87	4.80	5.58	6.16	6.86	7.54	7.11	7.58	8.05	8.40	8.93
BB	0.57	1.07	3.39	4.96	6.49	7.74	8.88	9.84	10.73	11.51	11.26	11.87	12.28	12.60	12.98
BB−	0.99	3.09	5.30	7.53	9.49	11.39	12.98	14.51	15.77	16.84	16.81	17.52	18.24	18.95	19.63
B+	2.10	5.71	9.24	12.27	14.59	16.40	18.07	19.55	20.89	22.14	21.99	22.67	23.37	24.04	24.70
B	3.74	8.51	12.54	15.61	18.02	20.21	21.64	22.69	23.66	24.63	23.70	24.39	24.97	25.47	26.00
B−	6.89	14.08	19.38	23.05	25.79	27.83	29.42	30.49	31.23	31.87	32.27	32.94	33.37	33.92	34.40
C	21.18	31.39	37.99	42.57	46.53	49.09	50.84	52.62	54.79	57.30	57.62	57.96	58.35	58.69	58.74

Code Snippets in R

B

We use the programming language R, because it is free and very widely used in the field for prototyping. It can be downloaded from https://www.r-project.org/.

B.1 General Calculus

B.1.1 Bisection for Root Finding

The following code is a translation from an implementation in FORTRAN from Press et al. (1992, 347).

The implicit function must have the form $G(x, \ldots) = 0$ where ... stand for the list of parameters, e.g. `GenericBondZSpread(x,param=list())`.

Listing B.1 Fitting data to yield curve models

```
1  bisect<-function(x1,x2,param,FUN,epsilon=0.0000001,jmax=100)
       {
2  # x1, x2: interval boundaries. param: list of parameter of
3  # R-function, FUN: R-function G(x)=0, epsilon: tolerance,
4  # jmax: maximum number of iterations
5     fmid=FUN(x2,param)
6     f=FUN(x1,param)
7   if(f*fmid>=0.0) {
8     print("root must be bracketed between x1 and x2")
9     return()
10  }
11  if(f < 0.0) {
12    root=x1
13    dx=x2-x1
14  } else{
```

(continued)

227

```
15    root=x2
16    dx=x1-x2
17    }
18    for (j in 1:jmax){
19      dx=dx*.5
20      xmid=root+dx
21      fmid=FUN(xmid,param)
22      if(fmid<= 0.) root=xmid
23      if(abs(dx) < epsilon || fmid == 0.) {
24        return (root)
25      }
26    }
27    print("no convergence")
28    return()
29    }
```

B.1.2   Auxiliary Routines

Listing B.2 AuxTCvecFromT02TE

```
1   AuxTCvecFromT02TE<-function(T0,TE,h,c){
2   # Calculate payment dates and amounts for a fixed regular
        bond
3   # T0: reference date, TE: Maturity date,
4   # h: payment frequency, c: annual coupon
5     cvec<-c()
6     tvec<-c()
7     tE<-as.numeric(julian(as.Date(TE)))
8     t0<-as.numeric(julian(as.Date(T0)))
9     fl<-floor((tE-t0)*h/365)
10    for (i in 1:fl){
11      tvec[fl+1-i]<-(tE-i*365/h-t0)/365
12      cvec[fl+1-i]<-c/h
13    }
14    cvec[fl]<-cvec[fl]+1
15    return(list(t=tvec,c=cvec))
16  }
17  #Usage
18  AuxTCvecFromT02TE(T0="2020-05-21",TE="2027-11-29",h=2,c
        =0.03667)
19  $t
20   [1]  0.02876712 0.52876712 1.02876712 1.52876712 2.02876712
21   [6]  2.52876712 3.02876712 3.52876712 4.02876712 4.52876712
22  [11]  5.02876712 5.52876712 6.02876712 6.52876712 7.02876712
23  $c
24   [1]  0.018335 0.018335 0.018335 0.018335 0.018335 0.018335
```

(continued)

```
25    [7] 0.018335 0.018335 0.018335 0.018335 0.018335 0.018335
26    [13] 0.018335 0.018335 1.018335
```

Listing B.3 veclint
```
1   veclint<-function(tvec,param=list(tgrid,vgrid,opt=T)){
2   # Linear interpolation on a grid of a vector
3   # tvec: vector of points, tgrid: x-vector of grid point
4   # vgrid: vector of y-points; opt: add (0,0)
5     x<-param[[1]];y<-param[[2]]
6     if (param[[3]]){x<-c(0,x); y<-c(0,y)}
7     a<-as.data.frame(approx(x, y=y, xout=tvec, method="linear"
         ))
8     return(a$y)
9   }
```

Listing B.4 veclint
```
1   vecDfLint<-function(tvec,param=list(tgrid,vgrid,h=1)){
2   # tvec: vector of tenors to be interpolated, tgrid: time
         points,
3   # vgrid: vector of values, h: coupon frequency
4     x<-param[[1]];y<-param[[2]];h<-param[[3]]
5     if (param[[3]]){x<-c(0,x); y<-c(0,y)}
6     a<-as.data.frame(approx(x, y=y, xout=tvec, method="linear"
         ))$y
7     df<-c()
8     for (i in 1:length(tvec)){
9       df[i]<-(1+a[i]/h)^(-tvec[i]*h)
10    }
11    return(df)
12  }
```

B.2   Financial Calculus

B.2.1   Yield and Discount Curves

Listing B.5 Yield cureves

```
1    # ECB Svensson, yield curve model
2    ycSvensson<-function(param,t){
3    # param: list of parameters, t: term
4      b0=param[[1]]; b1=param[[2]]; b2=param[[3]];b3=param[[4]]
5      a1=param[[5]]; a2=param[[6]]
6      yc<-b0+b1*exp(-t/a1)+b2*exp(-t/a1)*t/a1
7      yc<-yc+b3*exp(-t/a2)*t/a2
8      return(yc/100)
9    }
10
11   ycHaugen<-function(t,param){
12   # param: list of parameters, t: term
13     return(param[4]+(param[1]+param[2]*t)*exp(-param[3]*t))
14   }
15   ycNelsonS<-function(t,param){
16   # param: list of parameters, t: term
17     return(param[1]+(param[2]+param[3])*(1-exp(param[4]*t))/
            param[4]*t-param[3]*exp(-param[4]*t))
18   }
19
20   # Linear interpolation
21   yc.lint<-function(t,param=list(tvec,yvec)){
22   # t: term, tvec: vector of terms,
23   # yvec: vector of yields
24     fv<-approx(tvec, y=yvec, xout=t, method="linear")
25     return(fv)
26   }
27
28
29   # discount rates from yc curve
30   df<-function(param,FUN,t){
31     yc<-FUN(param,t)
32     x<-(1+yc)^(-t)
33     return(x)
34   }
35   # discount rate from ECB curve
36   param<-c(BETA0,BETA1,BETA2,BETA3,TAU1,TAU2)
37   df(param,ycSvensson,t)
38
39   # discount rate from Haugen curve
40   param<-c(a1,a2,a3,a4)
41   df(param,ycHaugen,t)
42
43   # Usage
```

(continued)

```
44   yvec<-c
        (0.15,0.16,0.24,0.46,1.07,1.65,2.60,3.29,3.87,4.54,4.70)
45   tvec<-c(1/12,3/12,6/12,1,2,3,5,7,10,20,30)
46   yc.lint(t,param=list(tvec,yvec))
```

B.2.2   Bond Pricing

B.2.2.1 Yield to Maturity

Listing B.6 GenericDiscountingYield
```
1    GenericDiscountingYield<-function(yield,param=list(tvec,cvec
        ,price)){
2    # yield: self-explanatory, tvec: terms vector [years],
3    # cvec: vector of cashflows, price: ...
4    # if price=0 then the NPV is calculated
5        tx<-param[[1]]; cx<-param[[2]];bx<-param[[3]]
6        summ<-0
7        for (i in 1:length(cx)){
8            summ<-summ+cx[i]*(1+yield)^(-tx[i])
9        }
10       return(summ-bx)
11   }
```

B.2.2.2 Fixed Coupon Bond Price from Yield

Listing B.7 FixedCouponBondYield
```
1    FixedCouponBondYield<-function(yield,param=list(t0,TT,h,c,
        price)){
2    # yield: fixed for discounting, t0: as.Date(reference date)
3    # TT: Maturity date, h: payment frequency, c: coupon [per
        year]
4    # price: if price==0 the NPV is calculated
5        tvec<-c()
6        cvec<-c()
7        h<-param[[3]]
8        Price<-param[[5]]
9        TE<-as.numeric(julian(as.Date(param[[2]])))
10       T0<-as.numeric(julian(as.Date(param[[1]])))
11       fl<-floor((TE-T0)*h/365)
12       for (i in 1:fl){
13           tvec[fl+1-i]<-(TE-i*365/2-T0)/365
```

(continued)

```
14      cvec[i]<-param[[4]]/h
15    }
16    cvec[fl]<-cvec[fl]+1
17    dP<-GenericDiscountingYield(yield,param=list(tvec,cvec,0))
18    cP<-dP-tvec[1]*param[[4]]/h
19    return(dP-Price)
20  }
```

B.2.2.3 Floating Rate Note Price

Listing B.8 GenericFloatQuotedMargin

```
1  GenericFloatQuotedMargin<-function(qm,param=list(tvec,cvec,
      index1,index2,dm,price)){
2  # qm: Quoted Margin, Tvec: terms vector [years]
3  # cvec: vector of cashflows, index1: last known index value
4  # index2: next index value, dm: discount margin,
5  # price: price of bond [optional]
6  # if  price=0 then the NPV is calculated
7    tvec<-param[[1]];    cvec<-param[[2]];    index1<-param[[3]]
8    index2<-param[[4]];    dm<-param[[5]];    price<-param[[6]]
9    cvec<-cvec/sum(cvec)
10   pvec<-c()
11   nx<-length(tvec)
12   tx<-c()
13   tx<-c(0,tvec)
14   pvec[1]<-1
15   tx[1]<-(tx[2]-tx[1])*365.25/360
16
17   for (i in 2:nx){
18     pvec[i]<-pvec[i-1]-cvec[i-1]
19     tx[i]<-(tx[i+1]-tx[i])*365.25/360
20   }
21   summ<-0
22   dfx<-1
23   for (i in 1:nx){
24     if (i==1) {
25       dfx<-dfx*(1+(index1+dm)*tx[i])
26       summ<-summ+(pvec[i]*(index1+qm)*tx[i]+cvec[i])/dfx
27     }
28     else {
29       dfx<-dfx*(1+(index2+dm)*tx[i])
30       summ<-summ+(pvec[i]*(index2+qm)*tx[i]+cvec[i])/dfx
31     }
32   }
33   return(summ-price)
34 }
```

Listing B.9 Par-interest-rate

```r
1   # Interest Rate
2   zint<-function(param,FUN=df,N){
3       s1<-N
4       s2<-0
5       for (i in 1:N){
6           t<-i*0.5
7           dff<-FUN(param,t)
8           s1<-s1-dff
9           s2<-s2+(N+1-i)*dff
10      }
11      return(2*s1/s2)
12  }
13
14  # Par-interest-rate
15  #
16  parIntRate<-function(cvec,tvec,param,FUN=yc){
17      dfx<-c()
18      for (i in 1:length(tvec)){
19          dfx[i]<-df(param,FUN,tvec[i])
20      }
21      cvec=cvec/sum(cvec)
22      s1=cvec[1]*dfx[1]
23      s2=tvec[1]*dfx[1]
24      for (i in 2:length(cvec)){
25          s1=s1+cvec[i]*dfx[i]
26          s2=s2+dfx[i]*(tvec[i]-tvec[i-1])
27          for (j in 1:(i-1)){
28              s2=s2-cvec[j]*dfx[i]*(tvec[i]-tvec[i-1])
29          }
30      }
31      z=(1-s1)/s2
32      return(c(z,s1,s2))
33  }
34
35      OECDPV<-function(n,z,param,FUN=df){
36      sum1<-0
37      sum2<-0
38      for (i in 1:n){
39          sum1<-sum1+FUN(param,t=i/2)
40          sum2<-sum2+(n+1-i)*z*FUN(param,t=i/2)/2
41      }
42      return((sum1+sum2)/n)
43  }
```

Listing B.10 parIntRate2

```
1  parIntRate2<-function(ir,param=list(tv,cv,df,fr,Pr)){
2  # ir: interest rate, tv: vector of tenors,
3  # cv: vector of cashflows; df: vector of discount rates,
4  # fr: frequency, Pr: price
5    tvec<-param[[1]];cvec<-param[[2]]; dfvec<-param[[3]]; h<-param
         [[4]]; P<-param[[5]]
6    N<-length(tvec)
7    price<-0
8    for (i in 1:N){
9      su<-0
10     for (j in i:N){
11       su<-su+cvec[j]
12     }
13     R<-su
14     price<-price+dfvec[i]*(cvec[i]+ir*R/h)
15   }
16   return(price-P)
17 }
```

B.2.2.4 Zero-Volatility Spread

Listing B.11 GenericBondZSpread

```
1  GenericBondZSpread<-function(zspread,param=list(cvec,tvec,
         dfvec,price=0)){
2  # Zero-Volatility Spread from cashflow
3  # zspread: self-explanatory, cvec: vector of cashflow
         amounts,
4  # tvec: vectors of payment dates, dfvec: vector of risk-free
         discount
5  # factors, price: self-explanatory
6    dfx<-c()
7    cvec<-param[[1]];tvec<-param[[2]];dfvec<-param[[3]]
8    for (i in 1:length(tvec)){
9      r<-exp(log(dfvec[i])/-tvec[i])-1
10 #     print(r)
11     dfx[i]<-(1+r+zspread)^(-tvec[i])
12   }
13   #cvec=cvec/sum(cvec)
14   summ<-0
15   for (i in 1:length(cvec)){
16     summ<-summ+cvec[i]*dfx[i]
17   }
18   return(summ-param[[4]])
19 }
```

B.2.3 Cashflow Pricing

The following pricing codes of functions are designed to be used as $G(x) = 0$. This is useful when using the iteration solver bisect of Listing B.1.

Listing B.12 DeltaPrice

```
1   DeltaPrice<-function(ir,tvec,cvec,dfvec,Svec,mu,h){
2   # ir: interest rate, tvec: vector of tenors,
3   # cvec: vector of cashflows; dfvec: vector of discount rates,
4   # Svec: vector of survival rates, mu: recovery rate,
5   # h: frequency
6     R<-c()
7     N<-length(tvec)
8     for (i in 1:N){
9       su<-0
10      for (j in i:N){
11        su<-su+cvec[j]
12      }
13      R[i]<-su
14      cvec[i]<-cvec[i]+ir*R[i]/h
15    }
16    R<-c(R,0)
17    sum<-dfvec[1]*( (1-Svec[1])*cvec[1] -(1-Svec[1])*mu*(cvec[1]+R
        [2]) )
18    sumrf<-dfvec[1]*cvec[1]
19    if(N>1){
20      for (t in 2:N){
21      sum<-sum+ dfvec[t]*( (1-Svec[t])*cvec[t] - (Svec[t-1]-Svec[t
          ])*mu*(cvec[t]+R[t+1]))
22      sumrf<-sumrf+dfvec[t]*cvec[t]
23    }}
24    return(c(sum,sumrf))
25  }
```

B.2.4 CDS Calculus

Listing B.13 SurvivalFromCDS

```
1   SurvivalFromCDS<-function(tvec,svec,dfvec,mu,simple=FALSE,h
        =1){
2   # Calculate Suvival rates from CDS rates
3   # tvec: terms vector, svec: swap rates vector,
4   # dfvec: zero-yields vector, mu: recovery rate, simple:
        option,
5   # h: payment frequency
6     S<-c()
7     dfi<-(1+dfvec[1]/h)^(-tvec[1]*h)
```

(continued)

```
8     S[1]<-1
9     S[2]<-(1-mu-svec[1]*0.5*tvec[1])/(1-mu+svec[1]*0.5*tvec
         [1])
10    dt<-tvec[1]
11    U<-dt*S[2]*dfi
12    V<-0.5*dt*(1-S[2])*dfi
13    if (simple){V<-0}
14    W<-(1-mu)*(1-S[2])*dfi
15    for (i in 2:length(svec)){
16       dfi<-(1+dfvec[i]/h)^(-tvec[i]*h)
17       dt<-(tvec[i]-tvec[i-1])
18       S[i+1]<-((1-mu)*(S[i]+W/dfi)-svec[i]*(0.5*S[i]*dt+V/dfi+
            U/dfi))/(svec[i]*0.5*dt+1-mu)
19       U<-U+dt*S[i+1]*dfi
20       V<-V+0.5*dt*(S[i]-S[i+1])*dfi
21       if (simple){V<-0}
22       W<-W+(S[i]-S[i+1])*dfi
23    }
24    return(S[2:length(S)])
25  }
```

Listing B.14 CDSfromSurvival

```
1   CDSfromSurvival<-function(tv,fv,Sv,mu,simple=FALSE,h=1){
2   # Calculate the swap rates from Suvival rates
3   # tv: terms vector, fv: zero-yields vector,
4   # Sv: survival rates vector, mu: recovery rate, simple:
        option,
5   # h: payment frequency
6     s<-c()
7     SX<-c(1,Sv)
8     Tv<-c(0,tv)
9     sx<-0
10    sz<-0
11    V<-0
12    k<-1
13    if (simple){k<-0}
14    for (i in 1:length(tv)){
15       dfi<-(1+fv[i]/h)^(-tv[i]*h)
16       dt<-(Tv[i+1]-Tv[i])
17       V<-k*0.5*dt*(SX[i]-SX[i+1])*dfi
18       sx<-sx+(SX[i]-SX[i+1])*dfi*(1-mu)
19       sz<-sz+dt*SX[i+1]*dfi+V
20       s[i]<-sx/sz
21    }
22    return(s)
23  }
```

Listing B.15 FixedBondDefautProb

```r
 1  FixedBondDefautProb<-function(mu,param=list(c,tvec,dfvec,
        Dvec,price=0,h=2)){
 2  # Bond price from cumulated default rates given recovery
 3  # mu: recovery rate, c: coupon p.a.,
 4  # tvec: vector of dates, dfvec: vector of discount rates,
 5  # Dvec: cululated default rates, price: if 0 then price
 6  # calculation, h: frequency
 7    d<-c(); S<-c()
 8    c<-param[[1]]/param[[6]];tvec<-param[[2]];dfvec<-param
        [[3]];D<-param[[4]]
 9    N<-length(tvec)
10    S<-1-D
11    d[1]<-D[1]
12    for (i in 2:N){
13      d[i]<-1-S[i]/S[i-1]
14    }
15    summ<-( S[1]*c+d[1]*mu*(c+1) )*dfvec[1]
16    for (i in 2:N){
17      a<-( S[i]*c+S[i-1]*d[i]*mu*(c+1) )*dfvec[i]
18      summ<-summ+a
19    }
20    summ<-summ+S[N]*dfvec[N]
21    return(summ-param[[5]])
22  }
23  # Usage, example recovery from price
24  a<-read.table("~/R/snptab.txt") # Standard and Poor's table
25  b<-a[a$V1=="B+",]
26  D<-b[2:16]/100
27  tt<-AuxTCvecFromT02TE(T0="2020-05-21",TE="2027-11-29",h=2,c
        =0.03667)$t
28  Dvec<-veclint(tt,list(1:15,D,T))
29  treasyc<-c(0.09,        0.11,    0.12,    0.14,    0.16,
        0.17,    0.21,    0.35,    0.53,    0.68,    1.16,    1.40)/
        100
30  tx<-c(1/12,2/12,3/12,0.5,1,2.,3,5,7,10,20,30)
31  dfvec<-vecDfLint(tt,param=list(tx,treasyc,opt=T,h=1))
32
33  FixedBondDefautProb(.3,param=list(0.03667,tt,dfvec,Dvec,
        price=0,h=2))
34  [1] 1.089181
35
36  para<-list(0.03667,tt,dfvec,Dvec,price=1.0559,h=2)
37  bisect(0,1,param=para,FUN=FixedBondDefautProb)
38  [1] 0.1166394
```

Listing B.16 DefautProbFromFixedBond

```
1   DefautProbFromFixedBond<-function(d,param=list(c,tvec,dfvec,
        price=0,h=2,mu)){
2   # Bond valuation with constant default rate
3   # d: default rate, c: coupon p.a.,
4   # tvec: vector of dates, dfvec: discount rates,
5   # price: 0 for price calculation, h: frequency,
6   # mu: recovery rate
7     S<-c()
8     h<-param[[5]]
9     c<-param[[1]]/h;tvec<-param[[2]];dfvec<-param[[3]]
10    mu<-param[[6]]
11    N<-length(tvec)
12    for (i in 1:N){
13      S[i]<-(1-d)^tvec[i]
14    }
15    summ<-( S[1]*c+(1-S[1])*mu*(c+1) )*dfvec[1]
16    for (i in 2:N){
17      a<-( S[i]*c+(S[i-1]-S[i])*mu*(c+1) )*dfvec[i]
18      summ<-summ+a
19    }
20    summ<-summ+S[N]*dfvec[N]
21    return(summ-param[[4]])
22  }
23  # Usage example: Discount rate from bond price
24  tt<-AuxTCvecFromT02TE(T0="2020-05-21",TE="2027-11-29",h=2,c
        =0.03667)$t
25  treasyc<-c(0.09, 0.11, 0.12, 0.14, 0.16, 0.17, 0.21, 0.35,
               0.53, 0.68, 1.16, 1.40)/100
26  tx<-c(1/12,2/12,3/12,0.5,1,2.,3,5,7,10,20,30)
27  dfvec<-vecDfLint(tt,param=list(tx,treasyc,opt=T,h=1))
28
29  par<-list(0.03667,tt,dfvec,0,2,0.4)
30  DefautProbFromFixedBond(0.0405,param=par)
31  [1] 1.057812
32
33  par<-list(0.03667,tt,dfvec,1.0559,2,0.4)
34  bisect(0,0.2,param=par,FUN=DefautProbFromFixedBond)
35  [1] 0.04099283
```

B.3   Examples

B.3.1   Survival Probability

Listing B.17 Example calculation of survival probabilities

```
1   # Maturities to be interpolated
2   tv<-seq(0.5, 10, by = 0.5)
3   # Interpolate zero yield values
4   fv<-approx    (tvec, y=dfvec,xout=tv, method = "linear")
5   # Interpolate swap rates values
6   sv<-approx    (tvec, y=svec,xout=tv, method = "linear")
7
8   # Calculate Survival probabilities
9   su<-SurvivalFromCDS(tv,sv$y,fv$y,mu,simple=FALSE)
10  # Plot probabilities
11  plot(tv,su,type="b",xlab="Residual Maturity [ years ]",ylab=
        "Survival Probability [ - ]")
12  grid(col="darkgrey")
13  # Calculate swap rates for control purposes
14  CDSfromSurvival(tv,fv$y,su,mu)
15   [1] 0.005686289 0.006867284 0.008971679 0.011258728
        0.015203733
16   [6] 0.019185617 0.023065278 0.026958271 0.030853117
        0.034754273
17  [11] 0.036428028 0.038104876 0.039784136 0.041465316
        0.041777889
18  [16] 0.042091483 0.042405927 0.042721085 0.043036847
        0.043353127
19  # Print survival rates
20  su
21   [1] 0.9952726 0.9885419 0.9773054 0.9616634 0.9341699
        0.8994780
22   [7] 0.8585344 0.8109468 0.7570808 0.6972649 0.6578288
        0.6163748
23  [13] 0.5729872 0.5277536 0.5044205 0.4812341 0.4581730
        0.4352149
24  [19] 0.4123359 0.3895110
```

B.3.2   Z-Spread

Listing B.18 Z-Spread from price

```
1   # USD Treasury rate as of 2020-05-21
2   treasyc<-c(0.09, 0.11, 0.12, 0.14, 0.16, 0.17, 0.21, 0.35,
        0.53, 0.68, 1.16, 1.40)/100
3   # USD Treasury rate support (grid)
```

(continued)

```
4    tt<-c(1/12,2/12,3/12,0.5,1,2.,3,5,7,10,20,30)
5    # Terms of specific bond
6    T0="2020-05-21";TE="2027-11-29";h=2;c=0.03667
7    # Create bond payment date vector
8    ts<-AuxTCvecFromT02TE(T0,TE,h,c)$t
9    cvec<-AuxTCvecFromT02TE(T0,TE,h,c)$c
10   # Linear interpolation of yield on bond payment dates
11   YC<-approx(c(0,tt),c(0,treasyc),xout=ts)
12   df<-c()
13   # Discount factors
14   for (i in 1:length(YC$x)){df[i]<-(1+YC$y[i])^(-YC$x[i])}
15   # parameter list of bond, price
16   param=list(cvec,ts,df,price=1.0559)
17   # Implicit equation solver
18   bisect(-0.01,0.05,param=list(cvec,ts,df,price=1.0559),FUN=
         GenericBondZSpread)
19   [1] 0.02567266
```

Listing B.19 Joint default

```
1    # Read S&P table
2    a<-read.table("~/R/snptab.txt")
3    lx<-length(a$V1)
4    doubl<-data.frame(nam=a$V1[1:lx],val=a$V3[1:lx]/100)
5
6    m<-matrix(nrow=lx,nco=lx)
7    gRho<-0.05
8    rho=min(gRho,1)
9    rho=max(rho,-1)
10   for (i in 1:lx){
11     for (j in 1:lx){
12       v1<-doubl$val[i]
13       v2<-doubl$val[j]
14       res<-v1*v2+rho*sqrt(v1*(1-v1)*v2*(1-v2))
15       print(c(v1,v2,res,i,j))
16       idum<-1
17       for (k in 2:lx){
18         if(res>=doubl$val[k-1] && res<doubl$val[k]){idum<-k}
19       }
20       m[i,j]<-as.character(doubl$nam[idum])
21     }}
22   m
```

Listing B.20 Minimum Interest Rate

```r
minIntRate<-function(cvec,tvec,dfx,P=1){
# cvec: vector of cashflows, tvec: tenors,
# dfx: vector of discount rates, P: price
  cvec=cvec/sum(cvec)
  s1=cvec[1]*dfx[1]
  s2=tvec[1]*dfx[1]
  for (i in 2:length(cvec)){
    s1=s1+cvec[i]*dfx[i]
    s2=s2+dfx[i]*(tvec[i]-tvec[i-1])
    for (j in 1:(i-1)){
      s2=s2-cvec[j]*dfx[i]*(tvec[i]-tvec[i-1])
    }
  }
  z=(P-s1)/s2
  return(z)
}
```

Reference

Press, W., Teukolsky, S., Vetterling, W., & Flannery, B. (1992). *Numerical recipes in FORTRAN: the art of scientific computing*. Cambridge, England: Cambridge University Press.

Index

Printed by Printforce, the Netherlands